HUMAN RIGHTS

HUMAN RIGHTS

Edited by
Ellen Frankel Paul
Jeffrey Paul
Fred D Miller Jr

BASIL BLACKWELL
for the
Social Philosophy and Policy Center
Bowling Green State University

© Social Philosophy and Policy 1984

First Published 1984
Reprinted 1986

Basil Blackwell Publisher Limited
108 Cowley Road, Oxford OX4 1JF, England

British Library Cataloguing in Publication Data

Human rights.
1. Civil rights.
I. Paul, Ellen Frankel   II. Paul, Jeffrey
III. Miller, Fred D.
323.4'01   JC571

ISBN 0-631-13699-1

Printed in Great Britain by
Whitstable Litho Ltd., Whitstable, Kent

CONTENTS

ACKNOWLEDGEMENT

Social Philosophy and Policy
wishes to thank
the Rockefeller Foundation
for the generous support that it provided
for the Conference at which
most of these papers
were originally presented.

INTRODUCTION

Human rights issues have been much discussed in recent years by political leaders who choose to make them part of their foreign policy initiatives, and by critics who shun such policies in favor of a more pragmatic approach. Political regimes of both the left and the right blithely proceed to persecute political dissidents, remaining little affected by the importunings of democratic politicians who decry such behavior as breaches of human rights.

The current political debate over human rights has regrettably failed to address fundamental philosophical questions about rights. It is the purpose of this collection to examine such foundational questions about rights, the answers to which are indispensable for evaluating policies which affect everyone's well-being. Do individuals have human or "natural" rights? Or rather, are all rights derived from the state? If individuals do have rights antecedent to their relationship to governments, where do these rights come from? From what attributes of human nature do these rights derive? How ought rights to be limited by other considerations, such as efficiency? What about instances in which rights appear to conflict? Political philosophers have frequently contended with one another concerning these questions.

In the Western political tradition, these questions have been answered in a variety of ways. For Lockeans and those persuaded by a prior argument, the rights that people have are derived from some feature of their humanity, from their propensity to labor, from their rationality, from their relationship to God, etc. In this collection, too, we will see representatives of this school of thought. For Gewirth, in his "The Epistemology of Human Rights", the rights we have are demonstrated by a "dialectically necessary method", so that if a person represents his purposes as good, and freedom and well-being are necessary to pursue those purposes, he has rights to that freedom and well-being, and ought on pain of self-contradiction to respect those same rights in others. Loren Lomasky's "Personal Projects as the Foundation for Basic Rights" and David Kelley's "Life, Liberty and Property" both share this propensity for discerning rights in properties or propensities of human nature.

Another equally strong current in Western moral and political philosophy has been far less hospitable to the notion of rights derived purely from human nature. Utilitarianism, particularly as represented by Jeremy Bentham, was inhospitable if not downright hostile to the idea of fundamental rights, that is rights not granted by governments but held by individuals as checks against the excesses of the state. In fact, Bentham called such claims "nonsense on stilts". But in two of the pieces included in this collection, utilitarianism is viewed as far less antagonistic to the notion of human rights. For Allan Gibbard and John Gray, the prospect of fusing utilitarian considerations with those human rights appears as definitely alluring.

The remainder of the papers in this volume, those by Bedau, Golding, Flathman, and Donagan, round out the discussion of human rights by providing treatments on both a more abstract level (e.g., Why do we have the rights we do?) and a more specific one (e.g., Is the right not to incriminate oneself a fundamental right?).

We hope that the papers collected in this volume will prove to be a valuable addition to the contemporary discussion on human rights.

Social Philosophy & Policy Vol. 1 Issue 2 ISSN 0265-0525

THE EPISTEMOLOGY OF HUMAN RIGHTS

ALAN GEWIRTH

Human rights are rights which all persons equally have simply insofar as they are human. But are there any such rights? How, if at all, do we know that there are?

It is with this question of knowledge, and the related question of existence, that I want to deal in this paper.

I. CONCEPTUAL QUESTIONS

The attempt to answer each of these questions, however, at once raises further, more directly conceptual questions. In what sense may human rights be said to exist? What does it mean to say that there *are* such rights or that persons have them? This question, in turn, raises a question about the nature of human rights. What is the meaning of the expression "human rights"?

Within the limits of the present paper I cannot hope to deal adequately with the controversial issues raised by these conceptual questions. But we may make at least a relevant beginning by noting that, in terms of Hohfeld's famous classification of four different kinds of rights,[1] the human rights are primarily claim-rights, in that they entail correlative duties of other persons or groups to act or to refrain from acting in ways required for the right-holders' having that to which they have rights.

It will help our understanding of this and other aspects of human rights if we note that the full structure of a claim-right is given by the following formula:

A has a right to X against B by virtue of Y.

There are five main elements here: first, the *Subject* (A) of the right, the person or persons who have the right; second, the *Nature* of the right; third, the *Object* (X) of the right, what it is a right to; fourth, the *Respondent* (B) of the right, the person or persons who have the correlative duty; fifth, the *Justifying Basis* or *Ground* (Y) of the right. (I capitalize each of these elements for the sake of emphasis and for easier recognition in what follows).

Let us now briefly analyze the human rights in terms of these five elements. Each element involves controversial questions about the interpretation of human rights, but for the present purposes I shall have to be content with a

[1] Wesley N. Hohfeld, *Fundamental Legal Conceptions* (New Haven: Yale University Press, 1964), 36ff.

brief summary. The Subjects of the human rights are all human beings equally. The Respondents of the human rights are also all human beings, although in certain respects governments have special duties to secure the rights. The Objects of the human rights, what they are rights to, are certain especially important kinds of goods. I shall subsequently argue that these goods consist in the necessary conditions of human action, and that it is for this reason that the human rights are supremely mandatory. It is also largely because the human rights have these Objects that they are uniquely and centrally important among all moral concepts, since no morality, together with the goods, virtues, and rules emphasized in diverse moralities, is possible without the necessary goods of action that are the Objects of human rights.

Let us, now, turn to the Nature of human rights, which was one of the conceptual questions I raised at the outset. This Nature is often expressed by formulations that are common to all claim-rights: that rights are entitlements, or justified claims, or the moral property of individuals. While recognizing some merit in each of these formulations, I wish to suggest another that is at once more comprehensive and more specifically tied to human rights. Such rights are *personally oriented, normatively necessary moral requirements*. Let me briefly elucidate the point of each part of this definition. The point of calling the human rights *personally oriented* is to bring out that they are requirements that are owed to distinct Subjects or individuals for the good of those individuals. This feature distinguishes human rights from utilitarian and collectivist norms where rights, if upheld at all, are consequential upon or instrumental to the fulfillment of aggregative or collective goals. The point of saying that the rights are *normatively necessary* is to indicate that compliance with them is morally mandatory. Such mandatoriness distinguishes the human rights from virtues and other goods whose moral status may be supererogatory, such as generosity or charity. Finally, in saying that the human rights are *moral requirements*, I wish to indicate three distinct but related aspects of human rights: they are requirements, first, in the sense of necessary needs; second, in the sense of justified entitlements; and third, in the sense of claims or demands made on or addressed to other persons. These three aspects involve the relations, respectively, between the Subjects and the Objects of the rights, between the Objects and their Justifying Basis, and between the Subjects and their Respondents.

What has been said so far, then, is that the Nature of human rights consists in personally oriented, normatively necessary moral requirements that every human have the necessary goods of action. From this it follows that the Justifying Basis or Ground of human rights is a normative moral principle that serves to prove or establish that every human morally ought, as a matter of normative necessity, to have the necessary goods as something to which he is personally entitled, which he can claim from others as his due.

These considerations have a direct bearing on one of the other conceptual questions I raised at the outset, about what it means for human rights to exist. The existence in question is not, in any straightforward way, empirical. Although Thomas Jefferson wrote that all humans "are endowed by their Creator with certain inalienable rights," it is not the case that humans are born having rights in the sense in which they are born having legs. At least, their having legs is empirically verifiable, but this is not the case with their having moral rights. The having or existence of human rights consists in the first instance not in the having of certain physical or mental attributes, but rather in certain justified moral requirements, in the three senses of "requirement" mentioned above.

There is, indeed, a sense in which the existence of human rights may be construed as consisting in certain positive institutional conditions. In this sense, human rights exist, or persons have human rights, when and insofar as there is social recognition and legal enforcement of all persons' equal entitlement to the aforementioned Objects, i.e. the necessary goods of action. But this positivist interpretation of the existence of human rights is posterior to a normative moral interpretation, since, as we have seen, the rights are in the first instance justified moral requirements. In the phrase, "there are human rights", "there are" is ambiguous as between positive and normative meanings. In the sense of "existence" that is relevant here, the existence of human rights is independent of whether they are guaranteed or enforced by legal codes or are socially recognized. For if the existence of human rights depended on such recognition or enforcement, it would follow that there were no human rights prior to or independent of these positive enactments.

The primary relevant sense of the existence of human rights, then, is the normatively moral justificatory one. In this sense, for human rights to exist, or for all persons to have human rights, means that there are conclusive moral reasons that justify or ground the moral requirements that constitute the Nature of human rights, such that every human can justifiably claim or demand, against all other humans or, in relevant cases, against governments, that he have or possess the necessary conditions of human action.

From this it follows that the epistemological question I raised at the outset is crucial to answering the ontological question of whether there are any human rights. That human rights exist, or that persons have human rights, is a proposition whose truth depends on the possibility, in principle, of constructing a body of moral justificatory argument from which that proposition follows as a logical consequence. This consideration also entails the epistemological point that to know or ascertain whether there are human rights requires not the scrutiny of legal codes or the empirical observation of social conditions but rather the ability, in principle, to construct such a moral argument.

The qualification "in principle" must be emphasized here. I am not saying that the very existence of human rights as a certain kind of morally justified norm is contingent on the actual success of this or that philosophical justificatory exercise. The existence of human rights depends on the existence of certain moral justificatory reasons; but these reasons may exist even if they are not explicitly ascertained. Because of this, it is correct to say that all persons had human rights even in ancient Greece, whose leading philosophers did not develop the relevant reasons. Thus, the existence of moral reasons is in important respects something that is discovered rather than invented. The failure of this or that attempt at discovery does not, of itself, entail that there is nothing there *to be* discovered.

The epistemological structure suggested by these considerations is unilinear and foundationalist, since the existence of human rights is held to follow from justificatory moral reasons and ultimately from a supreme moral principle. An alternative, coherentist structure would involve that the existence of human rights is not to be established in any such unilinear way but rather by a sequence of interrelated reasons that may themselves include judgments about the existence of human rights. This latter structure, however, besides being more complicated, may be convicted of vicious circularity, including the difficulty that it may not serve to convince those who on purportedly rational grounds have denied the existence of human rights. I shall deal below with some further aspects of this question.

There have, of course, been philosophers, such as Bentham and Marx, who on various other grounds have denied the very possibility of constructing a moral justificatory argument for human rights. Hence, they have denied that human rights exist in what I have said is the primary sense of such existence. Among the grounds they have given for this denial is the moral one that human rights are excessively individualistic or egoistic, so that their espousal leads, in Bentham's words, to overriding what is "conducive to the happiness of society,"[2] and, in Marx's words, to separating man from the values of "community" and "degrading the sphere in which man functions as a species-being."[3] I shall not deal further with these criticisms here, except to note that they involve the epistemological question of whether a rational justification can be given of a moral principle that holds that all persons equally have certain moral rights. Such a principle should be able to accommodate the social emphasis of thinkers like Bentham and Marx while avoiding their excesses.

In the remainder of this paper, then, I want to do two main things. First, I shall conduct a brief critical examination of some of the main recent attempts

---

[2] Jeremy Bentham, *A Critical Examination of the Declaration of Rights*, in *Bentham's Political Thought*, ed. B. Parekh (New York: Barnes and Noble, 1973), 271.

[3] Karl Marx, *On the Jewish Question*, in *The Marx-Engels Reader*, second edition, ed. R. C. Tucker (New York: W. W. Norton, 1978), 43.

on the part of moral philosophers to work out an affirmative answer to the epistemological question of whether the existence of human rights can be known, proved, or established. In criticizing each of these attempted answers, I shall elicit certain conditions that must be satisfied by a successful answer to the question. Second, I shall give my own answer and shall indicate why I think it fulfills these conditions.

II. PRIOR ATTEMPTS AT JUSTIFICATION: CONDITIONS FOR SUCCESS

Before considering the answers given by other philosophers, we should note that arguments for human rights are sometimes identical with arguments for distributive justice, or at least are presented in the context of arguments for distributive justice. The reason for this is that the concepts of rights and of distributive justice are closely related. One of the most traditional definitions of justice is that it consists in giving each person his due, and this is largely equivalent to giving each person what he has a right to. Hence, rights are the substantive content of what, according to many conceptions of justice, ought to be distributed to persons. The universality of human rights is further brought out in the definition's reference to "each person." This definition as such, however, does not include the additional, formal idea of the *equal* distribution of rights. But many traditional conceptions of justice do, of course, incorporate this further element of equality.

The answers I shall consider to the epistemological question of human rights will also coincide in part, then, with answers that have been given in arguments for egalitarian justice, which involve especially that all persons have a right to be treated equally in certain basic respects.

One traditional answer is intuitionist. Thus, Thomas Jefferson held it to be "self-evident" that all humans equally have certain rights, and Robert Nozick has peremptorily asserted that "individuals have rights."[4] Such assertion is not, of course, an argument for the existence of human rights; it would not serve at all to convince the many persons throughout history who have had different intuitions on this question. Hence, this answer fails to satisfy *the condition of providing an argument.*

The remaining answers to be considered do provide arguments of various sorts. One argument is "formal." It holds that all persons ought to be treated alike unless there is some good reason for treating them differently. The 'ought' contained in this principle is held to entail that all persons have a *right* to be treated alike, and hence to be treated as equals. This in turn is held to entail that all persons have rights to equal consideration. This principle is based on the still more general principle that cases which are of the same kind

---

[4] Robert Nozick, *Anarchy, State and Utopia* (New York: Basic Books, 1974), ix.

ought to be treated in the same way, and being human is held to be such a kind.[5]

The formal principle raises many difficult problems of interpretation. In particular, it leaves unspecified what constitutes a "good reason" for treating persons differently, that is, what sub-kinds are relevant to differential treatment; and, of course, very many differences, including intelligence, sex, religion, color, economic class, have been held to be thus relevant. The principle, then, can eventuate not only in egalitarianism but also in drastic inegalitarianism of many different sorts. Hence, the argument fails to satisfy what I shall call *the condition of determinacy*, since it may serve to justify mutually opposed allocations of rights.

The next three answers I shall consider bring in certain contents. One is the argument of Joel Feinberg, who sets forth the "interest principle" that "the sorts of things who *can* have rights are precisely those who have (or can have) interests."[6] Now, waiving the murkiness of the concept of "interests," I think this principle is true as far as it goes; but it does not, of itself, go far enough to provide an adequate basis for human rights. Feinberg's arguments for the principle establish at most that it gives a necessary rather than a sufficient condition for having rights. More generally, he does not show just how the having of interests serves to ground the having of rights. Surely, not every case of having an interest is a case of having a right to the satisfaction of the interest. Hence, the argument does not fulfill what I shall call *the condition of sufficiency*, of providing a sufficient ground for the ascription of rights. Moreover, since animals may have interests and humans may have unequal interests, the "interest principle" does not justify either rights that belong only to humans or rights that belong to all humans equally. Hence the argument does not satisfy *the condition of adequate egalitarian premises*, since it does not establish *equality* of rights among all humans.

Another answer that tries to base human rights on human needs or interests was given by William Frankena. He held that humans "are capable of enjoying a good life in a sense in which other animals are not.... As I see it, it is the fact that all men are similarly capable of enjoying a good life in this sense that justifies the *prima facie* requirement that they be treated as equals."[7] The sense in question is one which Frankena identifies as "the happy or satisfactory life."

[5] For this argument, see Ch. Perelman, *The Idea of Justice and the Problem of Argument* (London: Routledge and Kegan Paul, 1963), 15–16; S. I. Benn and R. S. Peters, *Social Principles and the Democratic State* (London: George Allen and Unwin, 1959), 110–11; W. K. Frankena, "Some Beliefs about Justice," in *Freedom and Morality: The Lindley Lectures*, ed. J. Bricke (Lawrence: University of Kansas, 1976), 66–68.

[6] Joel Feinberg, *Rights, Justice and the Bounds of Liberty* (Princeton, N.J.: Princeton University Press, 1980), 167. A similar principle was set forth by H. J. McCloskey, "Rights," *Philosophical Quarterly* 15 (1965), 126.

[7] W. K. Frankena, "The Concept of Social Justice," in *Social Justice*, ed. R. B. Brandt (Englewood Cliffs, N.J.: Prentice-Hall, 1962), 19.

It will be noted that this argument moves from an "is" ("the fact that all men are similarly capable . . .") to an "ought" ("the requirement that they be treated as equals"). The argument does not fulfill *the condition of logical derivability of "ought" from "is"*. For it fails to show how the factual similarity adduced by Frankena justifies the normative egalitarian obligation he upholds. One might accept the factual antecedent and yet deny the normative consequent, on the ground, for example, that the value of some person's happiness or goodness of life is greatly superior to that of other persons, so that their rights to happiness or to certain modes of treatment are not equal.[8] In addition, the argument may also fail to satisfy the condition of justified egalitarian premises, for it still remains to be shown that all humans are equal (or even sufficiently similar) in their capacity for enjoying happiness in the sense intended by Frankena.

His argument, also, does not satisfy *the condition of a rational justification of the criterion of relevance*. It fails to show why the factual characteristics in respect of which humans are *equal* or *similar* are decisively relevant to how they ought to be treated, as against those factual characteristics in respect of which humans are *unequal* or *dissimilar*, such as the capacity to reason or to attain command over others or to control their appetites or to produce valued commodities or to work toward long-range goals, and so forth. Hence, the degree to which some factual characteristic is distributed among persons cannot of itself be the justifying ground for the allocation of rights.

A more direct way of deriving rights from needs is to *define* human rights as justified claims to the fulfillment of important needs. This, in effect, is what is done by Susan Moller Okin when she defines a human right as "a claim to something (whether a freedom, a good, or a benefit) of crucial importance for human life."[9] She lists three kinds of important human needs – to basic physical goods, to physical security, to being treated with respect. She then says, "Using the definition of human rights given above . . . we can logically infer three fundamental human rights from these three needs."

This definitional way of inferring the existence of human rights suffers from at least two difficulties. First, just because human rights are *defined* as claims to important goods, this does not prove that anyone *has* such claims, in the sense that these claims *ought* to be fulfilled. Since human rights, as claim-rights, entail correlative duties, how does the *definition* of human rights as claims to the fulfillment of important needs serve to ground the substantive assertion that persons have duties to fulfill these needs? Why should any person who is reluctant to accept this duty regard Okin's definition as a sufficient justifying

---

[8] See the acute criticism by Gregory Vlastos, "Justice and Equality," in Richard Brandt, *Social Justice* (Englewood Cliffs, N.J.: Prentice-Hall, 1962), 52–53 (note 45).

[9] Susan Moller Okin, "Liberty and Welfare: Some Issues in Human Rights Theory," in *Nomos XXIII: Human Rights*, ed. J. Roland Pennock and John W. Chapman (New York: New York University Press, 1981), 235.

ground? Her argument, then, does not fulfill *the condition of rationally necessary acceptability to all rational persons.*

A related difficulty is that Okin's definition takes sides on controverted substantive issues about human rights. Some philosophers have held, for example, that the only human rights are the rights to freedom, which require only duties of non-interference on the part of Respondents. Why, then, should they accept Okin's definition as a basis for the positive duties she attributes to Respondents? For this reason, her argument does not satisfy *the condition of an adequate account of the Objects of rights.*

Let us next consider a fifth answer to the epistemological question. This is H. L. A. Hart's famous presuppositional argument. He says: "If there are any moral rights at all, it follows that there is at least one natural right, the equal right of all men to be free."[10] His point is that all special moral rights are grounded either in Respondents' freely choosing to create their obligations or in the fairness of having an equal distribution of freedom among persons who subject themselves to mutual restrictions. Hence, Hart's argument for the equal natural right of all humans to freedom is that this right is presupposed by all or at least some of the most important special moral rights.

This argument suffers form at least three difficulties. First, it does not satisfy what I shall call *the condition of justified premises.* Hart has not adequately established that there *are* the special moral rights that figure in the antecedent of his initial statement. He appeals especially to the rights created by promises. But it is not self-evident that an act of saying, "I promise," taken by itself, generates any rights or duties. If there is indeed such generation, it is because there is presupposed a background institution defined by certain rules. Hence, there must be a prior justification of this institution as authorizing the generation of valid rights and duties. Here, however, Hart's argument fails to satisfy the condition of determinacy. For there may be morally wrong institutions, so that even though they are constituted by certain rules, these do not authorize valid rights and duties. Hart, however, has not provided this more general justification of the institutions he invokes. Hence, since his implicit appeal to institutions may yield morally wrong as well as morally right results, his premise is not morally determinate.

A further difficulty of Hart's argument is that, like Feinberg's argument, it does not fulfill the condition of justified egalitarian premises. If special moral rights are to be used to show that there is an *equal* right of *all* men to be free, then such universal equality must be found in the special rights themselves. But Hart has not shown that all men equally derive rights from the transactions of promising, consenting, and imposing mutual restrictions. He presupposes,

[10] H. L. A. Hart, "Are There Any Natural Rights?," *Philosophical Review* 64 (1955), 175, 189–91.

without any justificatory argument, the very egalitarianism he seeks to establish. A believer in basic human inequality, such as Nietzsche, would deny that all men are equal with regard to the special rights. Hence, Hart's argument does not establish the egalitarian universalism he upholds.

A sixth argument for equality of rights is the procedural one given in Rawls's famous theory of justice. He justifies this equality by arguing that if the constitutional structure of a society were to be chosen by persons who are "in an initial position of equality" and who choose from behind a "veil of ignorance" of all their particular qualities, the principles of justice they would choose would provide that each person must have certain basic, equal rights.[11]

Amid its many complexities, this by now familiar argument fails to satisfy three important conditions. One is *the condition of truth*: persons are not in fact equal in power and ability, nor are they ignorant of all their particular qualities. Hence, to assume that they are (in some sort of "original position"), and to base on this equality and ignorance one's ascription of equal rights, is to argue from a false premise. In making this point I do not overlook that arguments based on counterfactual assumptions may be cogent and even powerful. But the cogency of Rawls's assumptions is reduced because of their exceptional extensiveness and the direct use he makes of them to justify an egalitarian conclusion. His argument also fails to satisfy the condition of rationally necessary acceptability to all rational persons, to which I have previously referred. For the total ignorance of particulars that Rawls ascribes to his equal persons has no independent rational justification. Hence, no reason is given as to why actual rational persons, who know their particular characteristics, should accept the equality of rights that is based on their assumed ignorance. In addition, Rawls's argument does not satisfy *the condition of non-circularity*, since he attains his egalitarian result only by putting into his premises an equality (of power and ignorance) which cannot itself be justified.

The seventh and final argument for equal human rights that I shall consider here is based on the doctrine that all humans are equal in dignity or worth. Thus the United Nations Universal Declaration of Human Rights (1948), in its first Article, says: "All human beings are born free and equal in dignity and rights." It is important to consider what is meant here by "dignity." Presumably, dignity is not an "empirical" characteristic in the way the having of interests or the capacity for feeling physical pain is empirically ascertainable. The sense of "dignity" in which all humans are said to have equal dignity is not the same as that in which it may be said of some person that he lacks dignity or that he behaves without dignity, where what is meant is that he is lacking in decorum, is too raucous or obsequious, or is not "dignified." This kind of dignity is one that humans may occurrently exhibit, lack, or lose, whereas the dignity in

---

[11] John Rawls, *A Theory of Justice* (Cambridge, Mass.: Harvard University Press, 1971), 11ff.

which all humans are said to be equal is a characteristic that belongs permanently and inherently to every human as such.

One difficulty with the attempt to derive human rights from such inherent dignity is that the two expressions, "A has human rights" and "A has inherent dignity" may seem to be equivalent, so that the latter simply reduplicates the former. Thus, for example, Jacques Maritain wrote: "The dignity of the human person? The expression means nothing if it does not signify that by virtue of natural law, the human person has the right to be respected, is the subject of rights, possesses rights."[12] If, however, the two expressions are thus equivalent in meaning, the attribution of dignity adds nothing substantial to the attribution of rights, and someone who is doubtful about the latter attribution will be equally doubtful about the former. Thus, the argument for rights based on inherent dignity, so far, does not satisfy the condition of non-circularity.

It is essential, then, to consider whether the attribution of inherent dignity can have a status independent of and logically prior to the attribution of rights. An important doctrine of this sort was set forth by Kant, who based his attribution of dignity (*Würde*) to the rational being on his autonomy or freedom, his capacity for self-legislation, for acting according to laws he gives to himself.[13] Now, Kant held that such autonomy is not an empirical characteristic since it applies only to rational beings as things-in-themselves and, hence, as not subject to the deterministic laws of natural phenomena. This doctrine, however, involves all the difficulties of the distinction between phenomena and noumena, including the cognitive non-ascertainability of the latter. Hence, the Kantian derivation of rights from inherent dignity does not satisfy *the condition of empirical reference* as regards the characteristics of humans to which one appeals.

There is more to be said on this matter of the relation of human rights to human dignity, but I shall be able to make my view of this relation clearer after I have set forth my own positive doctrine.

This concludes my examination of seven recent attempts to give justificatory arguments for equal human rights. The examination has indicated that a successful argument must satisfy at least twelve conditions: providing an argument, determinacy, sufficiency, adequate egalitarian premises, logical derivability of "ought" from "is," rational justification of the criterion of relevance, rationally necessary acceptability to all rational persons, adequate account of the Objects of rights, justified premises, truth, non-circularity, and empirical reference.

---

[12] Jacques Maritain, *The Rights of Man and Natural Law*, trans. by D. Anson (New York: Charles Scribner's Sons, 1951), 65.
[13] I. Kant, *Foundations of the Metaphysics of Morals*, sec. 2 (Akademie ed., 434–36).

III. THE JUSTIFICATORY ARGUMENT FOR HUMAN RIGHTS

I now wish to present my own answer to the justificatory or epistemological question of human rights. It will be recalled that the Justifying Basis or Ground of human rights must be a normative moral principle that serves to prove or establish that every person morally ought to have the necessary goods of action as something to which he or she is entitled. The epistemological question, hence, comes down to whether such a moral principle can be rationally justified.

It is important to note that not all moral principles will serve for this purpose. Utilitarian, organicist, and elitist moral principles either do not justify any moral rights at all, or justify them only as ancillary to and contingent upon various collective goals,[14] or do make rights primary but not as equally distributed among all humans. Hence, it will be necessary to show how the moral princple that justifies equal human rights is superior, in point of rational cogency, to these other kinds of moral principles.

Now, there are well-known difficulties in the attempt to provide a rational justification of any moral principle. Obviously, given some high-level moral principle, we can morally justify some specific moral rule or particular moral judgment or action by showing how its rightness follows from the principle. But how can we justify the basic principle itself? Here, by definition, there is no higher or more general moral principle to be appealed to as an independent variable. Is it the case, then, that justification comes to a stop here? This would mean that we cannot rationally adjudicate between *conflicting* moral principles and ways of life and society, such as those epitomized, for example, by Kant's categorical imperative, Bentham's utilitarianism, Kierkegaard's theological primacy, Stirner's egoism, Nietzsche's exaltation of the superman, Spencer's doctrine of the survival of the fittest, and so on.

The Problem of the Independent Variable

One of the central problems here is that of the independent variable. Principles serve as independent variables for justifying lower-level rules and judgments; but what is the independent variable for justifying principles themselves? Another way to bring out this problem in relation to morality is to contrast particular empirical statements and particular moral judgments. Consider, on the one hand, such a statement as "Mrs. Jones *is* having an abortion," and, on the other hand, "Mrs. Jones *ought* to have an abortion." We know, at least in principle, how to go about checking the truth of the first statement, namely, by referring to certain empirical facts that serve as the

---

[14] I have tried to show this elsewhere with regard to utilitarianism. See Alan Gewirth, "Can Utilitarianism Justify Any Moral Rights?" in *Nomos XXIV: Ethics, Economics, and the Law*, ed. J. Roland Pennock and John W. Chapman (New York: New York University Press, 1982), 158–178.

independent variables for the statement to be checked against. But how do we go about checking the truth of the second statement, that Mrs. Jones *ought* to have an abortion? Indeed, what would it *mean* for the second statement to be true? What is the independent variable for *it* to be checked against? For the first statement to be true means that it corresponds to certain empirical facts. But with regard to a judgment like "Mrs. Jones *ought* to have an abortion," what facts would *it* have to correspond to in order to be true? Is there any moral '*ought*' in the world, in the way in which the factual '*is*' is in the world, serving as the independent variable for testing or confirming the relevant statements? If not, then is the moral judgment in no sense either true or false?

The problem we have reached, then, is whether there is any non-question-begging answer to the problem of the independent variable in morality. I now want to suggest that there is. To see this, we must recall that all moral precepts, regardless of their greatly varying contents, are concerned with how persons ought to *act* toward one another. Think, for example, of the Golden Rule: "*Do* unto others as you would have them do unto you." Think also of Kant's categorical imperative: "*Act* in such a way that the maxim of your action can be a universal law." Similarly, Bentham tells us to *act* so as to maximize utility; Nietzsche tells us to *act* in accord with the ideals of the superman; Marx tells us to *act* in accord with the interests of the proletariat; Kierkegaard tells us to *act* as God commands, and so forth.

The independent variable of all morality, then, is human *action*. This independent variable cuts across the distinctions between secular and religious moralities, between egalitarian and elitist moralities, between deontological and teleological moralities, and so forth.

But how does this independent variable of action help us to resolve the difficulties of moral justification? Surely we can't take the various rival moral principles and justify one of them as against the others simply by checking it against the fact of human action. Moreover, since if action is to be genuinely the non-question-begging independent variable of morality, it must fit *all* moral principles, how does action enable us to justify *one* moral principle *as against* its rivals?

The answer to these questions is given by the fact that action has what I have called a *normative structure*, in that, logically implicit in action, there are certain evaluative and deontic judgments, certain judgments about goods and rights made by agents; and when these judgments are subjected to certain morally neutral rational requirements, they entail a certain supreme moral principle. Hence, if any agent denies the principle, he can be shown to have contradicted himself, so that his denial, and the actions stemming from it, cannot be rationally justifiable. Thus, together with action, the most basic kind of reason, deductive rationality, also serves as an independent variable for the justification of the supreme principle of morality.

Why Action Gives the Principle a Rationally Necessary Acceptability

It is important to note that because the principle is grounded in the generic features of action, it has a certain kind of *material necessity*. It will be recalled that some of the justificatory arguments for rights examined above failed because they did not satisfy the condition that they be acceptable to all rational persons as a matter of rational necessity. For example, why must any rational person accept Rawls's starting point in the "veil of ignorance"? Why, for that matter, is it rationally necessary for any rational person to accept the Golden Rule or any other moral principle that has hitherto been propounded?

The conditon of rationally necessary acceptability is fulfilled, however, when the independent variable of the argument is placed in the generic features of action. For this involves that, simply by virtue of being an agent, one logically must accept the argument and its conclusion that all persons equally have certain moral rights. Now, being an actual or prospective agent is not an optional or variable condition for any person, except in the sense that he may choose to commit suicide or, perhaps, to sell himself into slavery; and even then the steps he intentionally takes toward these goals involve agency on his part. Hence, if there are moral rights and duties that logically accrue to every person simply by virtue of being an actual or prospective agent, the argument that traces this logical sequence will necessarily be rationally acceptable to every agent: he will have to accept the argument on pain of self-contradiction.

There is a sense in which this grounding of the moral principle in action involves a foundationalist conception of justification. For, as we shall see, the argument begins with a statement attributable to any agent, that he performs some purposive action. This statement is based on the agent's direct aware-ness of what he is doing, and it leads, in a unilinear sequence, to his statement that he and all other agents have certain rights and correlative duties. I need not be concerned, in the present context, with further epistemological issues about the certainty or trustworthiness of the rational agent's direct awareness or about any presumed "data" on which this awareness might be based.

The argument's unilinearity, with its concomitant avoidance of circularity, is an important asset. In this regard, the justificatory procedure I shall follow does not have the defects of Rawls's method of "reflective equilibrium," according to which "considered" moral judgments and general moral prin-ciples are reciprocally tested against and adjusted to one another.[15] There are at least two difficulties with this method. First, the "considered moral judgments" of one person or group may differ markedly from those of another person or group, so that they do not provide a firm or consistent basis for justifying a moral principle. Second, the argument is circular since the principle is justified by the very judgments that it is in turn adduced to justify.

[15] Rawls, *A Theory of Justice*, 20–21, 48–51, 120, 579.

My argument, in contrast, begins not from variable moral judgments but from statements that must be accepted by every agent because they derive from the generic features of purposive action. Hence, my argument is not "foundationalist" in the sense that it begins from *moral* or *evaluative* statements that are taken to be self-justifying or self-evident. The present argument is one in which statements about actions, and not statements about values or duties, are taken as the basic starting point. And these statements entail, in a noncircular sequence, certain judgments about the existence of human rights.

The Argument for Equal Human Rights

I shall, now, give a brief outline of the rational line of argument that goes from action, through its normative structure, to the supreme principle of morality, and thence to equal human rights. In my book, *Reason and Morality*,[16] I have presented a full statement of the argument, so that for present purposes I shall stress only certain main points.

To begin with, we must note certain salient characteristics of action. In ordinary as well as scientific language, the word 'action' is used in many different senses: we talk, for example, about physical action at a distance, about the action of the liver, and so forth. But the meaning of 'action' that is relevant here is that which is the common object of all moral and other practical precepts, such as the examples I gave before. Moral and other practical precepts, as we have seen, tell persons to *act* in many different ways. But amid these differences, the precepts all assume that the persons addressed by them can control their behaviour by their unforced choice with a view to achieving whatever the precepts require. All actions as envisaged by moral and other practical precepts, then, have two *generic features*. One is *voluntariness* or *freedom*, in that the agents control or can control their behavior by their unforced choice while having knowledge of relevant circumstances. The other generic feature is *purposiveness* or *intentionality*, in that the agents aim to attain some end or goal which constitutes their reason for acting; this goal may consist either in the action itself or in something to be achieved by the action.

Now, let us take any agent A, defined as an actual or prospective performer of actions in the sense just indicated. When he performs an action, he can be described as saying or thinking:

(1) "I do X for end or purpose E."

Since E is something he unforcedly chooses to attain, he thinks E has sufficient value to merit his moving from quiescence to action in order to attain it. Hence, from his standpoint, (1) entails

---

[16] Alan Gewirth, *Reason and Morality* (Chicago: University of Chicago Press, 1978), chs. 1–3.

(2) "E is good."

Note that (2) is here presented in quotation marks, as something said or thought by the agent A. The kind of goodness he here attributes to E need not be moral goodness; its criterion varies with whatever purpose E the agent may have in doing X. But what it shows already is that, in the context of action, the 'Fact-Value gap' is already bridged, for by the very *fact* of engaging in action, every agent must implicitly accept for himself a certain *value*-judgment about the value or goodness of the purposes for which he acts.

Now, in order to act for E, which he regards as good, the agent A must have the proximate necessary conditions of action. These conditions are closely related to the generic features of action that I mentioned before. You will recall that these generic features are voluntariness or freedom and purposiveness or intentionality. But when purposiveness is extended to the general conditions required for success in achieving one's pusposes, it becomes a more extensive condition which I shall call *well-being*. Viewed from the standpoint of action, then, well-being consists in having the various substantive conditions and abilities, ranging from life and physical integrity to self-esteem and education, that are required if a person is to act either at all or with general chances of success in achieving the purposes for which he acts. So freedom and well-being are the necessary conditions of action and of successful action in general. Hence, from the agent's standpoint, from (2) "E is good" there follows

(3) "My freedom and well-being are necessary goods."

This may also be put as

(4) "I must have freedom and well-being,"

where this 'must' is a practical-prescriptive requirement, expressed by the agent, as to his having the necessary conditions of his action.

Now from (4) there follows

(5) "I have rights to freedom and well-being."

To show that (5) follows from (4), let us suppose that the agent were to deny (5). In that case, because of the correlativity of rights and strict 'oughts,' he would also have to deny

(6) "All other persons ought at least to refrain from removing or interfering with my freedom and well-being."

By denying (6), he must accept

(7) "It is not the case that all other persons ought at least to refrain from removing or interfering with my freedom and well-being."

By accepting (7), he must also accept

> (8) "Other persons may (i.e. It is permissible that other persons) remove or interfere with my freedom and well-being."

And by accepting (8), he must accept

> (9) "I may not (i.e. It is permissible that I not) have freedom and well-being."

But (9) contradicts (4), which said "I must have freedom and well-being." Since every agent must accept (4), he must reject (9). And since (9) follows from the denial of (5), "I have rights to freedom and well-being," every agent must also reject that denial. Hence, every agent logically must accept (5) "I have rights to freedom and well-being."

What I have shown so far, then, is that the concept of a right, as a justified claim or entitlement, is logically involved in all action as a concept that signifies for every agent his claim and requirement that he have, and at least not be prevented from having, the necesary conditions that enable him to act in pursuit of his purposes. I shall sometimes refer to these rights as *generic rights*, since they are rights that the generic features of action and of successful action characterize one's behavior.

It must be noted, however, that, so far, the criterion of these rights that every agent must claim for himself is only prudential, not moral, in that the criterion consists for each agent in his own needs of agency in pursuit of his own purposes. Even though the right-claim is addressed to all other persons as a correlative 'ought'-judgment, still its justifying criterion for each agent consists in the necessary conditions of his own action.

To see how this prudential right-claim also becomes a moral right, we must go through some further steps. Now, the sufficient as well as necessary reason or justifying condition for which every agent must hold that he has rights to freedom and well-being is that he is a prospective purposive agent. Hence, he must accept

> (10) "I have rights to freedom and well-being because I am a prospective purposive agent,"

where this "because" signifies a sufficient as well as a necessary justifying condition.

Suppose some agent were to reject (10), and were to insist, instead, that the only reason he has the generic rights is that he has some more restrictive characteristic R. Examples of R would include: being an American, being a professor, being an *Übermensch*, being male, being a capitalist or a proletarian, being white, being named "Wordsworth Donisthorpe," and so forth. Thus, the agent would be saying.

(11) "I have rights to freedom and well-being *only* because I am R,"

where "R" is something more restrictive than being a prospective purposive agent.

Such an agent, however, would contradict himself. For he would then be in the position of saying that if he did *not* have R, he would *not* have the generic rights, so that he would have to accept

(12) "I do not have rights to freedom and well-being."

But we saw before that, as an agent, he *must* hold that he has rights to freedom and well-being. Hence, he must drop his view that R alone is the sufficient justifying condition of his having the generic rights, so that he must accept that simply being a prospective purposive agent is a sufficient as well as a necessary justifying condition of his having rights to freedom and well-being. Hence, he must accept (10).

Now by virtue of accepting (10), the agent must also accept

(13) "All prospective purposive agents have rights to freedom and well-being."

(13) follows from (10) because of the principle of universalization. If some predicate P belongs to some subject S because that subject has some general quality Q (where this 'because' signifies a sufficient reason), then that predicate logically must belong to every subject that has Q. Hence, since the predicate of having the generic rights belongs to the original agent because he is a prospective purposive agent, he logically must admit that every purposive agent has the generic rights.

At this point the rights become moral ones, and not only prudential, on that meaning of "moral" where it has both the formal component of setting forth practical requirements that are categorically obligatory, and the material component that those requirements involve taking favorable account of the interests of persons other than or in addition to the agent or the speaker. When the original agent now says that *all* prospective purposive agents have rights to freedom and well-being, he is logically committed to respecting and hence taking favorable account of the interests of all other persons with regard to their also having the necessary goods or conditions of action.

Since all other persons are actual or potential recipients of his action, every agent is logically commmitted to accepting

(14) "I ought to act in accord with the generic rights of my recipients as well as of myself."

This requirement can also be expressed as the general moral principle:

(15) "Act in accord with the generic rights of your recipients as well as of yourself."

I shall call this the Principle of Generic Consistency (*PGC*), since it combines the formal consideration of consistency with the material consideration of the generic features and rights of action. As we have seen, every agent, on pain of contradiction and hence of irrationality, must accept this principle as governing all his interpersonal actions.

This, then, completes my argument for equal human rights. Its central point can be summarized in two main parts. In the first part (steps 1 to 9), I have argued that every agent logically must hold or accept that he has rights to freedom and well-being as the necessary conditions of his action, as conditions that he *must* have; for if he denies that he has these rights, then he must accept that other persons may remove or interfere with his freedom and well-being, so that he *may not* have them; but this would contradict his belief that he *must* have them. In the second part (steps 10 to 14), I have argued that the agent logically must accept that all other prospective purposive agents have the same rights to freedom and well-being as he claims for himself.

Since all humans are actual, prospective, or potential agents, the rights in question belong equally to all humans. Thus, the argument fulfills the specifications for human rights that I mentioned at the outset: that both the Subjects and the Respondents of the rights are all humans equally, that the Objects of the rights are the necessary goods of human action, and that the Justifying Basis of the rights is a valid moral principle.

How the Argument Fulfills the Conditions of Justification
It will also be recalled that in my critique of previous attempts to answer the epistemological question of human rights I listed twelve conditions that the attempts had collectively failed to satisfy. I do not have the time now to do any more than to indicate very briefly how my own argument satisfies each of these conditions. The condition of providing an argument is obviously satisfied. The remaining eleven conditions, which concern the requirements for a successful argument justifying or proving the existence of human rights, may be divided into four groups. First, the conditions of justified premises, truth, and empirical reference are fulfilled by my argument because I begin from actual, empirically discriminable agents who pursue their purposes and know the relevant circumstances of their action. Second, the argument also fulfills the conditions of adequate egalitarian premises and rational justification of the criterion of relevance, because the agents are equal as having purposes and it is this having of purposes which has been shown to be relevant to their claiming of rights. Third, the argument has fulfilled the conditions of non-circularity and logical derivability of 'ought' from 'is,' because it has shown how the claiming of rights with their correlative 'oughts' logically follows from being a purposive agent, while at the same time such agency has not been defined in terms of claiming or having rights. Fourth, the argument fulfills the remaining

conditions of determinacy, sufficiency, rationally necessary acceptability to all rational persons, and adequate account of the Objects of rights. For the argument has shown how every agent's needs for the necessary goods of action provide a sufficient basis for his claiming rights to their fulfillment; and the opposites of these rights are not derivable from the argument in question. Moreover – and the importance of this must again be stressed – the argument is necessarily acceptable to all rational person qua agents because it is logically grounded in the generic features that characterize all actions and agents.

Some Objections to the Argument

Many questions may be raised about this argument. They include objections made on behalf of egoists, amoralists, "fanatics," radical social critics, and historians, as well as charges that the idea of prudential rights (as found in step (5) above) makes no sense and that the argument's egalitarian conclusion is not in fact justified. I have dealt with these objections elsewhere.[17]

I wish, now, to consider two further objections against the first nine steps of my argument as given above. These steps culminate in the assertion that every agent logically must hold or accept that he has rights to freedom and well-being as the necessary conditions of his action. One objection bears on the Objects of these rights. My argument moves from step (4), "I must have freedom and well-being," to step (5), "I have rights to freedom and well-being." The argument is that if the agent denies (5) then he also has to deny (4). It may be objected, however, that this argument entails that whenever some person holds that he must have something X, he also has to hold that he has a right to X. But this, to put it mildly, is implausible. If someone thinks that he *must* have a ten-speed bicycle, or the love of some woman, it surely does not follow that he thinks, let alone has to think, that he has a *right* to these Objects.

My reply to this objection is that it overlooks an important restriction. My argument is confined to *necessary contents* – to what is necessarily connected with being an agent, and hence to the necessary goods of action. Hence the argument excludes the kinds of *contingent reasons* that figure in the objection. Persons do, of course, desire many particular things, and they may even feel that they *must* have some of these. But there is a difference between a 'must' that is concerned with Objects that are, strictly speaking, dispensable, and a 'must' whose Objects are the necessary conditions of action. The latter Objects, unlike the former, have an ineluctableness within the context of action that reflects the rational necessity to which the argument must be confined if its culminating obligatoriness is to be justified.[18] I shall deal with this further below, in connection with the dialectically necessary method.

[17] See *Reason and Morality*, 82–102; "Appendix: Replies to Some Criticisms," in *Nomos XXIV: Ethics, Economics, and the Law* (see above, n. 14), 178–190; "Why Agents Must Claim Rights: A Reply," *Journal of Philosophy* 79 (1982), 403–410.
[18] I have previously discussed this specific point in *Reason and Morality*, 77–78, 81–82.

A second objection bears on the Subjects of the rights. In my argument above I held that if the agent denies (5), "I have rights to freedom and well-being," then, because of the correlativity of rights and strict 'oughts,' he must also deny (6), "All other persons ought at least to refrain from removing or interfering with my freedom and well-being." I, then, showed that the denial of (6) entails a statement (9) which contradicts another statement (4) which every agent must accept, so that to avoid self-contradiction every agent must accept (5). It may be objected, however, that a statement like (6) may be accepted on grounds other than the acceptance of a rights-statement like (5). The grounds may be utilitarian or of some other non-rights sort. Consider, for example, (6a), "All persons ought to refrain from removing or interfering with the well-being of trees (or animals, or fine old buildings)." One may accept this without having to accept (5a), "Trees (or animals, or fine old buildings) have rights to well-being." In other words, one may accept that one *ought not to harm* certain entities without accepting that these entities have *rights* to non-harm. But since my argument above depended on the logical equivalence between a statment (5) that upholds rights and a statement (6) that upholds the 'ought' of not harming, the objection is that the need to accept (6) does not entail the need to accept (5). If it did, we should have to accept that trees, animals, and even old buildings have rights.

My answer to this objection is that it misconstrues the criterion of the 'ought' in (6). This 'ought' is not upheld on general utilitarian grounds or on other general grounds not primarily related to its beneficiary. Rather, it is upheld as signifying something that is due or owed to the beneficiary, something to which he is entitled by virtue of its being required for all his purposive actions.[19] Thus the 'ought' in (6) has a specificity and stringency which are not captured in (6a). Hence, my argument does not entail that entities other than human purposive agents have rights, since its 'ought' involves the more specific requirement of something that is owed or due. This more specific 'ought' can pertain only to human purposive agents as its beneficiaries. And such a strict 'ought', unlike other 'oughts' that are looser or less specific, is correlative with a rights-judgment.

The Dialectically Necessary Method

It will be helpful for further understanding of my argument if I comment on a certain procedural aspect of it. I have used what I call a *dialectically necessary method*. The method is *dialectical* in that it begins from statements presented as being made or accepted by an agent; it proceeds from within and is relative to his own first-person conative perspective, and it examines what his statements logically imply. The method is dialectically *necessary* in that the statements in

---

[19] See *Reason and Morality*, 66, 73, 79, 95.

question logically must be made or accepted by every agent. Thus, my method stands in contrast to an *assertoric method* whose statements are propounded by the writer or speaker himself as being objectively true without being relative to his own purview as an agent; and my method also stands in contrast to a *dialectically contingent method* where the statements are presented as being made by and relative to an agent or other interlocutor, but there is no logical necessity that he make or accept those statements. Rawls's argument uses a dialectically contingent method; this is why I hold that it fails to satisfy the condition of rationally necessary acceptability to all rational persons. This may also be true in part of Hart's argument. All the other arguments I examined above used an assertoric method.

It follows from my use of the dialectically necessary method that what my argument has established is not the *assertoric* proposition that all humans have certain rights *tout court*, but rather the *dialectically necessary* proposition that every agent logically must hold or accept that he and all other prospective agents have the generic rights. This relativity to agents and their claims does not, however, remove the stringency of the rights or the categoricalness of the moral principle that justifies them. For since agency is the proximate general context of all morality and indeed of all practice, whatever is necessarily justified within the context of agency is also necessary for morality, and what logically must be accepted by every agent is necessarily justified within the context of agency. Because of this actional context of morality, the moral principle that all persons equally have human rights can be stated assertorically as well as dialectically.

There are several reasons for using the dialectically necessary method. Certain inferences that would not be valid apart from the agent's first-person conative perspective *are* valid *within* that perspective. Consider, for example, the inference from (1), "I do X for end or purpose E," to (2), "E is good." Contrast this with an attempted inference from (1a), "Some agent A does X for end or purpose E," to (2), "E is good." Now, (2) does not follow from (1a); but (2) does follow from (1). The difference between these two inferences is that in the latter, from (1) to (2), "E is good" is stated by the agent himself from within his own context of conative, purposive action. In the inference from (1a) to (2), on the other hand, "E is good" is presented assertorically, as being stated by an objective observer of the agent and his action. But that the purpose for which someone acts is *in fact* good does not follow from its being his purpose, since many agents act for bad purposes. What does follow is that the agent *thinks* his purpose is good; and this is what is conveyed by the first-person perspective of the dialectically necessary method. The evaluation contained in the consequent – that E is good – is not adequately supported by the statement that someone performs a purposive action, *unless* that statement is made by the agent himself. For it is because it is *his* purpose, which *he* conatively endorses, that the evaluative endorsement contained in the consequent follows. The naturalistic arguments I considered above from human needs or interests also failed in part because they omitted this first-person conative standpoint of the agent.

A second reason for using the dialectically necessary method – this time bearing on its necessity – is that it restricts the argument to what every agent is logically or rationally justified in claiming from within his conative standpoint in purposive action. The point of this restriction is as follows. Morality is often the scene of severe dissensus, of conflicting claims and counter-claims about what is right or ought to be done. To resolve these conflicts in a rational way, what is needed is recourse to a context that is *logically binding* on every agent. Such is the context of action itself. For whatever the divergent purposes for which they may act or advocate acting, all agents are involved in the context of action; hence, if there are any practical judgments that logically must be accepted by every agent from within his own perspective of purposive agency, these judgments can serve as a kind of firm, rationally ineluctable basis for evaluating whatever further judgments or actions he may want to pursue. In this way, then, the use of the dialectically necessary method can yield valid criteria for morally right actions which every agent must accept on pain of self-contradiction. The rational appeal to consistency or self-contradiction thus serves as a second-order standard for evaluating all the divergent rules or norms which agents may uphold. The point is not that ethics is reduced to logic but rather that morally wrong actions, judgments, and rules are shown to be unjustified because they do not pass the most basic test of rational justification. Or, to put it otherwise, if certain substantive answers to moral questions can be shown to be so conclusive that logical inconsistency results from denying or rejecting them, this provides a culminating argument for accepting such answers as sound and for rejecting the opposed answers as unsound.

Human Dignity as the Basis of Human Rights

I wish to conclude this paper by returning to the argument for human rights based on human dignity that I briefly considered above. It will be recalled that I objected to Kant's version of this argument on the ground that his appeal to rational beings as things-in-themselves violated the condition of empirical reference. Now, however, we may reinterpret Kant's doctrine along the lines of the conception of action that I have briefly presented here. As we have seen, human action, as an empirically ascertainable phenomenon, has the generic features of voluntariness (whereby the agent controls his behaviour by his unforced choice with knowledge of relevant circumstances) and purposiveness (whereby he aims at certain goals he wants to attain and can reflect on his goals). By virtue of the voluntariness of his actions, the agent has a kind of autonomy or freedom. And by virtue of his actions' purposiveness, he regards his goals as *good*, as *worth* attaining.

An ineluctable element of *worth*, then, is involved in the very concept and context of human purposive action. Such action is not merely an unordered set of episodes or events. Rather, it is ordered by its orientation to a goal which gives it its value, its point. This is so even if the action is done for its own sake, so that it is its own goal. In either case, the goal or end has *worth* for the agent as something to be reflectively chosen, aimed at, and achieved. And this worth is not merely instrumental; it characterizes at least some of the agent's ends themselves as he conceives and pursues them.

Now, there is a direct route from the worth of the agent's ends to the worth or dignity of the agent himself. For he is both the general locus of all the particular ends he wants to attain and also the source of his attribution of worth to them. Because he is this locus and source, the worth he attributes to his ends pertains *a fortiori* to himself. They are *his* ends, and they are worth attaining because *he* is worth sustaining and fulfilling, so that he has a *justified* sense of self-esteem, of his own worth. He pursues his ends, moreover, not as an uncontrolled reflex response to stimuli, but rather because he has chosen them after reflection on alternatives. Even if he does not always reflect, his choice can and sometimes at least does operate in this way. Every human agent, as such, is capable of this. Hence, the agent is an entity that, unlike other natural entities, is not, so far as it acts, subject only to external forces of nature; he can and does make his own decisions on the basis of his own reflective understanding. This, of course, was Kant's point also. By virtue of these characteristics of his action, the agent has worth or dignity.

This attribution of dignity may be interpreted either dialectically or assertorically. Dialectically, the argument means that every agent must attribute worth or dignity to himself, since he is the locus and source of his attribution of worth to the purposes for which he acts. Assertorically, the argument means that, regardless of the specific worth or value of any of his particular purposes, every agent has worth or dignity because of his capacities for controlling his behavior and acting for ends he reflectively chooses.

The sequence from this dignity to rights might similarly be upheld in either of two ways. One is the dialectical way discussed above. By this method the agent would simply augment his statement that freedom and well-being are the necessary goods of his action with the affirmation that he must have these goods not only as an agent but as a person who has dignity or worth by virtue of his agency. The argument, with this corroborating qualification, would otherwise proceed as previously indicated. Its conclusion is that every agent must act in accord with his recipients' rights as well as his own, so that he must respect his recipients as well as himself.

The other way of moving from dignity to rights is assertoric. Since every agent has dignity, his status as an agent ought to be maintaned and protected. For dignity is an attribute or characteristic that, of itself, deserves respect and makes mandatory the support of the being that has it. This mandatoriness or 'ought,' moreover, is strict: it is correlative to an entitlement on the part of the agent who has dignity. In this way, dignity entails rights.

I think that the assertoric arguments incur much greater problems than do the dialectical ones, because of the former's difficulties in satisfying the conditions of empirical reference and of the logical derivability of 'ought' from 'is.' Each mode of argument, however, is based on the connection between human action and human rights emphasized here, and each serves to bring out an important element in the justification of human rights.

It is also important to note, however, that the connection between dignity and rights is not only retrospective, as based on inherent characteristics of human agents, but also prospective. A central reason for grounding human rights in the necessary conditions of human action is that this serves to emphasize that the ultimate purpose of the rights is to preserve for each person a certain fundamental moral status. All the human rights, those of well-being as well as of freedom, have as their aim that each person have rational autonomy in the sense of being a self-controlling, self-developing agent who can relate to other persons on a basis of mutual respect and cooperation, in contrast to being a dependent, passive recipient of the agency of others. Even when the rights require positive assistance from other persons, their point is not to reinforce or increase dependence but rather to give support that enables persons to be agents, that is, to control their own lives and effectively pursue and sustain their own purposes without being subjected to domination and harm from others. In this way, agency is both the metaphysical and the moral basis of human dignity. Consequently, when all humans are held to have rights to the necessary conditions of their action, the connection of the rights with human dignity is not merely asserted, but is explicated in terms of the needs whose fulfillment is required for the protection of such dignity.

Philosophy, University of Chicago

Social Philosophy & Policy Vol. 1 Issue 2 ISSN 0265-0525

COMMENT ON GEWIRTH
CONSTRUCTING AN EPISTEMOLOGY OF HUMAN RIGHTS: A PSEUDO PROBLEM?

ARTHUR C. DANTO

Those rights are human rights which, in Professor Gewirth's phrase, "all persons equally have simply insofar as they are human." His task is to demonstrate that there are human rights, and to demonstrate that such demonstration is necessary to the very existence of these rights. "That human rights exist . . . is a proposition whose truth depends upon the possibility, in principle, of constructing a body of moral justificatory argument from which that proposition follows as a logical consequence." As philosophers we should no doubt like to be able to prove the existence of human rights – prove that there are such rights in the event that the fool shall have said in his heart that there are none, even using his folly against him by showing his denial to entail *its* denial – but it is a bold claim that rights are things whose *esse est demonstrari*.

Yet something like this seems to be claimed. "For human rights to exist, or for all persons to have human rights, *means* (my italics) that there are conclusive moral reasons that justify or ground the moral requirements that constitute the Nature (Gewirth's capital) of humans rights . . ." And again, "The existence of human rights depends on the existence of certain moral justificatory reasons." This is a far stronger and philosophically a more exciting claim than one where we might say that without reasons there would be no actions, since reasons are presupposed by the very existence of an event being an action and are arguably the causes of actions. Here it is as though proof penetrates the being of what is proved, so there is an internal connection between them, and it is difficult to think of another case where anything like this would be true. Descartes in a way gives us an example, since he sets out to discover what he is and finds that he is the kind of being presupposed precisely by the possibility of such a search; and Heidegger discovers his essence in the very asking of the question what his essence is. In these cases the conditions of putting the question constitute an answer to it, and Gewirth's philosophical method resembles this somewhat. At least what he terms late in his paper "the dialectically necessary method" does, entrapping the denier of human rights in a kind of conflict, almost as though there were a dialectic between the conditions and the content of the argument. In whatever way the denial entails a contradiction, the affirmation entails a necessity, but the argument itself is more than a logical showpiece if the deep claims of the paper are sound, since what one argues for cannot be separated from – "depends for its existence on" – the argument itself, since *it* gives the "morally justificatory reasons" from which the rights argued for cannot be detached: a kind of logical lifeline to their reality.

The argument is to pivot on the anthropological premise that we have rights so far as we are agents, action being inseparable from our essence as thought is in the less plausible anthropology of Descartes: "a body-bearing soul cannot sustain from action," the *Gita* says, addressing those for whom abstention seemed both an existential option and a prescription for estopping karma. I want to grant this premise, pausing to stress only that it will be action just as action which generates the rights, not this or that particular action. Someone may interfere with my performance of a certain action, but this will not automatically violate my rights as a human as it would be were he to interfere with the conditions which make action as action a possibility. This is somewhat difficult to construe philosophically, for it is not as though a wedge can be driven between me, on the one side, and those conditions on the other, if we accept the anothropology. Still, it will only be at this very general level that interference with *human* rights is possible, since their connection is with the most general conditions of action as action. So it will not be a violation of her human rights, but (perhaps) her rights as a women if *W* is prevented access to abortion. Her humanity, as it were, is left intact, even if her choice is foreclosed – and, indeed, it would be hard to see what a society could come to if foreclosure of choice were as such in violation of human rights. All that would be in violation of that, in what I perceive as Gewirth's scheme, would be foreclosure of choosing – not a limit on freedom but freedom's elimination.

So we are being asked to locate human rights "in the necessary conditions for human action": the most general conditions there can be, given the anthropology, since there cannot be action if they do not hold. Without them, indeed, *morality* is impossible, "since no morality, together with the goods, virtues, and rules emphasized in diverse moralities, is possible without the necessary goods of action." The "necessary goods of action" are, as we shall see, just the conditions necessary for action which, from the agent's point of view, he *must* have. These are "the Objects of human rights." Hence, human rights are presupposed by every morality that presupposes action, as almost all do, and must be consistent with each morality, though moralities be inconsistent each with each.

I find appealing the thought that human rights lie outside every moral system because presupposed by morality as morality, since it makes an attack on human rights an attack on morality as such, and immediately yields up the universality claimed for human rights in the great enabling documents. It gives a common ground to which those who work on behalf of human rights can appeal, since they share it with abusers, and it offers them a neutral place to stand which enables Amnesty International, for example, to justify its claim that there are human rights and that these rights are not politically parochial or ideologized. Universality is, I think, a more important philosophical achievement to aim for than equality, since I should think equality falls out just from the meaning of the concept: if human rights are what we are entitled to on grounds of our humanity, they must be the same for humans as humans, humanity not being something which admits of difference or degree. This is what makes the analogy to distributive justice a poor one. There will be such justice only in certain societies organized on principles of equity. But human rights must be invariant to all, admitting that there are wide variations in their recognition and protection. Universality follows from the grounding of human rights in the most general conditions for human action, so if that fails it is a noble failure, and we must look elsewhere for grounds. I think it does fail, or at least I am unsure it succeeds, which brings me, then, to the argument which is the *pièce montée* of Professor Gewirth's logical banquet.

The concept of action is to play a crucial logical role in the argument by enabling passage across the fact/value gap, which Gewirth claims it does. To act is to do something for some end E, which entails that from the agent's point of view "E is good." "E is good" cannot divest itself of quotation marks, being something said or at least thought by an agent, doubtless too bent on E to recite even to himself that it is good, and there will be a severe problem of disquotation, since it will not follow from "E is good," said by him from within his point of view, that E is good, and even within quotations this need not be a moral use of "good." All that "E is good" conveys is that the E-directed agent *ipso facto* makes a value judgment on behalf of E, there being no action save for some end and the end in every instance is regarded as the good from the perspective of him who acts for its sake. "For the agent," "from the agent's point of view," "within the context of action," "from the agent's standpoint," are qualifiers as necessary as and discharging much the same function as quotation marks, and no more than they are they eliminable from the argument, since it is with reference to and on the basis of them that the "dialectically necessary method" does its work. Each component of the argument "begins as being made or accepted by the agent; it proceeds from within and is relative to his own first-person conative perspective." So it really is a Cartesian kind of argument, turning on certain features of the grammar of the first-person case. True, Gewirth says "the statements in question logically must be made or accepted by every agent." That is to say, each agent may voice them from within his own perspective, since their content and structure pretty much define what one's own perspective is. But problems arise when I speak of others from outside their perspective, as inevitably I must, they not being me. What is valid from the first-person perspective may not be valid at all from the perspective of third-persons, just because there are asymmetries between first and third-person grammar which are damaging unfortunately just where Gewirth needs them. I may say, for instance, that to the degree that *he* – some third person – acts, he makes a value judgment. But "he makes a value judgment" is not a value judgment but the ascription of one, or really a judgment of fact, it being a fact that people do make value judgments, or even must make them if they act. So in the third-person we do not cross the fact/value gap, but the fact/fact gap, if that, and to no remarkable philosophical moment. From the third person's perspective it may be crossed, but from mine it is not, and, of course, conversely.

The structure of discourse, here, resembles too closely the celebrated paradox of Moore not to remark the analogy. I cannot say of myself that I believe what is not the case, but of another I can say that he believes what is not the case. "I believe that p but p is false" is a kind of incoherent statement, though not formally contradictive, but all suggestion of incoherence vanishes when we move from "I" to "he." It is sometimes said that to believe that p is to believe p is true, but what this finally must mean is not a psychological necessity but a verbal one: there may be things I can believe which I cannot say. Saying (or thinking) is what generates incoherences, such as they are, as much in doxastic domains as in the domain of action as depicted by Gewirth. But were someone to say that he has crossed the belief/truth gap he would be rash, even if he lamely were to add: "I mean from within the perspective of the fact that I believe there are external objects I cannot coherently doubt that there are." It would be rash just because to the degree that we have the first-person/third-person differences, we appreciate that it is quite possible to believe what is not the case, and so taking it for granted that I am a third-person to a possible other, it is possible to construe me as a third-person to myself. True once more, there are things I cannot *say* coherently. I cannot say, for instance "I cannot say anything" as the utterance is blasted by the conditions of its utterance. But *that* does not guarantee a status of logical loquacity on me. No gap I can recognize has been crossed, and to the degree that its traversal is a condition for the sort of argument human rights depends on, Gewirth has not furnished it.

Let us, now, consider the central components (3) and (4), "My freedom and well-being are necessary goods," and its modal rephrase, "I must have freedom and well-being." Now (3) is said to follow from (2), and perhaps it does from the first-person perspective, but I wonder whether they in any sense connect in the third-person form: it is from the outside quite possible that certain things are necessary to a person without it following that he necessarily has them: men need oxygen, for instance, but it is possible for them to lack it.

And it has to be possible for rights to be violated, even if this means depriving humans of goods necessary to them. Gewirth moves somewhat too easily in and out of first-person reasoning. Freedom and well-being are defended as necessary conditions of action, but their being necessary *goods* at best follows from within the first-person perspective, as does the speaker's having rights to those goods, in (5). I can basically see someone arguing that if x is good (as it must be – for me – if I pursue x), then whatever I need in order to get x is derivatively good – for me. But I don't see it following that I have *rights* to what I need in order to get x unless I have a right to x. And even within the first-person perspective I fail to see that it follows from something being good that I have a right to it. A rapist may well declare that what he takes by force is good, and his taking it by force is good as well – but that he has a right to what he has taken or a right to take it is virtually to deny that it was rape.

To what sort of freedom do I have a right? If it is the sort of freedom held to be a necessary condition for action as action, it is, I should think, metaphysical freedom, and while I may regard this as a good and somewhat emptily claim a right to it, it is difficult to see what depriving me of it could consist in short of depriving the world of *me*. A prisoner still can act, is still capable of action as action, and an extreme voluntarist like Sartre would echo the *Gita* in saying that the burden of freedom cannot be shifted off, however much I despise the constraints within which it is exercised. So, very likely what is meant is liberty, a political good rather than a metaphysical condition, or the kind of freedom slaves by definition lack. These freedoms do come close to what I consider human rights to be, and it is precisely freedom of conscience that Amnesty International identifies as having to be violated if the individual's rights of concern to the organization are violated. Yet it is difficult to see these as necessary conditions for action as action, or necessary goods, for it is plain that persons act in their absense, and fight for them when they lack them, and it would be cruel to say that they have them on the grounds that they are agents. In whatever sense the agent, from his point of view, *must* have such goods, it is consistent that others materially impede his enjoyment of them, since rights are thwarted at every turn. I would, of course, agree that they ought not to be if I ought to have those rights, and this is not just a matter of first-person perspective from within which Gewirch coaxes a first-person contradiction, but from the structure of deontology itself.

There is a marvelous, dilapidated cube once drawn by Saul Steinberg which dreams of itself as geometrically impeccable: with vertices a polyhedron might be proud of, sharp edges and invariant faces, and everything lettered and numbered *comme il faut*. I respect it for having its vision, as I respect Professor Gewirth for having his vision of the efficacy of reason to ground the rights of man. It would be a great day for reason beyond question, but, perhaps only from my point of view, the argument I have barely addressed seems very inadequate. Something as fragile and threatened as human rights are needs some better protection than an argument with itinerant operators, dependent upon the eccentricities of first-person implicatures and the internal presuppositions of points of view. Professor Gewirth has doubtless encountered these objections before, as they are obvious, and perhaps has answers to still them. So I shall be curious to hear what they can be. Before I defer to Gewirth, I would like to give a short characterization of a very different approach.

In the afterwash of 1968, I found myself a member of a group charged with working out disciplinary procedures for acts against my university. It was an exemplary group from the perspective of representation so urgent at the time: administrators, tenured and non-tenured faculty, graduate and undergraduate students, men and women, whites and blacks. We all wondered, nevertheless, what right we had to do what was asked of us, and a good bit of time went into expressing our insecurities. Finally, a man from the law-school said, with the tried patience of someone required to explain what should be plain as day, and in a tone of voice I can still hear: "This is the way it is with rights. You want'em, so you say you got'em, and if nobody says you don't then you do." In the end he was right. We worked a code out which nobody liked, but in debating it the community acknowledged the rights. Jefferson did not say that it was self-evident that there were human rights and which they were: he said we *hold* this for self-evident. He chose this locution mainly, I think, because he was more certain we have them than he was of any argument alleged to entail them, or of any premises from which their existence was to follow. This is the way it is with rights. We *declare* we have them, and see if they are recognized. After that it is a matter of lobbying or something more extreme than that, but having taken a stand on the moral limits of our personhood, we have no choice.

But what really does Gewirth's logical soliloquizer do at the crucial step (5) than *make a claim*, declare his rights to the goods of action, to what he *must* have not in the sense of necessity that action would be impossible without them, but that he needs them in order to act in conformity with his vision of humanity? Under the illusion, perhaps, that he has crossed the divide between fact and value, he may think he is just describing a fact when in truth he has only shifted mood. And if rights are what we must claim or which must be claimed on our behalf, well, there are no rights save in the framework of declaration and recognition. But then the project of constructing an *epistemology* of human rights reveals itself, to use a phrase which has been too *vieux jeu* for far too many decades now to be brought out without a degree of self-consciousness, a *pseudo problem*. That's just not the way it works.

Philosophy, Columbia University

Social Philosophy & Policy Vol. 1 Issue 2 ISSN 0265-0525

REPLY TO DANTO

ALAN GEWIRTH

I want to comment briefly on seven points in Professor Danto's discussion of my paper.

1. He says that according to my conception of the existence of human rights, their *esse est demonstrari* – that is, for human rights to exist is for them to be demonstrated. He also says that, according to my thesis, "what one argues for cannot be separated from . . . the argument itself . . ."

Now this is true in one sense but not in another. There is an ambiguity in Danto's use of words like "demonstrari" and "argument." These words may refer either to particular, contingent *attempts* at demonstration and argument or to rationally necessary *structures* of demonstration and argument. Danto's remarks might suggest that it is in the former sense that I tie the existence of human rights to argument. But, on the contrary, it is obviously the latter meaning that I use when I say: "That human rights exist . . . is a proposition whose truth depends on the possibility , *in principle*, of constructing a body of moral justificatory argument from which that proposition follows as a logical consequence," and that "for human rights to exist . . . means that there are *conclusive* moral reasons that justify or ground the moral requirements that constitute the Nature of human rights . . ." (emphasis added). The existence of such reasons is independent of whether this or that particular justificatory argument is successful; such reasons are discovered, not invented. Hence, what I argue for, that human rights exist, can be separated from my own or anyone else's *attempts* at argument.

My general point is that rights are a kind of attribute that belong to persons; but they are not empirical attributes; rather, they are normative attributes, in that they entail requirements about how persons ought to be treated. Hence, we ascertain that persons do have these attributes not by empirical inquiry, but rather by ascertaining relevant, appropriate normative reasons.

2. Danto says that my argument does not cross the fact/value gap, as I hold that it does. But his basis for this assertion is unclear. He recognizes that the fact/value gap *is* crossed from within the agent's first-person perspective; thus Danto writes, "To act is to do something for some end E, which entails that from the agent's point of view 'E is good' . . . All that 'E is good' conveys is that the E-directed agent *ipso facto* makes a value judgment on behalf of E . . ." But

this is just what I hold and all that I need to hold. I was making a point about the crossing of the fact/value gap only from within the agent's *first-person* perspective, not from any *third*-person perspective.

Hence, when Danto draws an analogy between the fact/value gap as I use it and what he calls "tne belief-truth gap," this analogy does not apply. For he here takes "truth" as something that is objective and not relative to the agent's (or anyone else's) belief-perspective. But in my reference to the fact/value gap I take "value" as being relative to the *agent's* perspective, i.e. the fact that he acts for end E entails that, *within* his perspective, E is good. This confinement to the agent's perspective simply means that the agent, by virtue of acting for E, *regards* E as good.

3. Danto questions my move from step (4), "I must have freedom and well-being," to step (5), "I have rights to freedom and well-being." The reason he gives for questioning this is that, "I don't see it following that I have rights to what I need in order to get X unless I have a right to X," and he gives rape as an example of an X to which an agent would *not* claim a right. But Danto, here, overlooks the difference between contingent and necessary ends or goods, and, hence, also the way in which right-claims enter the argument. The agent does not claim a right to freedom and well-being merely because they are necessary to his performing some one particular action as against another. Rather, he claims a right to freedom and well-being because they are the necessary conditions of his performing *any* and *every* action, either at all or with general chances of success. Hence, the object of his right-claim has a kind of necessity and universality that does not pertain to any of his particular actions as such.

This point is closely connected to my use of the dialectically necessary method. The agent is assumed to be rational in the sense that he recognizes that the argument is to be confined to his *necessary* beliefs about what is *necessarily* involved in his action, because such beliefs provide an objective standpoint from which his contingent, controversial beliefs and purposes can be rationally evaluated. Hence, the agent in my argument is logically justified in claiming a right only to the necessary conditions of his action or successful action in general, but not to the particular objects or ends of his particular actions. The establishment of such particular rights must wait upon further justificatory argument that can come only after a general moral principle about rights has been established.

4. Danto asks, "To what sort of freedom do I have a right?" He considers just two possibilities, which he calls "metaphysical freedom" and "political freedom"; and he points out that the former is so inherent in being human that no one can be deprived of it except by being killed; while political freedom cannot be a necessary condition of action because persons can act even in its absence.

Now, the freedom I am primarily concerned with here is neither meta-physical freedom nor political freedom, but rather freedom of action. This freedom consists in controlling one's behaviour by one's own unforced choice, and hence without external interference, while having knowledge of relevant circumstances. Persons can, of course, be deprived of this freedom by violence, coercion, deception, and in other ways. Such freedom is a necessary, general condition of each particular action. If someone is deprived of it on one occasion, he may, of course, still have it on other occasions; but still, for every particular action its presence is a necessary condition.

There is also, however, a connection between such freedom of action and political freedom. This connection is especially involved in my thesis that freedom and well-being are necessary conditions not only of *action* but also of *successful* action in general, where such success consists in achieving the purposes for which one acts. For the absence of political freedom may sharply restrict persons' range of successful actions: not only slaves but also other subjects of repressive regimes.

5. Danto says: "Something as fragile and threatened as human rights needs some better protection than an argument with itinerant operators, dependent upon the eccentricities of first-person implicatures and the internal pre-suppositions of points of view." Here, as elsewhere in his comments, Danto overlooks that my argument is restricted to the *necessary* structure of action, as my use of the dialectically necessary method requires. Thus he overlooks, for example, that in what he calls the "eccentricities of first-person implicatures" these "implicatures" must be accepted by all agents because they derive from the generic features of purposive action. Hence, they have a kind of necessity and universality which gives the argument for human rights the sort of firm status that Danto correctly says they need.

6. Danto suggests that there is no need for any epistemological argument to answer the question of how we know there are any human rights. Referring to Jefferson, he says that "he was more certain we have them than he was of any argument alleged to entail them . . . This is the way it is with rights." But Danto is mistaken if his point, here, is that belief in human rights is so widespread in our culture or tradition that no justificatory argument is needed. If Bentham or Marx or Nietzsche, or their followers, are held to be included in our culture or tradition, then it contains important elements that are antithetical to the idea of human rights. And if they are not so included, then our culture or tradition is confronted by important, ongoing currents of thought and action that are antithetical to the idea of human rights. In either case, then, one cannot soundly maintain that belief in human rights is so strong in our culture or tradition that no attempt at argument or proof is needed.

7. Danto offers, as his own candidate for the basis of rights, a kind of performative theory whereby the unchallenged claiming of rights is sufficient

to establish their existence: "you say you got 'em, and if nobody says you don't then you do." Here, Danto substitutes for "the eccentricities of first-person implicatures" the vagaries of second-person declarations. But he ignores such questions as these: what if someone, like, say, Brezhnev or Pinochet, says you *don't* have the rights? Does this, therefore, go any way toward *establishing* that you don't? When Danto, then, says that "there are no rights save in the framework of recognition," he incurs the ambiguity I noted near the beginning of my paper, where "there are" can refer either to social recognition or to moral justification. To make rights dependent entirely on declaration and recognition would mean that slaves and other oppressed groups would have no rights even in the sense of moral justification. In place of this shaky, rhetorical basis for rights, I have tried to show that human rights have a firm foundation, which no agent can disavow, in the necessary conditions of human action.

Social Philosophy & Policy Vol. 1 Issue 2 ISSN 0265-0525

PERSONAL PROJECTS AS THE FOUNDATION FOR BASIC RIGHTS

LOREN LOMASKY

A theory of basic moral rights ought to aim at telling us who the beings are that have rights and of what those rights consist. It may, however, seek to achieve that goal via an indirect route. In this paper I shall attempt a strategy of indirection. The first stage of the argument is a consideration of why moral theory can allow any place at all to rights. Acknowledging rights can be inconvenient. An otherwise desirable outcome is blocked if the only ways in which it can be attained involve the violation of rights. Why not jettison rights and thereby render these outcomes achievable? The answer that will be suggested trades on it being a deep fact about human beings that they can and do order their lives by reference to long-term commitments and aspirations. In my terminology, they are *project pursuers*. If people were rational animals all of whose interests were flickering and evanescent, an ethic entirely resting on maximization of impersonal value would be appropriate. But because projects entail commitments to values not subject to trade-offs, the introduction of rights is plausible.

That is the first major stage of the argument. The second builds on it and tries to show that the recognition of rights or their equivalent is morally required, that only an ethic in which basic rights are acknowledged can be properly responsive to persons' status as project pursuers. More particularly, it is suggested that rights take the form of constraints imposing minimal forbearance on others such that one has reasonable expectations of being able to pursue one's projects amidst a world of other project pursuers. Basic rights, then are largely, but not necessarily entirely claims to noninterference.

I

What is it that we do when we ascribe moral rights to a being? At least in part it is to single out certain interests of that being as possessing special urgency. It is not necessary that he in fact prize these interests, that he *take an interest* in them. That is why it makes sense to ascribe rights to very young children, wastrels, and lunatics. Nor is it the case that one who cares deeply that some state of affairs obtain thereby acquires some right to its production.[1] The connection is not so neat as that, though, as I shall argue having interests safeguarded by rights is systematically associated with the ability to take an interest. But if there are any rights, then there must be interests which occupy a privileged moral position. They are interests that one may legitimately claim (or have claimed on one's behalf by another) as one's due.[2]

Looked at from the perspective of one transacting with a rights holder, rights are seen as establishing boundaries that may not be crossed at one's will. One's actions must rather be gauged so as not to encroach on those interests of others which are enjoyed as a matter of right. Ronald Dworkin speaks of rights as *trumps*;[3] Robert Nozick describes them as providing *side constraints* upon action.[4] The two locutions have similar if not identical force;[5] they announce to individuals and governments alike, "Even if some goal of yours is intensely desired, you may not pursue it in a manner involving the violation of someone's rights."

Because rights do constrain conduct, they may be barriers to getting to where one wants to go. This can be galling to reformers, revolutionaries, and nation states with vast designs for social reconstruction. It is, then, not entirely surprising that the chief service paid by ambitious governments to the cause of human rights is lip service. But why, morally speaking, should it be otherwise? Is it not simply unreasonable to be bound by side constraints that prevent movement from a situation of lesser overall well-being to one of greater, perhaps markedly greater, well-being? There is a need to explain why it is rational to accept a social order that rejects the attainment of otherwise good results simply because they involve rights violations.

The beginning of an answer can be found in the observation that rights rule out certain trade-offs in which the interests of one person are sacrificed for the

---

[1] See Thomas Scanlon, "Preference and Urgency," *Journal of Philosophy* 72 (1975): 655–669. For a contrary position see Michael Tooley, "Abortion and Infanticide," *Philosophy and Public Affairs* 2 (1972): 37–65.

[2] Joel Feinberg, "Duties, Rights and Claims," *American Philosophical Quarterly*, 3 (1966) 137–144; and "The Nature and Value of Rights," *Journal of Value Inquiry*, 4 (1970) 243–257.

[3] *Taking Rights Seriously* (Cambridge: Harvard University Press, 1977), Introduction, xi.

[4] *Anarchy, State, and Utopia* (New York: Basic Books, 1974), 29.

[5] A side constraint defines what is permissible within a game, practice or institution. It cannot be violated without stepping outside of that activity. Cashing out the metaphor of a trump, x can trump y but be overtrumped by z, all within the context of a particular game. So the restriction of encroachment imposed by a right taken as a side constraint is conceptually stricter than that of a right as trump (which can have a low position within an indefinitely extended hierarchy of trumps). This is borne out by a comparison of Dworkin's and Nozick's accounts of the place of rights. For Nozick rights are almost unabridgable, possibly giving way in a situation where "catastrophic moral horror" otherwise impends (*Anarchy, State, and Utopia*, footnote, 30). Dworkin's rights are less sturdy, how much less so not being clearly indicated. The model of side constraints is a simpler one to work with, and I shall adopt it for this paper even though that ducks the hard question of the absoluteness of moral rights.

sake of another. The infliction of an injury upon A even to prevent a yet greater misfortune befalling B is judged impermissible. This way of construing rights evokes familiar philosophical formulations: individuals are inviolable; persons are not interchangeable one with another; rational agents must be treated as ends in themselves and not merely as means. That so many strands of thought congregate at just this point suggests its importance. Unfortunately though, none of these formulations is so clear and persuasive as to be self-validating. Indeed, the reverse is the case; each is notoriously slippery. One is strongly drawn toward regarding this as the embarcation point for an explication of rights, but it is not obvious how to make headway.

I suggest the following strategy; let us proceed indirectly by examining the supposition that individuals' interests are perfectly interchangeable such that it is entirely proper to make any trade-off that increases our preferred measure of social good, say overall utility.[6] That moral stance will be seen to rest on a very different conception of persons and their ends than that which underlies a morality based on respect for human rights. If the former conception of persons is unacceptable, then interchangeability must be rejected. Its rejection is not equivalent to the justification of a rights-based morality, but it is to make the first crucial move in that direction.

One acts in order to attain some end which one values. It may be a distant consequence of the action not to be enjoyed for many years, or it may be the doing of the action itself. The two are not exclusive; the action may be chosen for its own sake, for the pleasure of doing that very thing *and* it may be done for the sake of valued consequences that will flow from it. Bodily movements like a twitch or knee jerk reflex can occur without there being any purpose to them, but action is inherently purposive.

One acts in order to attain some end which one values, but not all ends are equally valued. One may act to satisfy a transitory desire assigned little weight: pausing briefly to smell a flower, scratching a minor itch. Or it may be to promote some momentous good to which one is wholeheartedly devoted. Almost always, when a person pursues one good, it is at the expense of another that could have been secured in its place. If I stop to smell the flower, then I arrive at my destination somewhat later; if I spend my money on a philosophy book, then I cannot use it to buy roast beef. In the economists' jargon, the use of a scarce resource, including one's time, has an *opportunity cost* that is represented as the next most highly valued choice forgone. Because action has

---

[6] For convenience sake, I shall take the standard of value as utility. That is not necessary for the argument to go through. It could instead be a proxy function for utility such as real GNP or an index of Rawlsian primary goods. Alternatively, the standard of value could respond to actions as they promote survival of the fittest members of the species, fidelity to the Categorical Imperative, or obedience to Divine commands. All that is required is that the standard be equally and impartially applied to all moral actors.

costs, it is rational for a person to choose in a way that gives precedence to more highly valued goods over those of lesser value. The disagreeability of going to the dentist today will be weighed against the pleasure of playing tennis instead, but also against the misery of the toothache that might eventuate in the future. Skill in juggling alternative possibilities for action by reference to their respective opportunity costs is the virtue of *prudence*.

The prudent man, then, is someone who finds reason to trade-off lesser satisfactions for greater ones. He is instantly recognizable under the guise of *homo economicus*. Economizing activity is rational because it involves the maximization of goods at a time and over time. More precisely, it is the maximization of *one person's* good. That qualification suggests an extension: if it is rational to maximize satisfaction over time, then it is equally rational to maximize satisfaction over persons. This result is one important version of the many doctrines that have gone by the name 'utilitarianism.' Its basis is the proposition that the rationality of morality is isomorphic to the rationality of prudence.[7]

Modeling morality on prudence may be seen as revolving around a strengthened conception of *impartiality*. The prudent man treats impartially, *ceteris paribus*, satisfaction of a desire at one stage of his life and the attainment of some other satisfaction at another stage of his life.[8] He acts prudently if he seeks to achieve maximum value over the course of his life. By parity of reasoning, moral impartiality involves giving equal consideration to the welfare of all those who will be affected by one's actions. It takes as irrelevant *whose* ends are being advanced, just as prudence classifies *when* a desire is satisfied as, by itself, irrelevant. If persons' ends conflict, then moral rationality dictates that net overall well-being be maximized. Impartiality so understood is not only often argued to be commendable, but even to be constitutive of morality, to be a defining feature of assuming "the moral point of view."[9]

Before we accept or, as I shall argue, reject this notion of impartiality, it is important to scrutinize the theory of rational motivation it presupposes. One is to be moved to act on the basis of considerations that are neutral with respect to whose interests are advanced. If end E_1 is favored by person A and E_2 by B and if E_1 and E_2 cannot be jointly realized, it is impermissible for one to favor E_1 merely on the grounds that it is A who prizes E_1. Partiality for A may not be invoked as *any reason at all* for choosing to realize E_1, let alone as the decisive factor. Of course, one may *feel* disposed to prefer A's end to B's, one's *empathy* may be more engaged by A, one may *delight* in A's good but be cold to B's;

---

[7] A significant nonutilitarian presentation of this theme is Thomas Nagel's *The Possibility of Altruism* (Oxford: Clarendon Press, 1970).

[8] I avoid consideration here of problems involved with discounting over time.

[9] I repeat that this need not result in utilitarianism. Any standard of value applied impartially as a test of rightness among all persons meets this formal condition.

insofar however as the agent is choosing rationally, he must totally discount those bases for deciding between advancing E_1 and advancing E_2.

Suppose though that *I* am A and am to choose between advancing my end or deferring in favor of B's. Does this offer a morally relevant consideration? Not for the theory now under consideration. Temptations to favor oneself, to value one's own ends higher simply on the grounds that they are one's own, are to be counted as irrational from the point of view of morality. Such irrational partiality is analogous to the imprudent man's snatching at a near-term satisfaction at the expense of a competing more distant satisfaction that outweighs it. It may be psychologically explicable why I am drawn to advancing E_1, but that does not amount to a justification for advancing E_1. To be sure, there may be reasons which, most of the time, validate a person's pursuing his own ends. They are the ends about which he knows most, is causally best situated to pursue, etc. These sorts of considerations are often brought up in the literature concerning utilitarianism. In each case, an impersonal standard of value, one that holds irrespective of agents' particular concerns, is invoked to weigh the respective merits of promoting one's own ends or relinquishing them in favor of another person's. Only by way of such impartiality, it might be claimed, is morality able to fulfill its most important function: service as an arbiter in cases of interpersonal conflict. Only if there is one standard of value to be applied in scrupulously identical fashion among all persons is the Hobbesian war of all against all to be avoided. The end scoring highest according to this standard is, in all cases, to be preferred. If E_1, which is my end, loses out, then so be it.

II

While each of my ends is identically mine, they differ from each other in terms of the intensity of my desire for them. Intensity is one indicator of the gravity of an end within a person's life, but it is not the only or even the most important indicator. A craving for a second handful of peanuts may be well-nigh irresistible for an agent who is simultaneously aware that eating the peanuts is a negligible component of his good. To more accurately discriminate between relatively trivial and relatively momentous ends, it is necessary also to consider how they differ in terms of their persistence and centrality throughout large stretches of an individual's life. Those ends which reach indefinitely into the future, play a central role within the various endeavors of the person, and which provide structural stability to his life I call *projects*. Projects take diverse forms and are pursued by both saints and sinners. They include: working for the Dictatorship of the Proletariat, serving God, serving Mammon, raising one's children to be responsible adults, attaining excellence as a disco dancer, acquiring wealth beyond dreams of avarice. An important genus of projects includes those directed at becoming and remaining a certain kind of person: being a man of one's word, a lover of beauty, a compassionless executioner. What this sundry lot has in common is that each of these is irreducible to isolated episodes of satisfying desire. It is more the reverse; whether a particular state of affairs counts as an outcome to be valued is largely a function of the projects to which one is committed. Scratching one's ear because it itches has a certain value almost irrespective of the overarching aims of one's life. But turning down a higher paying job in order to devote oneself more fully to one's family cannot usually be successfully explained simply in terms of the intensity of some passing desire. It is a grave mistake within moral psychology, from which other serious mistakes follow, to analyze all choice as on the model of relieving an itch. Lives are not a sequence of discrete episodes of responding to whatever desire is perceived at that moment to be most insistent. Rather, lives have a structure that lends intelligibility to particular choices. At least that is so for project pursuers. It is not possible to explain a project pursuer's various purposive actions without a prior recognition of the agent's abiding commitments.

What this means is that a project pursuer cannot be an indiscriminate evaluator, one open to motivation from an unlimited number of directions. Instead, by committing himself to one or several ends above all others, he has thereby restricted the range of attainable situations that can serve as inducements to action. A project pursuer cannot be a volitional *tabula rasa*. His volitions have become channeled, not in every respect and not come what may (in part because what may come is a radical change of heart), but channeled nonetheless in virtue of the ends that he has chosen to serve. Projects are filters through which only some motivations pass. The fact that some action would conflict with project pursuit is in itself reason to reject motivation from that direction. I deliberately say *reason* and not merely *cause*; the claim is that one who has actively and autonomously chosen to devote oneself to a certain sort of life is rationally committed to evaluating outcomes in terms of their conduciveness to the ends which individuate that particular life.

Projects clash with impartiality. To be committed to a long-term design, to order one's activities in light of it, to judge one's success or failure as an acting being by reference to its fate; these are inconceivable apart from a frankly partial attachment to one's ends. If E_1 is bound up with A's conception of the type of person he is and the kind of life he has chosen to lead, then he cannot regard its attainment as subject to trade-off with B's E_2 simply on the ground that some impersonal standard of value ranks E_2 above E_1. Rather, A will appraise possible courses of action by reference to a personal standard of value. His central and enduring ends provide him reasons for action that are recognized as his own in the sense that no one who is not committed to those very ends will share the reasons for action that he possesses. Practical reason is *essentially differentiated* among project pursuers, not merely contingently differentiated by the unique causal constraints each person confronts from his own distinct spatio-temporal location. That E_1 can be advanced by A might provide A overwhelmingly good reason to act. That B could equally effectively advance E_1 might merit vanishingly little weight in B's moral deliberations. To put it slightly differently, practical reason is inherently and ineliminably indexical. A will regard the assertion, "E_1 is *my* deep concern," as a significant reason in itself for his seeking to advance E_1 rather than some competing end.

The foregoing should not be misunderstood. It is not being claimed that project pursuit insulates one from all reason to consider the well-being of others. It has not even been denied that one may have compelling reason to sacrifice a deeply cherished ideal for the sake of another's good. Rather, my point is that commitment to one's projects is incompatible with regarding some impersonal standard of value as sufficient to justify trading off ends to which one has undertaken commitments. It is to call into question the view that morality is a certain kind of skill in trading off lower utility outcomes for higher ones (plus the willingness to apply that skill whatever the circumstances). For beings who undertake commitments, not everything is open to trade-offs. The opposed view takes all ends as like commodities that have an established market price: x units of honesty trading for y units of hunger relief or z of ballet appreciation. A skilled commodity trader will transact at the price that maximizes returns. After all, he deals in items that, as it were, are held at arm's length. He holds onto them tentatively, always ready to barter them for a different package that adds up to greater value. This is an inappropriate model to apply to a morality that must come to terms with commitment to projects.[10]

Moral reasoning that is sensitive to the existence of personal projects should not be construed as narrowly egoistic. A's strong attachment to E_1 is matched by B's attachment to E_2 – and A can be fully aware that it is. If A is consistent, he will acknowledge that B's reluctance to sacrifice E_2 follows from B's status as a project pursuer. While A does not share B's commitment to E_2, both A and B may be equally able to conclude that B has overwhelmingly good reason to value the promotion of E_2 rather than E_1. Generalization over persons of rational motivation to pursue their own projects is, thus, also a species of impartiality, though different from the one previously criticized. Instead of propounding one impersonal standard of value invariant among persons, impartiality at this level recognizes as many standards of value as there are persons, each one providing reasons for action to that person. It involves the

---

[10] "Would you accept $1 million to kill your father and sleep with your mother?" Is the question crass and insulting because the price is too low? Because it is expressed in the wrong unit?

recognition that each individual will judge his actions from his own unique vantage point, and that each is acting rationally by so doing. Displacing impartiality to this higher level has the virtue of making sense out of commitment to projects.

At bottom, the two conceptions of morality that have been opposed rest on different analyses of the relations persons bear to their own ends. There is a metaphysical gulf that separates one from the other. Emphasis on the moral significance of project pursuit is based on a conception of personal identity over time which incorporates not only criteria of memory retention and bodily continuity but also persistent attachment to one's ends. As an active being, one's identity is not simply a given but is created and recreated continuously through *identifying* oneself with one's projects.[11] One understands a life as a life, and not merely a jumble of discrete episodes, by focusing on motivational patterns that persist over long periods of time and order a large number of particular variations. "This is someone who, three years ago, decided to plant tomatoes in his backyard garden," provides insubstantial information about the person's purposive dimension. But saying, "She is an ardent Zionist"; "He is a Cicero scholar," is to begin to explain a life.

A coherent life, coherent from both the outside *and* the inside, is not open to motivation from just any direction. Rather, it will systematically embrace some potential sources of value and stand aloof from others. Consider a variation on a theme from Kafka in which a person awakens one morning to find that he has the body of a loathsome insect. Suppose that instead of a bodily metamorphosis he had undergone an equally radical volitional transformation. That to which he was formerly drawn he is now indifferent; outcomes he had previously worked to avert now command his allegiance. And suppose further that such shifts occurred regularly and could assume an unlimited variety of forms. In such a scenario, the unity of the person as an acting, purposive being would have completely broken down. Indiscriminate evaluators of this sort are different in kind from project pursuers, and even if it makes sense to suppose them bound by some moral framework, it would be a morality different from that applied by and to project pursuers.

A less fanciful way to understand the difference that attention to projects makes in the conception of a person is as follows. If practical reason is essentially different among persons then, if E_1 is A's end, A recognizes not simply that there is reason for E_1's advancement but also that there is reason-

---

[11] Derek Parfit has skillfully argued that less hangs on personal identity than is commonly supposed. See his "Personal Identity," *Philosophical Review* 80 (1971): 3–27; "On 'The Importance of Self-Identity'," *Journal of Philosophy* 68 (1972): 683–690. Attention to the status of projects yields a similar conclusion: self-identity understood as a passively received endowment is metaphysically shallow; the identity one forges through one's extended undertakings is metaphysically and morally rich.

for-E_1's-advancement-by-A. Whatever reason B may have to cooperate in the pursuit of E_1, B's reason to advance E_1 is not identical to A's reason to advance E_1. Conversely, if projects are absent from moral theory, each person has equal reason to advance any end that is endorsed by the impersonal standard of value. That E_1 emerges because of some volitional act of A provides A no reason to advance E_1 that is not also reason for B to advance E_1. That is because the value E_1 holds out is not specifically value-for-A or value-for-B; it is simply (impersonal) value.

But then in what sense can E_1 be said to be A's end? True, it originated within the psycho-physical organism that is A. But once it comes into being, it stands equally as an object worthy of promotion by all agents able to help it along. The reason for its advancement is its utility score, not A's idiosyncratic attachment to it. An end that is equally an item of value for all persons though is, in no distinctive sense, A's. That is, E_1 is entirely common property.

The result is a breakdown in the individuation of persons along the purposive dimension. It was argued that one crucial element of identity over time is the identity created by a person through his commitments to some overriding ends and concomitant rejection of motivation by others. But if all persons have equivalent reason to bring about every state of affairs, then all distinctions along this dimension vanish. An impersonal standard of value entails complete conformity in rational motivation. The especially intimate relation between a person and his ends – his very own ends – ceases to exist. Of course, to the extent that agents do in practice deviate from this impersonal standard of motivation, they at least implicitly accept divergency among persons of reasons for promotion of particular ends. I claim that this is to be welcomed rather than described as a lamentable clash between self-interest and the demands of morality. A moral impartiality that finds no place for projects is theoretically deficient because it is unable to find room for, let alone justify, a unique relationship obtaining between an agent and his own ends.

III

If this paper were primarily a venture in descriptive metaphysics, it would be appropriate to argue at much greater length and with much more rigor for the claim that a correct analysis of what we fundamentally take persons to be must incorporate project pursuit. Instead, I shall assume that this claim has been rendered at least plausible by the preceding discussion and go on to draw some applications for a theory of basic rights. The one that immediately suggests itself is that enhanced sharpness can be given to the previously vague notion of individuals not being interchangeable one for another. According to moral theories that acknowledge an impersonal standard of value, there exists a universal human enterprise in which we are all summarily enrolled. It is the ceaseless and perpetual endeavor to maximize utility or to maximize whatever other good is sovereign. Each being is a soldier on the line, and though they stand in different positions and wield different armaments, their cause is the same. This is nicely captured by Charles Fried's assertion that, "men have [claims] on each other by virtue of their common humanity, to help maintain and further *their enterprise* as free rational beings pursuing *their life plan*."[12] Note especially the occurrence of 'life plan' in the singular. Implicit in this picture is that while individuals may fall by the wayside, the enterprise goes on. However, it then becomes utterly mysterious why there should be anything suspect about sacrificing one of the troops for another just so long as more impersonal value is thereby attained. Interchangeability is inextricably built into that picture: all else equal, one producer of value can be replaced by another producer of value without any effect on overall value. That which leaves overall value unchanged is, tautologously, morally neutral.

Alternatively, interchangeability no longer looms if one denies that there is a universal human enterprise in which all of us alike are participants. There can be as many enterprises as there are agents, and every agent applies a personal standard of value to those states of affairs that are within his power to promote or impede. Therefore, there is no one impersonal standard of value in terms of which all ends are commensurable. From what perspective could one justify the claim that A and all of A's ends ought to be sacrificed for the considerably greater charm of B and B's ends? Certainly not from the perspective of A, and even if this result would conveniently follow from B's appraisal of value, it would not be rationally binding on A. To generalize, no project pursuer can be shown to be rationally obligated to sacrifice for the sake of someone else's interests that which is essential to his own ability to construct a worthwhile life (here understood very roughly as a life in which the persistent attachment to one's projects can be expressed in fitting activity). Such sacrifice is *supererogation*, not *duty*, a distinction that emerges with some clarity in the context of a project-regarding ethic. Utilitarianism and other ethical systems that endorse an impersonal standard of value have a notoriously difficult time finding room for any distinction between duty and supererogation because they are alike in the relevant respect of being instances of value maximization.

If an impersonal standard of value reigns, then lives possess instrumental value insofar as they are productive of whatever this standard takes to be of intrinsic worth. However, it is hard to see how lives can be of more than instrumental value, how they can be other than servants to the standard. For a utilitarian, persons turn out to be convenient loci at which and by which utility can be generated. Because rightness of action is a function of utility produc-

---

[12] Charles Fried, *Right and Wrong* (Cambridge: Harvard University Press, 1978), p. 124. Emphasis added.

tion, it is necessarily utility that counts primarily, persons only derivatively. By way of contrast, an ethic in which project pursuit assumes a central place is one in which each project pursuer is constructing a life which has unique value because he gives it that value through his commitment to some ends as directive for him. Value emerges from commitment, not because the world is empty of value before an Existentialist Hero essays a venture of radical choice, but for the most prosaic reason that commitment engenders a personal standard of value in terms of which possible outcomes are appraised. The value that emerges is conceptually posterior to commitment, not prior to and thus conditioning choice.

Again: to require A to renounce E_1 and to enroll him as B's partner in the pursuit of E_2 is to make A an adjunct to B's projects. This is how I construe the locution of treating someone merely as a means and not as an end in himself. For A to regard himself as an end, A must conceive of his life as being individuated by the commitments he has undertaken; A treats B as an end in himself when A respects B's commitments by not attempting to force B to serve A's projects. It is to accord to each project pursuer moral space within which he can autonomously attempt to realize a connected and coherent conception of the good for him.

Rights are just this entitlement to moral space. By establishing boundaries that others must not transgress, they accord to each right holder a measure of sovereignty over his own life. Thus, an ethic incorporating basic rights has the *shape* of an account sensitive to the importance of project pursuit. Because people undertake commitments that in large part determine what will be an object of motivation for them, they have reason to reject a social calculus that holds all ends subject to trade-off for higher scoring ends. That is, they have reason to reject morality conceived of as an exercise in unconstrained maximization in favor of a morality that incorporates side constraints. This does not amount to a justification of basic rights, but it suggests that whatever may emerge as best candidate for being an acceptable theory of morality will at least include elements that are like rights in creating moral space for individuals.[13]

The diversity of ends to which project pursuers can commit themselves has been emphasized. Is there, however, a common thread that runs through this diversity, an end that every project pursuer has reason to acknowledge? At least one suggests itself: the value of being a project pursuer. A first approximation of an argument for that result is: if A values the promotion of E_1, then A

---

[13] A stringent methodological principle will take a moral theory to be justified only if it meets some high standard of consistency, plausibility, theoretical economy, etc. and if, in addition, it is shown that no other theory meets a yet higher standard. A *very* stringent methodological principle insists on a uniqueness proof: no theory T' inconsistent with T meets a standard as high as the one T does. I have no idea how to go about showing that a theory of basic rights satisfies either of these strictures. It is an open question whether an account in which rights are entirely absent may incorporate some distinct notion that does everything rights can do (or more).

is rationally obliged to value his own ability to realize E_1. That inference though will not go through as it stands. Suppose what A values is that someone or other swim the English Channel. It is a matter of indifference to A who swims it, himself or B, so long as someone does. Also, if one person swims it, that is as good as if two people swim it. Therefore, if neither B nor anyone else were to swim the Channel, A would value his own swimming; but if B were to swim the Channel, then A would place no value on his own ability to do so. It seems, then, that whether a project pursuer values his own ability to pursue his projects is contingent; it will often but not always accompany having a project.

The initial idea can be sharpened. Commitment to an end is not merely the purely theoretical reflection that it would be good if that end were realized. It is instead the practical judgment that there is reason to act in order to bring about that end: A recognizes that there is reason for the promotion of E_1 but additionally, and more to the point, that there is reason-for-the-promotion-of-E_1-by-A. The unique relation that binds an agent to his own ends involves having reason to bring about those ends. Otherwise they would not be ends (for action) but at most what Aristotle calls objects of wish (*boulesis*).[14] This is a trivial truth, but what is not trivial is that human beings are constituted as project pursuers. That latter fact is, I believe, a far-reaching aspect of philosophical anthropology.

If A's attachment to E_1 is not merely the wish that E_1 somehow be made to obtain but instead the commitment to act in order to produce E_1, then A values his own ability to act for the sake of his own ends. He values being a project pursuer.

This result is considerably stronger than may at first seem to be the case. It is not a necessary truth that one who assigns positive value to some outcome O also values the circumstance of his valuing O. For example, a cigarette smoker may desire to smoke cigarettes, may be motivated by that desire to smoke cigarettes, yet, at a higher level, disvalue the circumstance of his desiring to smoke cigarettes.[15] Volition at one level need not be in harmony with volition at a higher level. One may be moved to do x and simultaneously value someone's preventing the doing of x.[16]

What is interesting about project pursuit is that it is not susceptible to disharmony in this way. Suppose that A is motivated to pursue E_1 yet fervently

[14] *Nicomachean Ethics*, 1111 b 26.

[15] See Harry Frankfurt, "Freedom of the Will and the Concept of a Person," *Journal of Philosophy* 68 (1971): 5–20.

[16] That is one reason why I think a derivation of rights from the bare fact of agency such as offered by Alan Gewirth in *Reason and Morality* (Chicago: University of Chicago Press, 1978) must fail. It is, though, an instructive failure. If agency is too spare a foundation for the derivation of rights, agency that has more determinate content may get one further along. Project pursuit is here being offered as the candidate for flesh that ought to cover and thus vivify the bare bones of agency. See my "Gewirth's Generation of Rights," *Philosophical Quarterly* 31 (1981): 248–253.

desires to be rid of the appalling desire for E_1. Then A has reason to bring about the state of affairs: A's not being motivated to pursue E_1. If that has directive force for his life such that it has implications for the value he assigns to a wide range of possible actions, if in other words it has the status of a project for A, then A values the ability to act so as to bring about the eradication of the desire for E_1. Even though the ability to pursue E_1 is disvalued, the *ability to be a project pursuer* has positive value for A.

The reason why project pursuit makes a difference here is that projects are taken to be those persistent desires which order a life and in terms of which other items are valued or disvalued. A being who has projects is one for whom there is a highest level that confers positive or negative value on lower level choices.[17] Therefore, commitments undertaken at the level of projects resound through all lower levels and entail that positive value is assigned to being a project pursuer.

This may look a bit like sleight of hand. But it is not maintained that project pursuit is a metaphysical Valium that causes all disharmony to vanish. Tension among values to which a person is attracted is expected to persist within a life; there are, after all, acute dilemmas for practical reasons. To be a project pursuer is not to transcend tension but to confront it. One constructs a life of greater coherence rather than less by utilizing a personal standard of value that itself is being created and recreated through one's choices in order to impose an ordering relation upon felt sources of sometimes disharmonious motivation. Success is usually a matter of more or less rather than all or nothing. But without the basis for imposing coherence that projects provide, a person would be simply the battleground on which disparate inclinations war. The absence of projects is a state of extreme psychosis in which one sees the breakdown of the person as an active being whose life has a recognizable unity.

Project pursuers, whatever their projects may be, value their ability to pursue projects. That means that they value having moral space. Because rights demarcate moral space, every project pursuer has reason to want to be accorded the status of a rights holder. Unfortunately, wanting doesn't make things so. That A wants B to accord A the status of a rights holder does not by itself in any way provide B reason so to regard A. At least this much more is required to get the progression toward rights underway: B must be able to recognize that A wants to be treated as a rights holder. That is why, to take an obvious example, rights claims cannot meaningfully be addressed to animals or forces of nature whose intrusion may be as undesirable as the intrusion of other men. (Puzzle: Could one meaningfully address a rights claim to a solipsist?) Need confers rights only when what is needed can be recognized by the one who can meet the need.

---

[17] Or, if there is no highest level but rather an infinite hierarchy, projects are those valuations such that at every higher level they are positively valued.

Crucially though, even this is insufficient to generate rights. A might need to be able to pursue his projects, A might need that B refrain from interfering with A, and B might recognize that A needs B's noninterference; still, a rights claim against B will not go through unless B has some rational motivation to respond to A's valuing being accorded the status of a rights holder. One can imagine a race of beings each of whom values the ability to pursue projects and whose abilities to do so require at least noninterference by others. Yet each is such as to be totally unmoved by the plight of the others. Their frantic strivings to give effect to their projects are viewed with the studied unconcern we might have for the doings of goldfish in a tank. "Whatever *it* is acting to bring about is no concern of mine," one of them might say. I suspect this is how we would respond to each other if each person's project were so different in kind from the projects of every other person that it would be inconceivable how anyone could succumb to motivation from *that* direction.

It is at this point that the generation of a theory of basic rights runs up against its toughest task: how can one go beyond the bare recognition of project pursuers to derive rational motivation to respect them as project pursuers? The problem is acute here because what's being bumped up against looks disturbingly like the is-ought divide. How can it be crossed? I am unsure what the best path to take is. Therefore I suggest three. Perhaps some one of them can be validated, perhaps luckily the passage is overdetermined, or, what I suspect to be the case, perhaps the most credible account of the basis of rational motivation involves elements of each.

The first line to be taken is to note that we are not in fact the sorts of beings described above: beings whose empathy is totally disengaged by the plights of their fellows. Rather, human beings are social animals whose survival is predicated upon being the beneficiaries of altruistic concern of a limited yet real scope. The organism's biology is such that it is totally dependent on others of its species throughout much of its life cycle and significantly dependent throughout the remainder. Thus, there is a sociobiological explanation of why the tendency to be moved by the needs of others, especially the needs of kin, has survival value and becomes a characteristic of the species. On this quasi-Aristotelian account, being motivated to accord others what they are known to need whatever else they might value is part of what it means to be human. Human rights emerge because there is not merely project pursuit but *human* project pursuit.

It is difficult not to be made uneasy by this move. Trickery is almost palpable.[18] One builds into an essentialist construal of man what one wants to

---

[18] However, if apparent trickery were to become a bar to philosophical respectability, an immense amount of the tradition would be uprooted: the ontological argument, Berkeley's idealism, some contemporary strategies.

churn out when it comes time to do ethical theory. If motivation to acknowledge and respect rights cannot be explained in a manner that amounts to a *justification*, the recourse is to offer a *causal* explanation rooted in the genes. Finally, what is explained turns out to be not exactly what was wanted in the first place: someone who fails to be motivated by the needs of others is not guilty of a moral failure so much as he is a sufferer from biological abnormality. In spite of these cautions, there remains an element of the approach that may have merit. If human beings are the sort of creatures who in fact can respond empathetically to each other, then they are the sort who *can* be motivated by recognition that others are project pursuers. A necessary but not sufficient basis for grounding rights has been uncovered.

The second line of approach is suggested by Thomas Nagel.[19] He argues that the ability to recognize oneself as one person in a world of other persons is logically sufficient to provide the basis for transmission of rational motivation. A's having end E_1 provides motivational force for A's pursuit of E_1, but also A's recognition that B has end E_2 provides A at least some reason to act so as to advance E_2. I say 'some reason,' because if value is not completely impersonal, then A's reason for promoting B's attainment of E_2 is not the same as nor as strong as B's reason for promoting B's attainment of E_2. Nonetheless, A recognizes that there does exist reason for bringing about E_2; possibly that very recognition has some motivational force. It could be put in this way: to recognize R as a reason for E_2 is thereby to acknowledge that it is not totally and in every respect indifferent whether E_2 obtain. R *is* why E_2 should obtain; otherwise R could not be conceived of as a reason. It may, of course, be one that is overwhelmingly overridden by other factors. In particular, A could acknowledge that B has reason (understood personally) to act in order to bring about E_2; thus there is (impersonal) reason to bring about E_2; thus A has some reason (understood personally) to advance E_2; however, A's commitment to his own projects entails pursuing E_1 which is incompatible with E_2.

This construal of the transmission of practical reason has much appeal. It provides a bridge between someone's *having a reason* and *there being reason*, that is, a bridge between personal value and impersonal value. A theory in which the two are completely disjoint (or where one is absent altogether) is untidy; because we can make sense of personal value and impersonal value as both being value, there ought to be some link between them. Perhaps the transmissibility of reason is that link. A related theoretical virtue is that there are not two radically different ways of understanding reason for action: understanding a reason as mine, which is suffused with motivational force, and understanding it as thine, which is entirely bereft of motivational force. Finally, the Nagel position wins out on grounds of simplicity over a theory that

---

[19] *The Possibility of Altruism*, especially Chapters XI and XII.

has to introduce some mediating instrumentality to explain how recognizing that E_2 is B's end provides A any reason to advance E_2.

It is not clear, though, that this approach is powerful enough to buttress a robust theory of rights. The reason transmitted from B to A can be vanishingly small. A has some reason to accord B the status of rights holder, but it may be supposed that this reason is routinely engulfed and outweighed by far stronger reasons A has to pursue his own projects at the expense of B. The possibility envisaged is that every project pursuer has *some* reason to accord rights to others but none has *sufficient* reason to do so.

There are other possibilities though. Imagine a world of project pursuers in which each is able to recognize others, in which each is liable to interference by others, and in which each recognizes his own liability to interference. The imaginative powers required are not great; this is a passable portrait of the actual world. Because each project pursuer values the ability to be a project pursuer, each has reason to act to bring about circumstances in which he will be able to lead a coherent life responsive to his own conception of the good. Since interference jeopardizes project pursuit, each has reason to act so as to eliminate interference by others.

What strategy merits adoption? One candidate is that of enslaving or otherwise neutralizing all potential interferers. There are good empirical grounds for thinking that this is unlikely to work very well. There are very many of them, and their potency is not much less than one's own. That is why it was initially rational to seek out a strategy for promoting their noninterference. Worst of all is that the enslavement strategy tends to be self-defeating: if others become aware of the attempted enslavement, they have reason to take preemptive measures. So, acting to eliminate interference creates reason for others to interfere.

A more promising strategy is one that is truly strategic, one responsive to transactors having reasons for action that mutually modify each other. A variation on Hobbesian social contract emerges. Everyone needs noninterference from others and each is in a position to interfere. If the situation is like this, then all agents have reason to trade their own noninterference for the like noninterference of others.

A variation is needed rather than vintage Hobbes. One problem familiar since Hume is that the conventional undertakings involved in contract are unintelligible unless the parties to it already acknowledge logically prior reason to regard certain doings as the undertaking of (morally) binding commitments. This is clearly so in the case of explicit contract, where A and B take their pledges as providing reason for subsequent compliance, and also for implicit understandings in which the parties successfully convey their intentions to be bound by reciprocal acknowledgments of the entitlements of others. Therefore, the use of contract in the theory of basic rights is better understood as a means by which rights are *acknowledged* rather than *established*. They are given force in a social context rather than created *ex nihilo*.

What is it that is acknowledged? It is that each has reason to value non-interference with his own projects and that this reason will have motivational force for others. If an earlier suggestion was cogent, this motivational force is implicit in the recognition of others as project pursuers who value their own ability to pursue projects. Willingness to forgo encroachments conditional on the like forbearance by others provides conditions such that this motivation is not drowned out by other factors. Respect for rights is feasible when granting moral space to others does not thereby jeopardize one's own moral space.

This is only a sketch of what an understanding of basic rights by way of project pursuit could look like. Much more deserves to be said. In particular, there has been no discussion of the reasons individuals can have for endorsing one project rather than another. That should not be construed as suggesting that all projects are of equal worth or that value attaches to being a project pursuer irrespective of the project pursued. The utmost seriousness surrounds deliberations over which long-term commitments are to guide one's actions, but this would be nonsensical if one project were as good as any other.

A theory of the good will offer criteria for the evaluation of projects. Because constructing that theory poses many difficulties, it is fortunate that an account of rights need not await a comprehensive theory of the good. Rights provide leeway for the autonomous development of one's own life, and therefore a satisfactory account of rights will admit that persons have the right to lead lives that fall short of being the morally best lives open to them. [20] Rights are not the whole of morality. They provide side constraints that limit the range of the permissible but do not uniquely determine it. For that reason the theory of rights is partly detachable from the theory of the good, such that work on the former need not be built upon the successful completion of the latter.

Independence is only partial. As noted above, the centrality of project pursuit rests on the assumption that how one commits oneself matters. Unless some theory of the good were feasible, the value of project pursuit would rest on a vacuum. However, rights theory can provisionally take the theory of the good to be a "black box" whose inner workings are unsolved. There is, though, a further possible connection between the two theories that at least deserves mention. It is credible to suppose that those projects of greatest value involve cooperative activity with other project pursuers. Many ends are such that it is either contingently or necessarily true that they can be advanced only through voluntary interaction among persons. If the good life requires co-operation, then each person has reason to bring about conditions in which

[20] See Jeremy Waldron, "A Right to Do Wrong," *Ethics* 92 (1981): 21–39.

cooperative ventures can be successfully entered into. Rights would emerge as preconditions for project pursuit of the highest value.

IV

The discussion of how rights are linked to project pursuit has also largely determined the form that basic rights take. Each project pursuer requires moral space within which to construct a life. Therefore, a regime of rights entails minimal constraints demanding the forbearance of others such that individuals can pursue projects amidst a world of similar beings, each with his own life to lead, and each owing respect to others. It would be idle to pretend that this conception is ideologically neutral; what has been offered is a scenario for the development of a classical liberal assessment of rights. Liberty, understood negatively as protection from coercive encroachments, is paramount. The defense I would offer to the charge of having connived to arrive at liberal rights is that liberalism is morally sound. Competing accounts of basic rights (including accounts in which basic rights are absent) must explain how they can lend to project pursuit the status that it merits. Alternatively, they can deny that we do possess a fundamental interest in being able to pursue projects. But if the preceding arguments are remotely persuasive, illiberal conclusions are dubious. Illiberalism can rest on any of the following assertions, each of which I believe to be mistaken:

(1) All value whatsoever is impersonal, measurable via some impersonal standard of value.

(2) An acceptable account of the nature of persons as active beings can dispense with project pursuit.

(3) Units other than individuals, say nations or economic classes, are the primary units of project pursuit.

(4) Project pursuers do not have reason to value their own ability to be project pursuers.

(5) It is not possible for individuals to establish conditions of reciprocal recognition and respect for the interest each project pursuer has in his ability to be a project pursuer.

If all of (1)–(5) are mistaken, then some variety of liberal (or libertarian) rights theory is correct.

Is it compatible with the foregoing to maintain that there also exist positive rights, justified claims against individuals or the state to sustenance? The answer, I think, is yes. A regime of thoroughgoing respect for autonomous construction of individual lives can be one involving more than noninterference. At least nothing said previously rules out that possibility. In particular, the conditions for successful civility could feature property rights that involve redistribution for the sake of enhancing the ability of less well-off persons to pursue their own projects. Whether maximally defensible property rights will take this form seems to be an empirical question, one that is historically conditioned. It is unduly dogmatic to maintain that, in all possible settings of civility, full capitalistic property rights are required in order that individuals are able to live as project pursuers.

Having said that, let me reiterate that this should not be taken as under-cutting the primacy of noninterference. Redistributive intrusions that are open-ended and that incessantly interfere with the ability of individuals to construct their own lives violate basic rights. Omniverous government is not compatible with liberty.

It may be argued that individuals equally need noninterference and also aid from others.[21] The two, however, are asymmetric. One can build noninter-ference into one's project pursuit by noting and refraining from specified actions that count as harms. However what others may need in the way of aid, and how much of it they might prove to need, is less easy to anticipate. That is not only because what counts as aid depends on what persons may bring themselves to want, but also because principles mandating the provision of aid are inherently intrusive. Whether A is in a position to provide aid to B depends as much on what B does as on precautions A takes. Therefore, rights grounded on the ability to pursue projects will endorse at most a tightly limited principle mandating the provision of aid. This result is also consonant with our moral intuitions, in which it is certainly the case that principles mandating the avoidance of harm are more stringent than are principles requiring the provision of aid.[22]

V

This paper is the prospectus of an attempt to understand basic rights by way of project pursuit, not its fully consummated outcome. The goal has been to make it seem plausible that some such program has promise. It is understood that many more questions have been left hanging than have been resolved. The restricted format can promote misunderstandings. Therefore, I conclude with four brief remarks concerning what I am *not* maintaining:

> (1) Just as I earlier acknowledged that not all projects are of equal worth, I now want to disavow that all projects should be taken as sacrosanct, untouchable. Hitler's remarkably consistent com-

---

[21] Gewirth so argues in *Reason and Morality* (Chicago, University of Chicago Press, 1978).

[22] This is discussed in my "Harman's Moral Relativism," *Journal of Libertarian Studies* 3 (1979): especially 284–289. See also Roger Pilon, "Ordering Rights Consistently: Or What We Do and Do Not Have Rights to Do," *Georgia Law Review* 13 (1979): 1171–1196.

mitment to genocidal havoc deserved to be squashed. It is intuitively plausible to maintain that one cannot have a right to pursue a project that inherently involves the frustration of other persons' projects. As it stands, this will not do. John has the right to marry Sue even if Fred's life is devoted to marrying Sue. Working out the details of what constitutes inadmissable interference is admittedly messy. At any rate, my argument has not been that all projects must be protected, but rather that human beings' capacity to commit themselves to projects is what undergirds the theory of human rights. The value of *being a project pursuer* must be acknowledged, not the value of any and every particular project.

(2) Rights theory would be much more comfortable if it could be held that rights are indefeasible, never overridden by other moral considerations (or by competing rights). Defeasibility opens the door to visionaries and scoundrels that side constraints were meant to shut. Unfortunately, the obstacles in the way of constructing a plausible theory of indefeasible rights seem insuperable. The problem with upholding rights though the heavens may fall is that the heavens may indeed fall. Nor is it apparent how to obviate the possibility of rights conflicting. Therefore, I am not willing to argue that rights are universally inviolable. However, it does seem reasonable to demand of a theory of rights that it not embrace systematically conflicting claims. Justifiable infringement[23] of rights will arise from untoward circumstances in a turbulent world in which not all eventualities can be foreseen rather than from internal theoretical opposition.

Admitting defeasibility is not to downgrade the centrality of project pursuit. Whether a right can justifiably be overriden will itself be construed as the question whether, in particular circumstances, upholding the right is at odds with the principle of valuing individuals' ability to be able to pursue their own projects. The consideration of defeasibility must take its bearings from the same landmarks as does the theory of rights.

(3) Basic rights as I conceive of them need not be instantiated in the same way in all social settings. They are not detailed prescriptions like positive rights, only written instead in Plato's (or Locke's) Heaven. If there is a basic right not to be punished unjustly, it can be upheld under legal systems with 12 man juries

---

[23] Judith Thomson helpfully distinguishes between *infringing* a right and *violating* a right in "Self-Defense and Rights," *The Lindley Lecture* (Lawrence: University of Kansas, 1977), 10.

or legal systems without them. Basic rights establish a range of moral permissibility that actual moral and legal systems can fall inside or outside of. On this conception, basic rights are not promiscuous in the social forms they countenance, but they do not entail any one determinate structure.

(4) There could be no rights if there were no project pursuers. It does not follow, nor do I believe, that all rights holders are project pursuers. So, for example, I have not precluded myself from making out a case for newborns enjoying a right to life. Speaking roughly, if any non-project pursuers have rights, they do so by riding on the coattails of project pursuers. To spell out how that might go must be left for another occasion.[24]

Philosophy, University of Minnesota at Duluth

[24] The question is addressed, but only in a very preliminary way, in my "Being a Person – Does it Matter?" *Philosophical Topics* 12 (1981); 139–152.

Social Philosophy & Policy Vol. 1 Issue 2 ISSN 0265-0525

WHY DO WE HAVE THE RIGHTS WE DO?

Hugo Adam Bedau

1. The question "Why do we have the rights we do?" obviously presupposes that we *do* have *some* rights; that is, that propositions of the form 'We have the right to *x*,' or of the form 'We have the right to do (or to have) *x*,' are true for certain values of *x*. The same issues would arise if the original question had been formulated, or were to be reformulated, as it sometimes is, in a purely existential manner, viz., "Why are there the rights there are?" I believe there is no difference between the two questions except a verbal one; at least, both of them share the same existential presupposition to the effect that there are certain rights. I mention this point for two reasons. One is merely to acknowledge the trivial but true point that the question in my title does have an existential presupposition. The second and more important point is that since I shall have very little to say about any actual rights, I would not want anyone to infer from my silence that I do not think we have any rights. I accept the presupposition of my original question, but I shall not dwell upon it.

2. One might ask my original question and mean by rights, *legal* rights, that is, rights identified through the legal provisions of some legal system. That is not the sense in which I pose the question. It is true that a legal positivist would be able to give no intelligible meaning to my question except by treating it as equivalent to asking, "Why do we have the legal rights we do?" However, since I am not a legal positivist, I want my question understood in another way.

It is also true that a certain kind of social activist might want my original question understood in a way that plays into the hands of the legal positivist. That is, one might construe the question "Why do we have the rights we do?" to mean "What have our predecessors done, what have we done, to get us the rights we have?" Understood in this way, there is a story to be told of class-struggle, of minorities fighting against majorities, of citizens against oppressive governments, and so forth. I don't for one minute dispute that there is such a story with regard to each of our rights. But the rights that will be explained in this way are legal (or constitutional) rights; only such rights can be the product of struggles of this sort. Such struggles do not explain what I want explained (or if they do, I do not see how they explain it, and so I shall ignore this kind of explanation).

The usual and perhaps simplest way to indicate what I have in mind is to say that the rights in question are *moral* rights. Thus, the presupposition of my original question is that some propositions of the form, 'We have the right, morally speaking, to do x,' or of the form, 'According to correct moral theory, we have the right to do x,' or perhaps, 'We have the moral right to do x,' are true for some values of x.

3. Given that my opening question has the existential presupposition I have mentioned, it seems natural to point out that this presupposition itself gives rise to a further question, namely, "What moral rights do we have?" And from this fact it might appear that in order to answer my first question, I should turn, perhaps first, to answer this second question. But I ask my original question in the hope and belief that we can answer it without knowing what our rights are, without reaching prior agreement on what those rights are, and without having in hand a list of the rights we have. Is this possible? I don't know, and I concede that I can think of arguments that might persuade us that it is not. But I can also think of an argument (perhaps 'argument' is too strong; very well, call it instead a 'consideration') in favor of the opposite view. Here it is.

Reflection on the original question suggests that it contains a certain ambiguity which permits reading it either as referentially transparent or as referentially opaque. That is, we can read the original question as asking "Given that we have a certain right, viz., R, why do we have *that* right?" Understanding the question in this manner, it seems not only natural but necessary to identify what that right is before trying to explain why we have it. But we can also read the original question as asking instead "Given that we have some (unspecified) right or other, why do we have it?" My intention is to try to pursue my original question in something like this latter reading, where we leave unspecified what the rights in question are.

4. Even if I may be allowed to proceed to answer my original question without first supplying a list of the rights we have, because my reasoning of a moment ago proves to be persuasive, one might still insist, in a fashion somewhat parallel to the objection just disposed of, that we cannot try to answer that original question until we know what a right is. One can imagine such a critic, inspired perhaps by the memory of G. E. Moore, insisting that we cannot sensibly attempt to ask *why* we have the rights we do without first knowing exactly *what* a right is, or without first having in hand an "analysis" of the concept of a right, or a "definition" of the term, 'right,' or of some such expression as 'a person, A, has the right, R, to do x.'

As with my previous objection, I sympathize with it, but I do not accept it. My reason here is that the force of the objection depends largely on the assumption that *what* a right is and *why* we have the rights we do are completely independent issues, or at least so nearly independent that we can profitably try to answer the former without concurrently exploring any ideas about the latter. At one time I was convinced myself that this assumption of independence was an absolutely necessary condition of progress in most areas of philosophy; but I am not convinced any longer. Instead, however, of trying to give an argument or any consideration against that assumption, I beg indulgence in putting it to one side. If it *is* false, then there is no need to derail an investigation into why we have the rights we do by turning first to explain exactly what a right is. It is enough, instead, merely to be alert to possible equivocations and obscurities in the concept of a right and to the need to avoid trading on them in the course of discussing the original question. At any rate, I shall attempt to proceed with no more than these cautions in mind.

5. We have so far considered in a preliminary way the priority and inter-relation among three questions, viz., my original question (Why do we have the rights we do?) and two subsequent questions (What rights do we have? What is a right?). How independent are the sets of issues that each question provokes? I confess I do not know, but I suggest that they may not be wholly independent of each other. Would you, as a philosopher, accept an argument to the effect that we have the rights we do because of p, q, and r, if it then turned out that your favorite right – your favorite interpretation of x in the propositional schema, 'We have the right to x' – now turns out not to be a right after all (i.e., 'We have the right to x' turns out to be false for this value of x)? This is exactly the experiment, if we choose so to view it, that Michael Tooley once performed with the right to life.[1] When it turned out on his account of the matter that normal human infants during the first year of life never have a right to live, considerable reluctance was manifested by philosophers in accepting the reasons he had given as correctly explaining why any creatures really have this right. How can this be surprising, or wrong-headed? If the response to Tooley's account of why we have the right to life is typical, as I think it is, rather than an exception, then we have to allow for some give and take between these seemingly independent questions, some subtle coordination between what we believe are our rights antecedent to the reasons we have for that belief, and also between both these matters and what we will count as a right. Whether or not the Rawlsian Method of Reflective Equilibrium is correct,[2] the give and take between our normative and theoretical reasoning that inspires it in the first place surely cannot be denied or ignored.

6. The foregoing serves as a preface to the observation that it is now much more difficult than it once was, say, two centuries ago, to answer my original question. This is so because thinkers abound today who claim that if we have any moral rights at all, then we have certain rights hitherto unnoticed and unclaimed. For example, Henry Shue is the latest and most unrelenting

[1] Michael Tooley, "Abortion and Infanticide," *Philosophy and Public Affairs*, Fall 1972, 2 (1), 37–65.

[2] John Rawls, *A Theory of Justice* (Cambridge, Mass.: Harvard University Press, 1971), §§9, 87; and Norman Daniels, "Wide Reflective Equilibrium and Theory Acceptance in Ethics," *Journal of Philosophy*, May 1979, 76 (5), 256–282.

philosopher to argue that all human beings possess what have come to be called welfare rights,[3] an idea not to be found in the seventeenth century[4] even if it has become a popular one in the twentieth. Other thinkers, such as John Noonan,[5] argue that unborn human beings have the right to life, and perhaps other rights as well, rights that Locke or Paine would have understood well enough but that they would have denied are possessed by unborn humans. Not only that, other contemporary thinkers, such as Peter Singer[6] and Tom Regan,[7] argue that infra-human creatures, such as horses and mice, have rights, the very same rights in at least some instances (viz., the right to life) that we do. *Mirabile dictu*, some thinkers even go so far as to entertain (I hesitate to say 'assert') the proposition that some vegetation has rights.[8] Can the day be far off when it is heard that natural objects – sea coasts, beaches, forests, streams, perhaps individual rocks – or even artifacts, such as individual buildings, also have rights?[9] Even if these rights are not alleged to be identical in all cases with the rights we are said to have, they may well be identical in some cases. In sum, there are strong forces at work to expand into new areas the kind of status and protection, of freedom from interference and of the imposition of responsibilities and duties upon others, that rights-possession (and perhaps nothing else) typically affords.

Given this efflorescence in claims or imputations of rights, anyone undertaking to answer my original question confronts a difficult predicament. For it seems very unlikely that one can answer my original question in a manner that is wholly neutral to all such substantive normative claims. Perhaps it *is* possible, just as I am ready to assume that the concept of a right that is being deployed across this ever-expanding area of alleged rights-possession remains the same. But it does seem to me highly unlikely that the best argument to explain why we have the right, say, to worship as we please, is also an argument sufficient to tell us why the Presidential Grove of *Sequoia sempervirens* has the right (if it does) to exist undisturbed.

[3] Henry Shue, *Basic Rights* (Princeton, N.J.: Princeton University Press, 1980).

[4] Richard Tuck, *Natural Rights Theory* (Cambridge, England: Cambridge University Press, 1979); and M. P. Golding, "The Concept of Rights: A Historical Sketch," in E. and B. Bandman, eds., *Bioethics and Human Rights* (Boston, Mass.: Little Brown and Co., 1978), 44–50.

[5] John T. Noonan, *How to Argue About Abortion* (New York: The Committee in Defense of Life, Inc., 1974).

[6] Peter Singer, *Animal Liberation* (New York: New York Review, 1975), and "Animals and the Value of Life," in Tom Regan, ed., *Matters of Life and Death* (New York: Random House, 1980), 218–259.

[7] Tom Regan, *All That Dwell Therein* (Berkeley, Calif.: University of California Press, 1982).

[8] Christopher D. Stone, *Should Trees Have Standing?* (New York: Avon Books, 1974); and William T. Blackstone, "The Search for an Environmental Ethic," in Tom Regan, ed., *op. cit.*, 299–335.

[9] Roderick Nash, "Do Rocks Have Rights?" *The Center Magazine*, November–December 1977, 10 (6), 2–12. I am indebted to Tom Regan for this reference.

7. All this also suggests that there may be several different kinds of answers to my original question. At one extreme there is the view that for every value of x in the propositional matrix, 'We have the right to x,' such that the resulting proposition is true, there is a different argument necessary to establish its truth. There is no reason I know of why this plurality of arguments (assuming a plurality of different rights) should not be necessary; but no one will deny, I think, that the prospect is unsatisfying as well as daunting. Another possibility, rather less intimidating, is that there are types of rights, certain families of rights with close affinity to each other, such that one type of argument is appropriate to explain why we have all the rights of one type, another type of argument appropriate to explain all the rights of another type, and so on. Elsewhere, I have relied upon this approach, at least its opening stage, which is to characterize rights in groups or families.[10] Here, however, I want neither to repeat that schema nor to press forward that kind of analysis. It may be fruitful, it may even be necessary, but for present purposes it is sufficient merely to mark it out as one possibility, and a familiar one at that.

8. So far, I have said little directly about *human* rights. Although everything I have said so far is relevant, I believe, to any possible comprehensive theory of human rights, it is time now to narrow the discussion to the proper subject. I propose to do this initially by considering a bad argument that some might be tempted to offer as an answer to my original question.

A few decades ago analytic or linguistic philosophers were much attracted by what I will call here "the game analogy." That analogy suggests the following argument about the nature of rights, including human rights:

(1) Rights are derived from certain rules.
(2) The rules are whatever those in authority decide or decree them to be.
(3) Good rules can be contrasted with bad rules according to how well compliance with them would advance the purpose of the game.
(4) All and only players in the game have these rights.

Now if we accept these four propositions and construe the rights in question as human rights, it is easy to see how they provide an answer to our original question. We have the rights we do, according to the game analogy, as a consequence of certain moral rules; we have the rights we do because of the way the rules that generate them advance the purpose of the game of human life.

---

[10] H. A. Bedau, "Human Rights and Foreign Assistance Programs," in Peter G. Brown and Douglas MacLean, eds., *Human Rights and U.S. Foreign Policy* (Lexington, Mass.: D. C. Heath, 1979), 29–44; and "International Human Rights," in Tom Regan and Donald VandeVeer, eds., *And Justice For All* (Totowa, N.J.: Rowman and Littlefield, 1982), 287–308.

Whatever else might be said for or against the game analogy in the present context, it seems to me to suffer from two fatal objections. The first is that it is not merely difficult to carry through the analogy of human life to a game – even a very complex and subtle game – it is impossible. Human life and being a person are not constituted by any rules, even if social, political, and economic life are regulated by certain rules. The second objection is that even if the first objection is wrong, or can be explained away, there are two further basic problems: The only plausible candidates for the purpose of the game of life will yield such a poverty-stricken set of rules that the human rights generated by them will seem woefully insufficient to most reflective observers; even if this turns out to be rebuttable, all the rights the game analogy can generate will be merely *special* rights, not general or universal (which is to say human) rights. Just as the rules of baseball provide for special rights for persons in certain positions, and only in such positions, e.g., the right of the batter at the plate to three strikes, or his right to take first base if his body is hit by a pitched ball, so the so-called human rights generated by the rules in question will not be general. They will apply only to persons in virtue of their holding a certain status, or playing a certain role – viz., that of person – rather than in anything intrinsic or essential to their nature.

So, even if the game analogy can explain why some persons have certain rights, and thus is relevant in some contexts to answering my original question, it is not relevant when that question is understood to refer only to human rights.

9. Although earlier I refused to turn aside from the main issue to give a definition of rights, or an analysis of the concept of a right, it is necessary to say something further about how human rights differ from other rights. I think it comes to this: If any human being has the right to do x, and this right is a human right, then every human being has the same right. That is, a human right is a universal right with respect to the class of human beings. Consequently, if I have the right to do x because you gave me the right, or because you sold me something z and my buying z gives me the right to do x, or because I am born to a certain status or role or position to which the right to do x is attached, then my right to do x cannot be a human right.

This fact suggests the following generalization. If the argument establishing the conclusion that I have the right to do x follows only from premises at least one of which refers to some property of me that is *not* a property of every other human being, then the right in question is not a human right and the argument establishing my right to do x cannot be an argument that tells me why I, or anyone, has the right to do x as a human right. A human right, whatever else it is, is something that you and I cannot fail to have; but any right established by the kind of argument considered above is unquestionably a right that you or I can fail to have – indeed, as things stand, there are (or at least seem to be) many rights (and not only legal rights) that you have but I lack, and vice versa.

10. As an illustration of an argument that does not satisfy the foregoing generalization (not that it was designed to do so), consider Rawls's argument that a person has the right to commit civil disobedience under certain conditions.[11] Rawls cites three such conditions: roughly, (i) when the law or policy that is the object of the person's protest imposes a grave injustice on someone, (ii) when the person has already made a good faith effort to use available lawful remedies to remove this injustice, and (iii) when the protester is willing to grant to anyone else the right to use similar methods of protest to advance his conception of justice. According to Rawls, if these three conditions are satisfied, you or I have the right to commit civil disobedience.

Rawls does not call this right a human right, although given the nature of the case one might be tempted to think that it really is one, whatever it is called. I think that would be a demonstrable error. The right to commit civil disobedience as established by the previous criteria cannot pass the test I proposed earlier to distinguish human rights from other rights. Here is why.

It is quite easy for a person *not* to have the right to commit civil disobedience. In fact, as things actually stand, most people do not have this right; the reason is that they do not hold views consistent with criterion (iii) above. For instance, I think it is plausible to believe that most members of the Ku Klux Klan do not have the right to commit civil disobedience, if for no other reason than simply because they would not grant this right to blacks, or to newly immigrated Asian-Americans, or to other non-whites.

One might reply to my objection by pointing out that nothing I have said undercuts the fact that it is possible for any human being to have this right. All that is required for any human being to have this right is for the human being to undertake illegal, non-violent protest with intentions consistent with the above criteria. This rebuttal is correct, but it does not establish the point. Because it is *possible* for conditions to exist under which any given person would have a right, it does not follow every person *does* have the right. A right possibly held by anyone is not identical with a right actually held by everyone; and only rights of the latter sort can be truly human rights. Therefore, the only explanations that qualify are explanations that account for rights actually held by everyone, not merely rights potentially or possibly held by anyone.

11. Arguments that tell us why we have the human rights we do seem to be divisible into two sorts. First, there are those that give an explanation solely by reference to what G. E. Moore would have called "natural" or non-moral facts about right-bearers. Second, there are the arguments that give an explanation by reference in part to something moral, some moral facts (and hence "non-moral" in Moore's sense) about rights-bearers.

[11] John Rawls, "The Justification of Civil Disobedience," in H. A. Bedau, ed., *Civil Disobedience* (New York: Pegasus, 1969), 240–245, and his *Theory of Justice*, §57.

As an example of the second sort of theory, consider Rawls's doctrine of natural duties.[12] Commentators have frequently noted that Rawls has no manifest doctrine of natural or human rights; rather, on his view, such moral rights as persons have are officially supposed to be logically derivative from the principles of justice generated in the original position. Some friendly critics (notably, Ronald Dworkin[13] and Norman Daniels[14]) have debated whether this manifest absence of any natural rights conceals a deeper and hidden doctrine of moral rights; we need not enter into that debate here. What commentators seem not to have noticed is that Rawls's explicit theory of natural duties can be used to generate counterpart rights, which could presumably be called natural rights (and if called natural rights, then why not called human rights?). The argument goes like this.

According to Rawls, each person has at least three natural duties to other persons: the duty not to be cruel; the duty to help another in need; and the duty to support and practice justice. But my duty not to be cruel to you could be regarded as a sufficient reason for saying that you have the right to humane treatment from me. All that is needed to warrant such an inference is a suitable version of the principle of the correlativity of rights and duties. This principle, to be sure, is controversial;[15] but that need not trouble us here. My point is merely to show two things. First, it is possible to use a doctrine of natural duties, such as Rawls's, to generate natural or human rights. Second, on such an account of how human rights are generated, we have an instance of what I called above the second sort of theory, namely, a theory that explains the rights we have by reference to some moral fact about us, in this case, our natural duties.

12. Can arguments of this second sort be correct? Could the best explanation for why we have the rights we do be an explanation by reference to some moral fact about persons? I don't see any reason why all such arguments must be unsound. But if *only* such arguments are sound, then the role of human rights in moral theory is far less interesting and important than many philosophers, moralists, and other theorists seem to have thought. The reason for this deflating conclusion should be obvious: It is, now, not our rights but our duties that wear the trousers (*pace* J. L. Austin). If this is so, then the interesting and important moral fact about human beings is that they have certain duties; the further fact that they also have human rights is derivative, secondary, and not fundamental.

---

[12] Rawls, *Theory of Justice*, §19.

[13] Ronald Dworkin, *Taking Rights Seriously* (Cambridge, Mass.: Harvard University Press, 1978), 159–183, especially pp. 171 ff.

[14] Norman Daniels, "Reflective Equilibrium and Archimedian Points," *Canadian Journal of Philosophy*, March 1980, 10 (1), 83–103, at 96–98.

[15] See David Braybrooke, "The Firm but Untidy Correlativity of Rights and Obligations," *Canadian Journal of Philosophy*, March 1972, 1 (3), 351–363.

13. Consider now a very different kind of argument of the second sort identified above. H. L. A. Hart once defended the view that if there are any moral rights, then there is at least one natural right.[16] His position can be restated and amplified as follows: Since everyone has many moral rights, everyone has at least one natural or human right, the equal right to be free (or, *pace* Rawls, the right of equal liberty).

This argument can usefully be viewed as a modern version of an argument that Hobbes relies on but seems not to have actually formulated. Hobbes relies on the idea that having a special moral right (as he allows anyone does who has ever been party to a contract) presupposes having a prior general moral right to make a contract in the first place.[17] This right to contract with another cannot, of course, itself be generated by some prior contract on pain of infinite regress. It must be a right, therefore, that everyone has *de novo*; it must be a "natural" right, as indeed it is on his theory. This right, moreover, is not merely a liberty (though it is that, viz., a right in the sense that a person who has it is under no obligation not to act in certain ways). It is a right that is meaningless unless it imposes a correlative duty on others not to interfere with acts that count as exercising this right.

14. The Hobbes-Hart arguments have what (*pace* Kant) might be called a transcendental character, in the sense that they appeal to human or natural rights to explain the actual moral world of familiar and indisputable special rights. In doing so, they provide an answer to my original question, by saying, in effect: We have the moral or human rights we do because they are the presuppositions of certain other moral acts and moral facts.

How adequate are the foregoing arguments as a foundation for human rights? They seem to have at least two limitations. One is that no one has the fundamental right these arguments establish who does not (or could not) act in the requisite fashion to secure a special right. In addition, the special rights in question are of a rather narrow sort. The other objection is that the right that these arguments establish is nothing more than is needed to serve the role of presupposition for the special rights in question. As a result, there looms an enormous gap between the result of these arguments and the rights usually thought to be fundamental, and natural or human. These objections are not fatal, of course, but they should suffice to encourage most friends of human rights to look further for better arguments.

15. Let us turn, now, to arguments of the first sort, in which the account of why we have the rights we do rests wholly upon reasons containing no moral principles, concepts, or facts. Half a century ago, during the heyday of philosophical anxiety over what Moore called "the naturalistic fallacy," many

---

[16] H. L. A. Hart, "Are There Any Natural Rights?" *Philosophical Review*, April 1955, 64 (2), 175–191.

[17] Thomas Hobbes, *Leviathan* (1651), Bk. I, ch. xiv, paras. 6–8.

philosophers would have insisted that no argument of the sort in question could possibly be sound. There was no way, we were assured, that any sound argument could consist wholly of non-moral premises and yet yield a moral judgment or principle as its conclusion. *A fortiori*, there could be no sound argument that consists wholly of non-moral premises and yet yields an account of why we have any human rights. In recent years, several philosophers have directly challenged this alleged impossibility of any derivation of an "ought" from an "is," by advancing what they contend are sound arguments of this sort.[18] One philosopher in particular has sought to cast his explanation of why we have human rights into this form of argument. I refer to Alan Gewirth, who has championed this line of reasoning in several places in recent years.[19]

Gewirth has argued that from a set of factual, descriptive, empirical statements by or about any agent and his intentional or purposive acts, it follows that there are certain human moral rights. All that is required for this inference, Gewirth claims, is a clear view of what it is to be a purposive, intentionally acting person and what the presuppositions and consequences of such action are. Gewirth summarizes what he calls his "dialectically necessary argument" when he says, "From the standpoint of the agent, his statement, 'I do X for purpose E' entails not only 'E is good' and 'My freedom and well-being are necessary goods,' but also 'I have rights to freedom and well-being.' "[20] These rights can be seen to be human moral rights because they are "generic," in the sense that all human action has these features, and because every human being is an actual or potential human agent.

16. This brief account of Gewirth's position does not do it justice, and others have already subjected it to persuasive criticism elsewhere.[21] For present purposes, it is enough to note that there is reason to doubt whether Gewirth really has explained why we have the human rights we do from reasons that contain no moral considerations. This is easy to see in the passage I have quoted, in which Gewirth insists that " 'I do X for purpose E' entails . . . 'E is good.' " Let us concede to Gewirth that the use of the term, 'good,' in this context does not mean 'morally good' or any equivalent notion. Let us also concede that if I do X for purpose E, then I *must believe* that E is good; it does seem self-contradictory for any agent to insist that he does X for purpose E but

[18] See especially John R. Searle, "How to Derive 'Ought' from 'Is'," *Philosophical Review*, January 1964, 73 (1), pp. 43–58.

[19] Alan Gewirth, *Reason and Morality* (Chicago Ill.: University of Chicago Press, 1978) and his *Human Rights* (Chicago, Ill.: University of Chicago Press, 1982).

[20] Gewirth, *Reason and Morality*, 102; cf. his *Human Rights*, 22–24.

[21] See especially the criticisms by Richard B. Friedman, Arval A. Morris, and Martin P. Golding, in J. Roland Pennock and John W. Chapman, eds., *Human Rights – Nomos XXIII* (New York: New York University Press, 1981), 148–174; Edward Regis, "Gewirth on Rights," *Journal of Philosophy*, December 1981, 78 (12), 786–794; E. M. Adams, "The Ground of Human Rights," *American Philosophical Quarterly*, April 1982, 191–196, at 193–194; and Paul Allen, "A Critique of Gewirth's 'Is-Ought' Derivation," *Ethics*, January 1982, 92 (2), 211–226.

does not believe that E is good, or doubts whether E is good, or knows that E is not good. Yet there is no contradiction in believing that E is good, when E turns out not to be good (as Gewirth is well aware). Any agent, therefore, who does X for purpose E, therewith believing that E is good, may yet be wrong in his belief. So how does Gewirth nevertheless think that when an agent says 'I do X for purpose E,' this entails 'E is good' as well as 'I have rights to freedom and wellbeing'? He thinks these entailments are rescued by treating them as "dialectically necessary" rather than as "assertoric." Not surprisingly, his view in the end is that "the existence of human rights can be proved only dialectically, within the context of agents' necessary claims, but not assertorically."[22]

It seems odd to regard such an argument and its conclusion as a successful effort to prove that human rights can be derived from wholly non-moral premises. The reason is that the assertoric propositions, 'I have rights to freedom and wellbeing' and 'Every agent has rights to freedom and wellbeing,' have not been derived or established at all. For all we know from Gewirth's argument, these two propositions may be false. Yet some such assertoric propositions must be true if we have human rights. To put this another way, Gewirth's argument at best shows that any moral agent in effect must say, 'If I am to act, then I and every other agent have the human moral right to freedom and wellbeing.' But it is difficult to see how this hypothetical proposition constitutes an explanation of why we have the rights we do, if we have any rights. So for this reason, quite apart from others that have been urged by others critics, it seems to me mistaken to think that Gewirth's account is an adquate answer to my original question.

17. There may be another way to understand arguments like Gewirth's, and it suggests that my original dichotomy between two types of arguments for human rights (viz., those that proceed from wholly non-moral premises, and those that proceed from at least one explicitly moral premise) may be a distortion and oversimplification. One of the philosophically interesting features of many arguments in recent years in political, social, legal, and moral philosophy is that they are not designed with avoiding the naturalistic fallacy foremost in mind. These arguments stress admittedly quasi-moral facts, or not wholly non-moral facts, about human nature, our capacity for reason, our species-unique needs, or (as in Gewirth's case) the generic features of human action and purpose. While it is clear that an appeal, say, to human nature in order to derive human rights does not move as frankly within the circle of morality as does an appeal to natural duties or moral rights, it is also clear that such an appeal does not take place entirely outside that circle, as would an appeal, say, to some evolutionary features of the human brain or to the genetic composition of a typical member of our species. And this suggests a rather

[22] Gewirth, *Human Rights*, 23.

different way of looking at possible types of arguments than does the dichotomy with which I began.

From this different perspective, philosophers seem to have at their disposal a range of possible considerations from which explanations might be drawn to tell us why we have the rights we do. At one extreme are plainly moral facts, which yield arguments that move within the circle of morality. At the other extreme are plainly non-moral facts, which yield arguments that are fatally vulnerable, if any arguments are, to the naturalistic fallacy. In between, however, are other arguments that appeal to quasi-moral facts about persons, their nature, reason, needs, and purposes. These arguments appeal to concepts that are not wholly non-moral because built into their very description and analysis will be certain norms, or the adequate basis for certain norms, that will serve to dictate or direct certain kinds of conduct by anyone who understands the original concept and who applies it to himself and his world.

To be sure, these arguments are not all alike, because there are considerable differences in the nature of the critical concepts under deployment. For example, Sartre made an argument to the effect that any attempt to establish human rights by reference to human nature would be utterly doomed to failure, because there is no such thing as a fixed human nature in the first place.[23] On this view, anything that could conceivably be said to be your nature, or my nature, would be a product of unique socialization and adventitious self-determination. Since no two persons experience the same socialization and act in the same self-determinative ways, no two persons could have the same human nature. But if no two persons have the same human nature, then human rights *semper et ubique et ab omnibus* cannot be derived from any argument that rests crucial weight on that concept.

However persuasive you may find that line of objection, it seems to me to be far less effective when reformulated as an argument against common human capacities. For I take it as an anthropological fact, resting in turn on biological facts, that members of the human species share a certain equipotentiality for socialization and self-determination that can be best expressed in terms of common human capacities. If so, then the concept of human capacities, however implicitly freighted it may be with moral considerations that render it unfit for status as a wholly or purely non-moral notion, is also invulnerable to the existentialist's critique mentioned above. If I am right, this suggests a certain strategy in the search for the best possible answer, or type of answer, to my original question.

18. Of all the arguments in recent years known to me that are designed to draw upon what I have called the middle portion of the spectrum of possible

---

[23] Jean-Paul Sartre, *Existentialism and Human Emotions* (New York: Philosophical Library, 1957), 9–51.

rights-entailing reasons, the most radical and in its own way ambitious such argument is by A. I. Melden.

Essential to Melden's argument for human rights is "the conception of a normative status that [the person] has with respect to others."[24] So much all philosophers will accept, I am sure. But Melden goes on to strike a distinctive and controversial note when he says that this status and the right(s) of which it is a part are "to be understood, if at all, only in terms of [their] place in the scheme of related concepts in which [they have a] place."[25] He goes on to point out that "The concept of a right is embedded in a complex network of associated concepts"[26] (though one might doubt, contrary to Melden, whether this fact is any less true of other concepts about persons, social life, or the natural world, or as though the truth of this point about rights is somehow unusually illuminating with respect to what rights are and why we have them). Like Hobbes before him, though without ever mentioning Hobbes in this connection, Melden seems to see promise-making as the paradigm act of human beings in creating and transferring rights. And so he says, "the right of the promissee and the obligation of the promiser is possible only if there is a basic right that any person has, as moral agent, to go about his affairs in the pursuit of his interests."[27] Thus, Melden's answer to my original question is this: We have the rights we do because of our status as moral agents, with the interests that agency projects and pursues; and we cannot explain or elucidate what it is to be a moral agent without eventual reference to our rights.

I pass over the problem that arises on this theory raised by the fact that the human rights generated by this kind of explanation, at least as Melden understands it, are few in number even if quite sweeping and abstract in character (viz., "the right of a person to go about his own affairs in the pursuit of his interests"). I am concerned only with what is distinctive about the kind of explanation he offers. After explicitly raising the spectre of Moore's naturalistic fallacy, Melden implies he thinks that his argument evades it, when he says:

> The philosophical understanding of the rights of human beings must come to rest on nothing less, and on nothing else than, this enormously complicated and moral form of human life itself . . . Instead of looking for a basis for human rights, we need to see more clearly in its rich and complex detail just what it is for persons to have the rights they have as human beings. It is here that all explanations come to an end.[28]

---

[24] A. I. Melden, *Rights and Persons* (Berkeley, Calif.: University of California Press, 1977), 79, and cf. 231.

[25] *Loc. cit.*   [26] *Ibid.*, 103.

[27] *Ibid.*, 134, and cf. 167, 203.   [28] *Ibid.*, 199–200.

Now the obvious trouble with this culminating passage is that it comes perilously close to saying that there is no such thing, after all, as explaining why we have the rights we do. There is, instead, the telling of a long and complex tale about what it is to be a human person, in which human rights will unfailingly show themselves in their characteristic roles; but the desire or need, and the very possibility, for any further explanation will evaporate. To borrow Wittgenstein's metaphor, which Melden so plainly has in mind, our spade is eventually turned when it strikes bedrock, except that here the bedrock consists of the intricate webbing of mutual understanding we have of ourselves and of others in a community of persons. Thus, Melden not surprisingly concludes by saying "any account would be in serious error if it attempted to provide a set of necessary and sufficient conditions for the possession of a human right."[29] To say that is equivalent to rejecting as ultimately misguided my original question, or at least to rejecting the natural way to construe it and the way one might say it has been implicitly construed up to this point (even though no mention has been made until now of "necessary and sufficient conditions").

19. I cannot, here, undertake to do full justice to Melden's theory.[30] Suffice it to make two observations. Melden is surely right in insisting that we cannot understand what human rights are and why we have the ones we do apart from, or independent of, any reference to what we believe to be distinctively human activities, interests, capacities, and the like. That much seems to me beyond doubt. But whether the explanation for those rights, so far as there is to be any explanation at all, lies in nothing more than a complex story about the form of life (*pace* Wittgenstein) peculiar to Western culture during the past few hundred years seems to me much more controversial.[31] That, of course, is not how Melden himself ever puts his position. Rather, he seems to think that the account he offers connects our rights to culturally-neutral and ideologically-independent concepts of the person and of the person's acts and their pre-suppositions. But this is simply not so. Once we allow that Plato and Aristotle, for example, had a concept of the person and of moral agency, then we will see that we will not find any notion of human rights inseparably related to personhood and moral agency. For we know neither Plato nor Aristotle had any conception of human rights. Whether one is prepared to regard this result, assuming one is willing to join me in finding it, as proof that Melden's projected theory is a failure, or proof only that human rights are securely

---

[29] *Ibid.*, 207.
[30] See also the criticism by Herbert Morris, "The Status of Rights," *Ethics*, October 1981, 92 (1), 40–51.
[31] Is it not more plausible to say that whereas the *discovery* of human rights is a relatively recent cultural phenomenon, the *foundation* or *source* of human rights must be as old and cultural-neutral as is our nature as rationally autonomous creatures?

embedded in a whole network of culture-bound concepts and principles, I shall leave unresolved.

20. So far, I have said nothing about the kind of explanation that a utilitarian might give for the rights we have. As a type of argument, at the most abstract level, it is simply another one of the many that derives the rights it acknowledges from a basic and more fundamental moral principle, in this instance, some form of the principle of utility. So much was plain in both Bentham and J. S. Mill, despite their hostility toward the very idea of natural or human or moral rights.

In contemporary ethical theory, utilitarians in their view of human rights tend to be good Benthamites.[32] Richard Brandt, for example, one of the foremost contemporary defenders of utilitarianism, invites human rights onto the moral scene only insofar as they can be seen as constitutent elements in an ideal code of morality.[33] Any explicit appeal to human rights plays no independent role in his theory. Insofar as human rights are thought of as absolute moral prohibitions or requirements, he accords them no status whatever. Even as weaker prohibitions or requirements – the only sort of moral rights a theory such as his can accommodate – they are conspicuous by their absence. No doubt an ideal moral code of the sort Brandt envisions would contain provisions for equal *legal* rights of many sorts; but this could not be made sense of as a reflection of antecedent *human* rights. To this extent, Brandt's theory has nothing to offer the student of human rights interested in answering my original question.

I think this is true generally of utilitarianism; it is simply not relevant to the task before us. This is somewhat confirmed by the way some long-time and conspicuous sympathizers with the utilitarian project, such as Jan Narveson[34] and David Lyons,[35] have lately abandoned it in order to foster support for moral rights quite apart from any connection of those rights to the criterion of welfare maximization.

21. It should not go unremarked here that the two writers who have done more than most to generate discussion about fundamental moral rights –

[32] Something of an exception to this generalization is Richard Hare, who has recently attempted to show how his utilitarianism can give a ground to human rights. See his *Moral Thinking* (Oxford: Clarendon Press, 1982), §§9.1–9.6, and his "Utility and Rights: Comments on David Lyons, Essay," in J. Roland Pennock and John W. Chapman, eds, *Ethics, Economics, and The Law – Nomos XXIV* (New York: New York University Press, 1982), 148–157.

[33] Richard Brandt, *A Theory of the Good and the Right* (Oxford: Clarendon Press, 1979). Brandt mentions moral rights, so far as I have been able to determine, in only three passages, at 195 and 292, as well as 267 (the solitary passage cited in his index).

[34] Jan Narveson, "Human Rights: Which, if Any, Are There?" in Pennock and Chapman, eds., *Human Rights*, 175–197.

[35] David Lyons, "Utility and Rights," in Pennock and Chapman, eds., *Ethics, Economics, and the Law*, 107–138.

Robert Nozick[36] and Ronald Dworkin[37] – have not tried to explain why we have the rights we do. Not only that, they have not even explained why they have not tried to explain this. Instead, they have been silent on the topic, despite confidently deploying the rights they think we have against countervailing considerations in various political, moral, and legal settings. Perhaps they have views so far unannounced that will fill the void; perhaps not. In any case, the influence of their views, or at least their recent popularity, does not seem to have been diminished from what it might have been owing to this omission. There is a lesson in this about how not to conduct adequate philosophical investigations of human rights. It seems to me that a theory of human or other non-legal rights that does not undertake to explain why we have the rights we do is really no theory at all, or at best only a fragment of a theory.[38] However suitable it may be for a political, legal, or sociological thinker to ignore my original question, it seems far too central to be ignored by philosophers.

22. Are we, now, any closer than we were at the start to having a good answer to my original question? Do we have even a clearer idea about what would count as a good answer, and why? It is hard to say. Let me close with some last suggestions in light of what has gone before.

The best explanation for the human rights we have must take its cue from the role these rights play in our lives, not only in our actual lives but in any possible human life, any life we could recognize as a life you or I might have lived. Human rights, like other rights, are themselves not ends or intrinsic goods; rather, they are instruments or conditions of such goods and so must be consistent in their possession and exercise by individual persons with a great plurality of specific ends individually chosen. Our common human predicament and roughly similar environmental circumstances and biological structure guarantee that our needs and capacities are far more homogeneous than heterogeneous. This is why these capacities and needs, joined to the distinctively human facts of being a person, figure so prominently in all the important recent efforts (only some of which I have been able to mention) that attempt to explain the source or foundation or rationale of our rights.

The great unresolved issue for philosophical reflection in this area is whether human rights can play a fundamental and underived role as the building-blocks of moral, social, legal, and political theory, or whether they cannot because their status is secondary and derived. However this issue may be resolved, a further question is whether human rights can do their job in

---

[36] Robert Nozick, *Anarchy, State, and Utopia* (New York: Basic Books, 1974).

[37] Dworkin, *op. cit.*

[38] I have discussed the idea of a theory of human rights more fully in "Human Rights: Some Theory-Oriented Reflections," presented at the Xth Interamerican Congress of Philosophy, October 1981.

relative isolation from other distinctively moral and quasi-moral concepts and principles or only in close conjunction (and perhaps even competition) with them.

23. When I began these remarks, I thought I would be able to say why we have the rights we do. I have not done so, and I see that I cannot. I draw some slight comfort from the realization that I appear to be in good, perhaps the best, company.

Philosophy, Tufts University

Social Philosophy & Policy Vol. 1 Issue 2 ISSN 0265-0525

INDIRECT UTILITY AND FUNDAMENTAL RIGHTS

JOHN GRAY

A TRADITIONAL VIEW OF UTILITY AND RIGHTS

According to a conventional view, no project could be more hopelessly misconceived than the enterprise of attempting a utilitarian derivation of fundamental rights. We are all familiar – too familiar, perhaps – with the arguments that support this conventional view, but let us review them anyway. We may begin by recalling that, whereas the defining value of utilitarianism – pleasure, happiness or welfare – contains no mention of the dignity or autonomy of human beings, it is this value which utilitarianism in all its standard forms invokes as the criterion of right action. Worse, insofar as utilitarian policy must have as its goal the maximization of welfare conceived as an aggregate summed over the utilities of everyone affected, legal and political utilitarianism seems bound to have a collectivist bias, trading on the dangerous fiction of a social entity and ignoring the distinctness of separate selves with their several incommensurable claims.

It seems that, if individuals can appear in the utilitarian calculus at all, it will only be as ciphers, abstract place-holders for units of welfare. For, as an aggregative value, utility must be indifferent to distribution, and insensitive to the preeminently distributive considerations marked by claims about rights. So, if whatever has utility can be broken down into units or elements which are subject to measurement or at least comparison by a common standard, then it will always be possible that a very great loss of welfare for one man or a few men can be justified if it produces a great many small increments of welfare for a vast multitude of men. It seems impossible, then, that utilitarian policy should be able to protect the interests of individuals or minorities, when these obstruct the general welfare or the welfare of large numbers. If there were such things as utility monsters – individuals capable of inordinately greater happiness than the ordinary run of human beings – it might even be utilitarianly allowable to sacrifice the welfare of the great majority to that of a favored few.

The conventional arguments rehearsed so far all express the difficulty utilitarian ethics faces in accommodating fundamental rights. Admittedly, utilitarianism in its applications in jurisprudence may (as it did in Austin) allow for the institution of legal rights of various sorts – civil rights as entrenched in a

constitution, or rights governing the practice of contractual exchange, say –
but these will be seen as institutional devices for the purpose of maximizing
general welfare, and not as embodying the irreducible moral claims of individuals. Even if we do not go so far as Dworkin in defining fundamental rights
as constraints on the pursuit of general welfare,[1] it seems plain that if they are
to be worth anything such rights must be more than merely shadows cast by
calculations of utility. For, if individuals have fundamental rights, they must be
able to stand upon them or invoke them to resist the claims of general welfare.
On any viable conception, in other words, fundamental rights must do more
for their bearers then secure a place in the calculus of utilities. Bentham's
maxim, "Everybody to count for one, nobody for more than one," may
disqualify some moral conceptions of an elitist or a particularist sort, but it will
not confer immunity against enslavement or summary execution if such
polices prove to be beneficial in utilitarian terms. Basic rights cannot be
reduced to utilitarian devices or strategems without being emptied of their
distinctive moral content as expressions of individuals' claims in justice.

As they are commonly rehearsed, these arguments hold no matter how
utility is conceived. It does not matter if welfare is given a hedonistic content as
in Bentham, an ideal construal as in G. E. Moore, or a eudaimonistic interpretation as in J. S. Mill, and it does not matter whether the utilitarian
principle enjoins us to maximize whatever has utility or else to minimize
whatever has disutility. In any case, intuition and common sense are unequi-
vocal that maximizing welfare may demand the infliction of losses on individuals which cannot be sanctioned by considerations of justice. This is, after
all, only a consequence of the disparity between utility as an aggregative
principle and the distributive character of principles about rights and justice.
At its deepest, this disparity expresses a most fundamental divergence in the
force of moral principles; a divergence between those goal-based or teleological principles which enjoin us to promote some value, and those rights-
based or duty-based principles which impose deontological constraints on the
promotion of values. The impossibility of a utilitarian derivation of fundamental rights is only a consequence of this fundamental distinction.

INDIRECT UTILITARIANISM: A NEGLECTED SPECIES OF
UTILITARIAN THEORY

Against the view which I have sketched in the preceding section, I wish to
explore the possibilities of a neglected form of utilitarianism which may not be
vulnerable to the standard objections. The form of utilitarian theory I have in
mind is *indirect utilitarianism*, a species often and rightly ascribed to Henry
Sidgwick, a proto-version of which may be found in Hume, and a very explicit

[1] See Ronald Dworkin, *Taking Rights Seriously* (London: Duckworth, 1977), Chapter Twelve.

and systematic version of which is expounded by J. S. Mill. As it is found in these writings, and in the work of our contemporary, Richard Hare,[2] indirect utilitarianism has several features. First, and most fundamentally, the principle of utility figures here not as a prescriptive principle, but as a general standard of evaluation. Indirect utilitarianism may be defined as that species of utilitarian theory in which a strong distinction is marked between the critical and the practical levels of moral thought, and in which the principle of utility is invoked, solely or primarily, at the critical level. Utilitarian appraisals apply, not directly to conduct, but to all the considerations which govern conduct – not only social rules, but the whole body of sentiments, attitudes and dispositions which lead us to do one thing rather than another. In its most general applications, indeed, utility may serve as a standard for the assessment of any state of affairs, whether or not it can be affected by any human action. But in its application to the human realm, it will apply especially to the codes of conduct to which we subscribe.

Next, given that its role in the indirect view is not that of a decision procedure for resolving specific practical dilemmas, utilitarian assessment bears especially on the codes and conventions which inform practical deliberation, and it issues, typically, in proposals for the revision and reform of these codes. Thirdly and lastly, indirect utilitarian policy is commended on the ground that direct utilitarianism has a self-defeating effect. Direct utilitarianism, which means here any view in which the decisive reasons cited for or against any act or policy are reasons having to do only with its utilitarian consequences, such utilitarianism is viewed as being generally and sometimes necessarily counterproductive. Indirect utilitarianism embodies and exploits the apparent paradox that utility maximisation will not be achieved by adopting the strategy of maximizing utility. Indeed, its central contention is that utility is best promoted if we adopt practical precepts which impose constraints on the policies which we adopt in pursuit of utility.

Each of the writers I have mentioned accords his own degree of emphasis to each of the features of indirect utilitarianism I have listed, and each has a somewhat different account of the source of direct utilitarianism's self-defeating effect. Let us, in order to exhibit more clearly some variations on the theme of indirect utility, consider each of those writers briefly. We may begin with David Hume, in whose *Treatise of Human Nature* may be discerned an indirect utilitarian analysis of the emergence and functions of rules of justice. For Hume, an indirect strategy in respect to the promotion of welfare is forced upon us by certain general facts of the human circumstance. These facts – which could conceivably have been otherwise, but which are for us so little

² See R. M. Hare, "Ethical Theory and Utilitarianism", in *Contemporary British Philosophy 4*, ed. H. D. Lewis (London: Allen & Unwin, 1976 and more recently, Hare's *Moral Thinking* (Oxford: Clarendon Press, 1981).

alterable as to be among the natural necessities of social life – are, above all, the limited sympathies and partial views of human beings and the natural scarcity of most human goods. As Hume observes, "Here, then, is a proposition which, I think, may be regarded as certain, that it is only from the selfishness and confined generosity of men, along with the scanty provision nature has made for his wants, that justice derives its origin."[3] The precepts of justice which these features of men's natural predicament necessitate are three are are characterised by Hume as "the three fundamental laws of nature, that of the stability of possessions, of its transference by consent, and of the performance of promises." "It is on the strict observance of those three laws," Hume tells us "that the peace and security of human society entirely depend; nor is there any possibility of establishing a good correspondence among men where these are neglected."[4] And, in the most explicit and crucial passage of his exposition, Hume asserts:

> . . . if men pursued the public interest naturally, and with a hearty affection, they would have never dreamed of restraining each other by these rules; and if they pursued their own interest without any precaution, they would run headlong into every kind of injustice and violence. These rules, therefore, are artificial and seek their end in an oblique and indirect manner; nor is the interest which gives rise to them of a kind that could be pursued by the natural and inartificial passions of men. To make this more evident, consider that, though the rules of justice are established merely by interest, their connection with interest is somewhat singular, and is different from what may be observed on other occasions. A single act of justice is frequently contrary to public interest; and were it to stand alone, without being followed by other acts, may in itself be very prejudicial to society . . . Nor is every single act of justice, considered apart, more conducive to private interest than to public; and it is easily conceived how a man may impoverish himself by a single instance of integrity, and have reason to wish that, with regard to that single act, the laws of justice were for a moment suspended in the universe. But, however single acts of justice may be contrary either to public or private interest, it is certain that the whole plan or scheme is highly conducive, or indeed absolutely requisite, both to the support of society and the well-being of every individual.[5]

---

[3] David Hume, *A Treatise of Human Nature*, Book Three, Part Two, Section II, 547 (Pelican ed.: London, 1969).

[4] *A Treatise of Human Nature*, Book Three, Part Two, Section VI, 5.

[5] *A Treatise of Human Nature*, 548–549.

It is easy to quibble with particular moves in Hume's argument. It may be that he does not need an assumption of natural human selfishness or limited generosity, but only the natural fact of diverse and conflicting human purposes, to show the importance of the stability of property. It may be that his precepts of justice would be necessary, even if there were not a natural scarcity of the goods for which men strive; for time would remain scarce and instability of property no less crippling a defect of human arrangements. But, though he may not need them, these general facts of human life are as clear to us as they were to Hume, and they do the job he wanted of them. The unalterable facts of our confined generosity and limited rationality and of natural scarcity by themselves disqualify any strategy of promoting general welfare directly. Given our human limitations, we have no hope of promoting general welfare except against a background of well-established rules of justice. Even when its operations appear to result in significant welfare losses, justice is to be viewed as an indispensable condition of welfare rather than as a competitor with welfare. We have no alternative to accepting justice as a system, if we aim to promote welfare, even if we suppose ourselves capable of identifying cases where its operations appear disutilitarian. As Hume observes in the third appendix to his *Enquiry Concerning the Principles of Morals*:[6]

> All the laws of nature, which regulate property, as well as all civil laws, are general, and regard alone some essential circumstances of the case, without taking into consideration the characters, situations and connections of the person concerned, or any particular consequences which may result from the determination of these laws, in any particular case which offers. They deprive, without scruple, a beneficent man of all of his possessions, if acquired by mistake, without a good title; in order to bestow them on a selfish miser who has already heaped up immense stores of superfluous riches. Public utility requires that property should be regulated by general inflexible rules; and though such rules are adopted as best serve the same and public utility, it is impossible for them to prevent all particular hardships or make beneficial consequences result from every individual case."

Hume's thesis is that whereas any single act of justice may be contrary to public or private interest, the usefulness of the whole system depends on its not being continuously threatened by utilitarian calculation. Hume exploits the indirect utilitarian paradox that we protect our interests and promote our welfare as best we can, not by treating the rules of justice as at any moment defeasible by reference to private or public welfare, but precisely by treating them as almost always invulnerable to such overthrow or abridgement. The

---

[6] David Hume, *An Enquiry Concerning The Principles of Morals*, Appendix III. See 179–280 of *Essential Works of David Hume*, ed. R. Cohen (New York: Bantam Books).

utility which acts of justice possess they possess as instances of a system of
rules or as aspects of a practice and this utility is lost if the costs of a particular
act are used to support a breach of the system of rules of which it is a part.
Unless those who apply them are governed by a disposition to implement rules
of justice regardless of their apparent disutilities, such rules will fail to yield the
utility we want of them.

In large part, then, Hume commends a strategy in which rules of justice
constrain utilitarian policy in virtue of the unalterable facts of our human
limitations. In part also, to be sure, Hume's entire view of human nature
inclined him to regard the rules of justice as spontaneously generated moral
conventions, serving general welfare but never designed for that purpose. In
Hume, indeed, a full understanding of the needs and circumstances which
give rise to a moral practice issues in an endorsement of it precisely on
utilitarian grounds, so that his moral and political thought bears a decidedly
conservative aspect. In Hume, perhaps, utility figures both as a principle for
explaining human life and as the ultimate canon of justification in conduct, and
these two uses of the principle are often hard to disentangle.

A much greater degree of self-consciousness as to the character and uses of
the principle of utility is to be found in J. S. Mill. More clearly and explicitly
than any other writer I know, Mill is at pains to emphasize that utility is a
principle of general evaluation and not a principle which yields in any straightforward way judgments about what ought to be done. Further, in his doctrine
of the Art of Life as set out in *A System of Logic*,[7] Mill develops a taxonomy or
classification system for practical life which enables him to distinguish between
the utilitarianly best thing to do (that which is, as Mill terms it, maximally
expedient) and what it is that a man has an obligation (defensible in utilitarian
terms) to do and which enables Mill to accord priority in the latter over the
former.

Mill's argument – as expressed in *A System of Logic*, the last chapter of
Utilitarianism, and the essay *On Liberty* – has three moves. To begin with,
Mill distinguishes the principle of utility from precepts for the guidance of
action and divides practical life into three areas, branches, or departments,
which he calls Prudence, Nobility (or Aesthetics), and Morality. Mill's first
claim is that, except where their maxims conflict and need arbitration, it is the
principles of the various departments of the Art of Life, and not Utility itself,
which ought to guide conduct. These secondary principles or *axiomata media*

---

[7] *A System of Logic*, Bok 6, Chapter 12. I have examined Mill's indirect utilitarianism in much
greater detail in my paper "J. S. Mill on liberty, utility and rights", which appears in *Nomos* XXIII
eds. J. Roland Pennock and J. W. Chapman (New York: New York University Press). A complete
statement of my interpretation of Mill on liberty and utility appeared in February 1983 as *Mill On
Liberty: A Defense* (London: Routledge and Kegan Paul, International Library of Philosophy
Series).

are, however, all derived according to Mill from Utility. Second, Mill contends that only Morality should come into the sphere of social control and enforcement, the other two spheres coming into the self-regarding area. For Mill, morality is an instrument of collective self-defense and has as its purpose the protection of men's vital interests from invasion and injury. Neither Prudence nor Nobility can sensibly be made the subject of enforcement. Thirdly, Mill argues that as a matter of utilitarian policy Morality should be maximally permissive as to liberty. There is a standing presumption against limiting liberty, itself derived from Utility, and this should be defeated only when an important interest is threatened and the costs of enforcement are not prohibitive. This third argument yields Mill's famous Principle of Liberty, which states that liberty may rightfully be restricted only when serious damage to the vital interests of others is at issue.

Mill's version of indirect utilitarianism is striking for a number of reasons. Inasmuch as the Principle of Utility applies as the supreme standard of evaluation in all branches of conduct and not just in ethics, it is not itself a moral principle and it does not of itself give us a criterion of right conduct. In Mill's own formulations, the Principle of Utility has primarily an axiological force specifying that pleasure or happiness, and that alone, has intrinsic value. Even if we add to Utility Mill's consequentialist Principle of Expediency, we still do not have a criterion of right action. For Mill, in fact, such a criterion falls out as a theorem from his whole theory of morality. The criterion of conduct fundamental in that theory is a criterion of wrongful conduct as that conduct, prejudicial to the interests of others, which it is maximally expedient should be made punishable. Conduct not other-regarding cannot be wrongful, however harmful it may be, though it may be grossly imprudent or otherwise lamentable.

Mill's proposal is that as a matter of utilitarian strategy concern for best consequences be displaced as a criterion of right action. What, though, justifies our adopting this strategy? Mill's view, as expressed in *On Liberty*, *Utilitarianism*, and elsewhere in his writings, is that pursuing utility directly by making it the goal of our policies is likely to be self-defeating in two ways. First of all, Mill adduces in *Utilitarianism* the psychological paradox that in men happiness is best achieved by pursuing and achieving ends valued for their own sakes. Here Mill trades on the complex Aristotelian and Humboldtian conception of happiness argued for in several places in his writings; for men, at any rate, happiness is not a long series of many episodes of pleasure, but a whole life in which self-chosen activities are pursued with a decent measure of success; happiness is not a passive state, nor is it the same for all men; it is found in activities and pursuits which will for each man have some distinctive and peculiar features. For the individual then, if Mill's post-Benthamite moral psychology has any credibility, "happiness" is barely a coherent goal at all.

Each of us finds happiness, when he does, in the successful pursuit of his own projects. But also, Mill avers, the direct pursuit of happiness is likely to be collectively self-defeating. There are problems in the coordination of human activities which make the Principle of Utility quite unfit to serve as framing the terms of social cooperation. It is by reference to some of these that Mill commends adoption of his Principle of Liberty rather than Utility itself as the salient maxim for regulating the coercive aspects of social life. His defense in utilitarian terms of the adoption of a maxim other than the Principle of Utility for the regulation of social life has always puzzled interpreters. We can see that Mill could coherently give a utilitarian defense of a maxim other than Utility, *and even support giving it a weight greater than Utility*, if direct application of the Principle of Utility proves, indeed, to be self-defeating.

In Sidgwick, as in Hume, indirect utilitarian analysis has largely conservative conclusions. Sidgwick holds that, though it is reasonable for a Utilitarian to wish to see a world in which all men have become Utilitarians, the attempt to bring about such a state of affairs may have serious costs and, in fact, may be indefensible in utilitarian terms. As Sidgwick puts it in a justly famous section of the *Methods*:

> . . . on Utilitarian principles, it may be right to do and privately recommend, under certain circumstances, what it would not be right to advocate openly; it may be right to teach openly to one set of persons what it would be wrong to teach to others; it may be conceivably right to do, if it can be done with comparative secrecy, what it would be wrong to do in the face of the world; and even, if perfect secrecy can be reasonably expected, what it would be wrong to recommend by private advice or example. These conclusions are all of a paradoxical character . . . Thus the Utilitarian conclusion, carefully stated, would seem to be this: that the opinion that secrecy may render an action right which would not otherwise be so should itself be kept comparatively secret; and similarly it seems expedient that the doctrine that esoteric morality is expedient should itself be kept esoteric. Or, if this concealment be difficult to maintain, it may be desirable that Common Sense should repudiate the doctrines which it is expedient to confine to an enlightened few. And thus a Utilitarian may reasonably desire, on Utilitarian principles, that some of his conclusions should be rejected by mankind generally; or even that the vulgar should keep aloof from his system as a whole, insofar as the inevitable indefiniteness and complexity of its calculations rend it likely to lead to bad results in their hands.

[8] Henry Sidgwick, *The Methods of Ethics* (London: Macmillan, 1893), 487–489.

Sidgwick's argument, here, is important in that it illuminates a point of correspondence between indirect utilitarianism and the more sophisticated versions of act-utilitarianism. There is nothing in the passage which I have quoted to which an intrepid act-utilitarian such as J. J. C. Smart would be bound to take exception: for in the writings of Smart and others, a distinction is explicitly made between that which it is utilitarianly rational to do, and that which it is reasonable in utilitarian terms to approve, praise, or commend. One of the points which will occupy me in the next section of this paper is how indirect utilitarianism is to be distinguished from sophisticated act-utilitarianism and from rule-utilitarianism, so I will not now pursue this question further, save to make one comment. After the passage I have quoted, Sidgwick goes on at once to assert that "Of course . . . in an ideal community of enlightened Utilitarians this swarm of perplexities and paradoxes would vanish; as in such a society no one can have any ground for believing that other persons will act on moral principles different from whose which he adopts."[9] We see, here, Sidgwick resisting a major insight of indirect utilitarianism, grasped by J. S. Mill, the insight that maxims other than (and more specific than) Utility would be indispensable even in a world of enlightened utilitarians. Sidgwick is an important expositor of elements of indirect utilitarian theory, nonetheless, in that he acknowledges (what an act-utilitarian must presumably contest) that efficacious pursuit of the utilitarian goal entails according to aspects of our ordinary moral life a measure of immunity to utilitarian appraisal and criticism. At any rate in our present phase of development, according to Sidgwick, our moral code will achieve its maximum usefulness only if it is largely protected from utilitarian erosion. The limitations Sidgwick places on the teachability and public avowal of utilitarian ethics, and his candid description of utilitarian ethics as an esoteric morality, all derive from his insight that utility will be lost if men make its pursuit their dominant motive.

SOME QUESTIONS AND CLARIFICATIONS

In the preceding two sections I have given the merest sketch of indirect utilitarian theory, supported by historical references to writers in whom elements of indirect utilitarian analysis can be discerned. It may be worth trying here, before I go on to develop the bearing of the indirect view on questions of fundamental rights, to confront some obvious questions about the character and claims of indirect utilitarian thought. In the first place, there are some difficult questions about the thesis that direct utilitarian policy has a self-defeating effect. Is this thesis advanced as embodying a generalization of some sort, to which there might be important exceptions? Is the claim that there is a range of cases, not covering the whole of practical life, in which direct

⁹ Sidgwick, *Methods of Ethics*, 489.

utilitarian policy is *necessarily* self-defeating? Or is it rather that there is such an overwhelming likelihood that direct utilitarian policy will be counter-productive that we have good reason to adopt a more oblique strategy? The question is a hard one for the indirect view because if there is only a likelihood that a direct policy will be self-defeating, and if we can identify those cases where the probability of such a result is small, then the power of the indirect view to support constraints on utility-promotion that are defensible in utilitarian terms will plainly be weakened.

A related question must, here, also be asked which poses a serious objection to the indirect view. It might be objected that there is a contradiction in the claim that direct utilitarian policy has a self-defeating effect.

According to this objection, the only reason an ideally well-informed and properly motivated act-utilitarian agent could fail to achieve maximum utility would be that he miscalculated. If he does not miscalculate, and acts instead on the best information available to him, then surely it is a necessary truth that his act produces the best possible consequences. In short, either he produces best consequences, or he fails to do so: what is unintelligible and incoherent is the indirect utilitarian claim that in achieving best consequences, there was some achievable utility foregone such that the net utility produced by his action was less than it could have been. Plausibly, however, this common-sensical objection ignores a very simple distinction. The distinction is between the utility achievable by an ideal utilitarian agent in an act-utilitarian world denuded of moral practices of the ordinary sort and the utility that can be achieved by a utilitarian agent who is constrained by a moral code. The indirect utilitarian argument is that, whereas a perfect utilitarian agent may act so as to achieve best consequences in any circumstances and so always maximizes utility, he will achieve a different and higher maximum of utility if his actions (and in some measure his deliberations) are constrained by weighty principles of morality and justice that are more specific than Utility itself and bar any direct appeal to it. In other words, the sum of an agent's utility-maximizing acts will not be a utility-maximizing sum, if indirect utilitarianism is right that the utilitarian agent will be able to do better in a partially non-utilitarian world.

Why is it, though, that even a perfectly rational utilitarian will not do particularly well in a wholly utilitarian world? Without going into the extremely complex arguments which others have developed in this area,[10] I think one very general sort of reason stands out as explaining the self-defeating effect of direct utilitarianism. I refer to the fact that, among the necessary conditions of social cooperation, are moral practices which direct or simple utilitarianism is

[10] I refer especially to D. H. Hodgson's pioneering *Consequences of Utilitarianism* (Oxford: Clarendon Press, 1967). A good guide to this area is D. H. Regan's excellent *Utilitarianism and Cooperation* (Oxford: Clarendon Press, 1980).

bound to corrode or supplant. These are, above all, the practices of truth-telling and promise-keeping, without general participation in which social cooperation is simply an impossibility. This strand of argument has been expressed, simply and concisely, by G. J. Warnock:

> Paradoxical though it may at first seem to say so, this end ("the betterness, or non-deterioration of the human predicament") is *not* most effectively to be pursued by general adoption of the sole over-riding object of pursuing it . . .
>
> Can one say that what simple Utilitarianism essentially defeats is the possibility of *cooperation?* It seems that, if two or more persons are effectively to cooperate . . . there must be such a thing as being prepared to be, and recognized as being, *bound* to specific require-ments of the cooperative 'ethics', or to specific undertakings. It is not, one may thankfully observe, essential that such bonds should abso-lutely never, with or without excuse, be broken; but it is essential that they should not in general make absolutely no difference, count simply for nothing one way or the other. But, if general beneficence is to be our sole criterion, they would inevitably count for nothing; they would be accepted with reservations, hence not relied upon, hence more readily disregarded and less relied upon, and so on to the point of wholly vanishing significance. And thus, towards the betterment of the human predicament, the simple recipe of general beneficence must be, while admirably intentioned, very minimally efficacious.[11]

The argument advanced by Warnock parallels that of Hodgson,[12] but Warnock's conclusions are rather different from Hodgson's. In *Consequences of Utilitarianism*, we recall, Hodgson had used the corrosive effects of direct utilitarian policy on indispensibly useful social practices as reason for abandoning utilitarianism *tout court*. In Warnock, on the other hand, there is the recognition that, if Hodgson-type arguments are sound, there is no reason why utilitarianism should not be able to accommodate them by adopting what I have called the indirect strategy. We come now, I think, to the nub of the indirect view, and to the claim which distinguishes it from standard varieties of act and rule utilitarianism. If, as Hodgson and the indirect view both maintain, direct utilitarian policy erodes the practices necessary to social cooperation, then these practices must be supported on utilitarian grounds as *imposing constraints on utilitarian policy*. They cannot be merely the rules of thumb of which Smart speaks: rather, insofar as they do constrain utilitarian action and deliberation, they possess what might be called "second-order" utility of their

---

[11] See G. J. Warnock, *The Object of Morality*, 31, 24.
[12] Hodgson, op-cit. footnote 10 above.

own, which they must lose if they are to be regarded as always vulnerable to utilitarian overriding. Indirect utilitarianism is distinct from even a sophisticated act-utilitarian view, then, because it requires that certain practices and conventions be accorded enough weight for their claims to be able to resist erosion by utilitarian appraisal. And, insofar as we can identify and weigh at the critical level those practices which do have second-order utility, we will not be irrational rule-worshippers if we subscribe to them even where a direct utilitarian policy would dictate that we breach them.

The indirect view has a no less important feature which distinguishes it from rule-utilitarianism. As we find it most clearly developed in J. S. Mill, the indirect strategy applies not only to social rules, but to entire codes of conduct, with all their attendant motives, dispositions, attitudes and sentiments. The indirect strategy demands not only that we institute or support social rules and practices having second-order utility, but also that dispositions and virtues be inculcated in respect to the proper application of social rules. These virtuous dispositions will not themselves have any utilitarian content, but will include such things as mercy, prudence, and so on. Because its compass is wider than social rules, the indirect view can cope with the central difficulty of rule-utilitarianism. Ought the rules which utility supports to be obeyed even when there is incontrovertible evidence of their producing a net utility loss? On the indirect view, social rules will not be liable to a rigoristic application, even though they will not on the other hand be subject to continuous utilitarian abridgement. For the virtuous dispositions which the indirect view also dictates that we inculcate in ourselves will lead us (without any necessity for utilitarian appraisal) to make abridgements of social rules in a wide range of cases where such breaches do in fact promote utility. The indirect view, inasmuch as its net is cast wider than the scope of social rules, can consistently treat social rules as more than rules of thumb and less than absolutist requirements.

It may be conceded that the indirect view is indeed distinct from the standard varieties of utilitarian theory, and yet it may be thought that it has difficulties of its own which make it less promising than the standard varieties. One obvious reason in support of this view, which I mention but cannot discuss, is that it may simply be denied (as it has been by J. L. Mackie and Peter Singer[13]) that direct utilitarianism has the self-defeatig effect to which I have referred. Even if this objection can be countered, it seems difficult to accept the claim that the Principle of Utility can have no prescriptive or action-guiding role within a utilitarianly sanctioned code of conduct. Even J. S. Mill allowed that appeal to Utility was unavoidable where the precepts of the various departments of the Art of Life made incompatible demands. More

---

[13] On this, see several useful references in Mackie's *Ethics: Inventing Right and Wrong*, bibliographical notes.

fundamentally, it might be objected, that the disseveration of the perspective of the moral agent from that of the observer or the legislator, which is fundamental to the indirect view, creates unnecessary difficulties for moral theory, and especially for consequentialist moralities. I do not aim to resolve any of these questions here, though I will address some of them in the last section of the paper. At this stage I wish only to reiterate the point made earlier about the role of practical constraints on the pursuit of utility functioning as means to its maximization. The key aspect of the indirect view is in the claim that insofar as they possess the "second-order"utility to which I alluded earlier, certain moral practices serve as *maximizing constraints* in respect of the promotion of utility. It is to an expansion and clarification of this claim, and an examination of its bearing on questions of fundamental rights, that I now turn.

THE INDIRECT UTILITARIAN DERIVATION OF FUNDAMENTAL RIGHTS

If the argument thus far has any credibility, one common line of criticism of any utilitarian theory of rights will be shown to be misplaced. This is the objection that even if utilitarian theory can accommodate rights as part of the body of rules of thumb which it generates, it cannot allow that rights should constrain the pursuit of general welfare. On the indirect view, if rights have the property of second-order utility, they have a utilitarian justification, especially where they operate as constraints on simple maximizing policies. Even if we grant the distinction between distributive and aggregative principles in which the standard objection to utilitarian rights theory is usually couched, we can see that it misfires. If direct utilitarian policy is counterproductive, we must accept practical constraints on it, and there is nothing to say that these will not include the distributive constraints imposed by principles conferring weighty moral rights on individuals.

It is one thing to argue, as I have done, that the indirect view allows for the institution of weighty moral rights as maximizing constraints on utilitarian policy; it is another thing altogether to show that the indirect view requires the adoption of rights principles. After all, the chief argument adduced in various forms by Hume, J. S. Mill and Sidgwick for an indirect strategy is a fallibilistic one. It is argued that we have no reliable means of identifying the act that has best consequences. Accordingly, we do better if we stick to general principles, even where our calculations seem to suggest that we are sacrificing some available welfare thereby. This fallibilistic argument, however, while it establishes the need for maxims more specific than Utility, in no way supports the case for rights.

In Hume and Sidgwick, as I have already observed, such fallibilism has conservative implications. It is bound to do so if it is supposed that the received moral code of any society, having stood the test of time, is likely to be wiser than any man or any one generation of men. Not that the indirect view is bound to lead to inflexible moral conservatism. Both Hume and Sidgwick were moral reformers in limited areas, and it is obvious that as society changes new dilemmas will be thrown up to which the received moral code may have no ready answer. Still, even a moderate moral reformism is a different animal from advocacy of fundamental rights. How might a defense of such rights be conducted according to the indirect view? Asking this question exposes an acute difficulty for all variants of the indirect view – the *epistemological* difficulty of establishing which moral practices possess second-order utility, and in what measure. Unless we can *know* which practices are to be preserved, which abolished, and which reformed so that social life contains an optimal mix of maximizing constraints, the promise of the indirect view will have proved to be in vain.

Consider J. S. Mill's argument for moral rights. In the last chapter of *Utilitarianism* – written as a separate essay before the earlier chapters and before *On Liberty* – Mill gives an account of justice as embodying the most fundamental of all classes of utility, security. Mill recognizes, of course, that justice is a broader category than that of rights, but his object in this chapter is to give good reason in utilitarian terms for acknowledging a weighty moral right to security as being possessed by all men. It is not that this right may never justifiably be violated: like many non-utilitarian theorists of rights, Mill is clear that none of the fundamental rights is indefeasible. Rather, within the compass of the account of justice he gives in utilitarian terms, Mill argues that security is to be accorded the status of a weighty moral right, in ordinary circumstances indefeasible by considerations of general welfare.

The argument of *On Liberty*, once it is seen as completing the theory of justice sketched in the last chapter of *Utilitarianism*, gives us further insight into Mill's utilitarian rationale for moral rights. In his *Liberty*, Mill adduces the human interest in individuality and autonomy, along with the fact of human fallibility and the role of unfettered intellectual speculation and practical experiment in furthering the growth of knowledge, to limit the sphere of coercive social control. Only where harm to others' interest is at stake can limitation of liberty ever be justified. Note that the Principle of Liberty, in disqualifying all restriction on liberty save where there is a question of harm to others, entails that the fact that a restriction on liberty may yield large benefits in terms of welfare or utility is *no reason at all* in favor of it, unless the limit on liberty *also* prevents harm to others. Mill's argument becomes intelligible and powerful once we see him as holding that utilitarian considerations themselves necessitate ranking the Principle of Liberty as a practical precept over any maximizing consequentialist principle.

Mill's argument, as I have so far expounded it, has a missing element crucial to his entire enterprise. This is his theory of the vital interests. Most of us are familiar with the large interpretative literature[14] spawned by analysis of the Principle of Liberty, and in particular by Mill's use of the concept of harm in it. It is, I think, generally accepted by now that Mill's conception of harm was one of harm to interests, so that the Principle of Liberty is to be stated as proscribing any limit on liberty except where harm to the interests of others may thereby be prevented. When *On Liberty* is taken in conjunction with the final chapter of *Utilitarianism*, however, there is more than we can say on Mill's conception of harm. The various restrictions Mill places on what is to count as harm for the purposes of the Principle of Liberty show him holding that, along with the vital interest in security, men possess another interest, that in autonomy, which is to be ranked over their other interests. Mill's submission is that this pair of interests is to be weighted over men's other interests in such a way that only damage to these interests can justify putting a limit on their liberty. Note here that Mill is not as some have argued, revising the content of utility or happiness, so that autonomy enters in as a particularly weighty ingredient of happiness. No doubt, as part of the more complex moral psychology he developed from the rudiments inherited from his father, Mill did believe that pleasures of activity are greater in human beings than is ordinarily realized. But his argument in *On Liberty* is not that autonomy figures as a matter of fact as a very weighty element in happiness, rather it is that autonomy ought as a matter of utilitarian strategy to be elevated along with security over the other human interests. This pair of vital interests functions in Mill's theory of the moral rights rather as the primary goods do in Rawls's theory of justice. We are to look to the vital interests and not to the utilities of

[14] See especially, J. C. Rees's contribution, "A Re-reading of Mill on Liberty", *Political Studies* 8 (1960): 113–129, reprinted with an important postscript (1965) in P. Radcliff (ed.), *Limits of Liberty*, (Belmont, CA: Wadsworth, 1966) 88–107. See also D. G. Brown, "Mill on Liberty and Morality," *Philosophical Review* 81 (1972): 133–158; "What is Mill's Principle of Utility?", *Canadian Journal of Philosophy*, 3 (1973): 1–12; "Mills Act-Utilitarianism," *Philosophical Quarterly*, 24 (1974): 67–68; "John Rawls: John Mill," *Dialogue*, 12 (1973): No. 3; "Mill on Harm to Others' Interests," *Political Studies*, 26 (1978): 395–399.

For David Lyons' cotributions, see his "Mill's Theory of Morality," *Nous*, 10 (1976): 101–120; "Human Rights and the General Welfare," *Philosophy and Public Affairs*, 6 (1977): 113–129. His recent paper, "Mill's Theory of Justice," which appears in A. I. Goldman and J. Kim (eds.), *Values and Morals* (Dordrecht, D. Reidel Publishing Company, 1978), 1–20; and his "Mill on Liberty and Harm to Others," *Canadian Journal of Philosophy*, Supplementary Volume V (1979): 1–19, are also important sources. Of crucial importance in developing the interpretation of Mill as an indirect utilitarian is Richard Wollheim's "John Stuart Mill and Isaiah Berlin: the Ends of Life and the Preliminaries of Morality," in Alan Ryan (ed.), *The Idea of Freedom* (Oxford: Oxford University Press, 1979), 253–269, and Wollheim's *The Sheep and the Ceremony: The Leslie Stephen Lecture, 1979* (Cambridge: Cambridge University Press), 28–33.

An extremely valuable source of recent interpretations is W. E. Cooper, Kai Nielson, and S. C. Patten (eds.), *New Essays on John Stuart Mill and Utilitarianism*, published as Supplementary Volume V (1979), *Canadian Journal of Philosophy*, in which the papers by David Lyons, J. P. Dryer, David Copp, L. W. Sumner and Fred Berger are particularly noteworthy.

the agents concerned when we are deliberating limits on their liberty. In Mill, however, this proposal is advanced as part of the utilitarian strategy.

SOME DIFFICULTIES IN MILL'S UTILITARIAN DERIVATION OF MORAL RIGHTS

Taking Mill's as the most explicit and systematic indirect utilitarian defense of fundamental rights, we have the following argument. As I wish to interpret it (following most recent interpreters), Mill's utilitarianism is continuous with Bentham's inasmuch as Mill retains a thoroughly want-regarding view of human interests. He does not deviate into some kind of perfectionist morality[15] but rather differs from Bentham in his empirical assessment of human moral psychology, assigning a greater weight than Bentham did to the active pleasures. Within the whole range of human interests, Mill advocates on grounds of utilitarian strategy, ranking the two interests of men in autonomy and in security above all the rest. If we see *On Liberty* as completing the argument for a moral right to security sketched in the last chapter of *Utilitarianism*, we may be justified in interpreting Mill as grounding two fundamental rights – the right to security of person and property, and the right to liberty – in the vital interests men have in security and in autonomy.

Now, quite aside from whether Mill's actual reading of human psychology is sound,[16] the structure of his derivation of fundamental rights poses a number of difficulties for him. First, even if we accept that there is good utilitarian reason to elevate the pair of vital interests over the rest, how does Mill propose that we trade off one vital interest with another when they compete? This is a problem of Mill's, obviously similar to that which Rawls has in respect to his primary goods, which cannot be circumvented by the expedient of linking the two vital interests in a conceptual way. For, even if the interests in autonomy and in security are not wholly distinct or separable, different institutions and different policies will promote them differentially. Granted the lexicographical priority of the pair of vital interests over all the others, Mill appears to need a decision procedure for resolving practical conflict within this pair.

Suppose, however, that we pass over this difficulty, and consider only the class of fundamental rights supposedly yielded by or grounded on the pair of vital interests. Are we allowed to maximize over fundamental rights, or to minimize over violation of such rights? Is it permissible, within Mill's structure of justification of fundamental rights, to follow a "utilitarianism of rights" approach, negative or positive? It has been perceived by Robert Nozick in his

---

[15] I employ the term "perfectionist" here in Rawls's sense. For an argument that J. S. Mill espoused a perfectionist morality, see V. Haksar, *Equality, Liberty and Perfectionism* (Oxford: Clarendon Press, 1979).

[16] Mill's argument was disputed on grounds of psychological realism by James Fitzjames Stephen in his *Liberty, Equality, Fraternity* (Cambridge: Cambridge University Press, 1967).

seminal discussion of this question,[17] that all of the morally objectionable features of the Benthamite calculus reappear within rights theory, unless we recognize some constraint on the violation of rights for the sake of greater rights protection on balance. This is a special problem for Mill, since on my interpretation he needs weighting principles for the two vital interests, and it seems inevitable that these will result in assessments of the associated rights as having differing degrees of importance.

This is, to be sure, a general problem in all theories in which it is allowed that fundamental rights may make conflicting demands in practice, and in which as a consequence these rights are not treated as embodying infinitely weighty side constraints. It seems that the latent maximizing structure even of Mill's indirect view imposes a greater pressure towards a utilitarianism of rights, however, than need be the case in a theory in which there is no such underlying commitment to maximize whatever has value. Only by contending once again that, as a rule of utilitarian strategy, we are justified in prohibiting trade-offs of a few weighty rights against many less weighty ones, can Mill avoid this maximizing commitment seeping into practical policy. The rationale would here be fallibilistic, as before: plausibly, we have no reliable means of identifying cases where such a trade-off of rights against rights is optimum in terms of on balance rights-protection. It seems implausible, all the same, to suppose that such fallibilistic reasons can support granting to the no trade-off rule about rights an absolutist status.

How serious are these difficulties for Mill's view? It seems to me that the difficulties I have canvassed regarding trade-offs between fundamental rights are confronted by any plausible theory of rights, whether or not it is animated by a maximizing commitment. Unless we treat fundamental rights as framing a complete structure of compossible side constraints,[18] we cannot avoid having some principles of weighting among them, and, if I am right that the maximizing commitment in respect of the vital interests surfaces here, then at least the decision between the conflicting rights is governed by some principle, and is not merely *ad hoc* or intuitionistic. Again, the teleological structure of Mill's derivation may even be a strength. We may characterize his indirect utilitarian derivation of basic rights as a rights-based political theory grounded in a goal-based moral theory. Dilemmas within the sphere of rights-protection are informed and governed, on this view, by considerations about the promotion of utilitarian interests. Mill's theory has at least the advantage that rights considerations are not treated as ultimate or foundational within it, and the problem it shares about conflicts of rights it has in common with all rights theories, including highly formalistic ones, which do not make the stipulation

---

[17]   See Robert Nozick, *Anarchy, State and Utopia*, 30 et seq.
[18]   Leibnitz's notion of compossibility is used in the content of rights theory by Hillel Steiner in his "The Structure of a Set of Compossible Rights", *Journal of Philosophy* 74 (1979), 767–775.

that no such competition of rights with each other, or defeat of one right by another, can ever occur. Mill's account, then, has the advantage that it reconstructs moral deliberation in questions to do with conflicts of rights in a fashion which renders it intelligible and shows it to be governed by principle.

CONCLUDING REMARKS

I close this avowedly exploratory paper by mentioning three hard problems for the indirect utilitarian derivation of fundamental rights as I have recon-structed it out of Mill's account of justice. The first problem concerns the strong distinction between the critical and the practical level of moral thought which the indirect view especially marks. It might be objected that this distinction has no peculiar connection with utilitarianism, or at any rate that the connection has yet to be exhibited in detail; there might be a large class of indirect moral theories, in some of which utility appraisals enter at the critical level, while in others it is judgments about rights which occupy that place.[19] I take it that Hare's Kantian derivation of utilitarian ethics is intended to answer this difficulty. A different but related point is that a wholly instrumental account of the value of rights, even of the sort given in the indirect view, does not seem to capture our sense of the moral importance of fundamental rights. Perhaps, if we cannot help but see in basic rights considerations which possess an irreducible or ultimate importance, such rights must enter our theory of them at the critical level and have a foundational role in the theory's applica-tions. The most adequate view of rights may not be, and certainly need not be, one in which claims of welfare are always defeated by rights: we might try, as A. K. Sen has done in some recent important work,[20] to elaborate a more complex moral structure in which both rights and welfare enter into a con-sequentialist theory. However this may be, the objection is that it needs to be shown that rights enter moral and political theory always and only as deriva-tions of some more fundamental principle. Against this objection, it may be worth observing that it is not an argument that is neutral in the area of moral epistemology. As Hare has pointed out, arguments of this sort appear to presuppose some sort of intuitionism in our moral knowledge, or at any rate they seem bound to rest content with the deliverances of our moral intuition as to the weight that rights principles are to have in our theory. It may be, however, that this translation of intuitive judgments into moral theory repre-sents a mistake in method.

This last point brings me to what is probably the most fundamental question about the approach explored in this paper. It may be objected that, in the indirect utilitarian approach, a claim for the primacy of theory over practice in

---

[19] This latter point is made by A. K. Sen in his "Utilitarianism and Welfarism", *Journal of Philosophy* 74 (1979): 463–488.

[20] See especially Sen's "Plural Utility", *Proceedings of the Aristotelian Society*, 1980/81.

moral life is made which we have no reason to accept. Especially in the indirect utilitarian view it is assumed that the role of theory is to reconstruct our primary moral judgments in a systematic and consistent fashion, and in so doing diminish the incoherences of actual moral life. In the indirect view, more than any other, however, it may be objected that this conception of the primacy of moral theory results in a kind of schiozophrenia in which as moral theorists we are bound to submit our commitments and attachments to an impartial scrutiny from which we are bound to exempt them in our role as moral agents. To argue this way[21] is to hold that the distinction between the critical and the practical levels of moral thought is misplaced, or at any rate that it cannot have the place in moral theory which the indirect view gives it. If this objection can be sustained, then not only indirect utilitarianism but much else in moral philosophy founders. This objection would seem, in fact, to place a severe limit on the scope and authority of moral theory itself. Whether this fact is an argument for my view, or a further consideration against it, may perhaps best be explored on another occasion.[22]

Politics, Jesus College, Oxford University

[21] I have in mind here, especially, Bernard Williams as an important sceptic about the systematizing aspirations of moral theory. See Williams' *Problems of the Self* (Cambridge: C.U.P., 1973) and *Moral Luck* (Cambridge: C.U.P., 1981).

[22] For their comments on a previous draft of this paper, I am indebted to David Gordon, Lester Hunt, Loren Lomasky, Murray Rothbard, Douglas Rasmussen, Jeremy Shearmur, Henry Veatch, and the participants in the Conference on Human Rights held at the Social Philosophy and Policy Center at Bowling Green, October 7–8, 1982. I am particularly grateful to my commentator, Prof. Robert Kocis, for his profound and subtle criticisms of my paper. I wish finally to thank Professor R. M. Hare for his detailed comments on my paper, and for his encouragement of the enterprise it attempts. None of those I have here acknowledged as helpful to me has any responsibility for my final argument.

Social Philosophy & Policy Vol. 1 Issue 2 ISSN 0265-0525

UTILITARIANISM AND HUMAN RIGHTS*

Allan Gibbard

INTRODUCTION

We look to rights for protection. The hope of advocates of "human rights" has been that certain protections might be accorded to all of humanity. Even in a world only a minority of whose inhabitants live under liberal democratic regimes, the hope is, certain standards accepted in the liberal democracies will gain universal recognition and respect. These include liberty of persons as opposed to enslavement, freedom from cruelty, freedom from arbitrary execution, from arbitrary imprisonment, and from arbitrary deprivation of property or livelihood, freedom of religion, and freedom of inquiry and expression.

Philosophers, of course, concern themselves with the theory of rights, and that is partly because of the ways questions of rights bear on fundamental normative theory. By far the most highly developed general normative theory has been utilitarianism. Now many opponents of utilitarianism argue that considerations of rights discredit utilitarianism, that utilitarianism yields conclusions about rights that we would normally regard as faulty, and that moreover, the reasons for regarding those conclusions as faulty turn out, upon examination, to be stronger than the reasons for regarding utilitarianism as valid. A valid theory cannot have faulty conclusions, and so thinking about rights shows utilitarianism not to be a valid normative theory.

Jeremy Bentham, the founder of the utilitarian movement in nineteenth century England, accepted the incompatibility of utilitarianism and "the rights of man," and rejected talk of the latter as "anarchical fallacies". His great successor John Stuart Mill, however, argued that a perceptive and far-sighted utilitarianism supports strong rights both of democratic participation and of individual freedom of action. Here, I want to examine utilitarian arguments for rights in general, with an eye toward the commonly recognized core of human rights.

On a utilitarian view of rights, the problem to be addressed is one of institutional design, and more broadly, of the design of social practices. Rights are not part of this problem, but part of its solution. At the most fundamental level, that is to say, institutions and practices are to be evaluated by their performance, and the standards by which performance is to be judged do not themselves involve rights. Rights, utilitarian liberals claim, are an important

* Work on this paper was supported by a Fellowship for Independent Study of the National Endowment for the Humanities.

part of the best solution to this problem of design. In the case of the core "human rights," the social practices in question are of two kinds, national and world. The ultimate hope is that protection of these rights may become a part of the effective constitution of every nation. The more immediate hope is that respect for human rights may be promoted and buttressed by the power of world opinion. A commonly recognized core of human rights, the hope is, can provide standards for worldwide public criticism of the ways governments treat those subject to their power.

It is notorious, though, that any utilitarian defense of rights threatens paradox. If I, a government official, am committed not to violate a commonly recognized core of human rights, then either I must think that violating those rights is never what is best calculated to promote the general good, or I must be prepared to sacrifice the general good in order not to violate those rights. Now it may seem implausible that the violation of commonly recognized human rights is never what is best calculated to promote the general good. In any case, it affords us little protection if rulers around the world are committed merely to respect human rights whenever doing so seems to them to fit the principle of utility. The situations in which commonly recognized human rights are violated are often ones of serious conflict and high passion, where the violators of human rights will almost always take their actions to be promoting the general good. Can a utilitarian, then, have a commitment to rights that is effective? Can he be genuinely committed not to violate certain rights, even if cases arise in which the course of action best calculated to promote the general good involves violating those rights? Or is that simply to renounce utilitarianism?

A main reason for treasuring these rights is the protection they offer: the prospect that their recognition will enhance human thriving and human happiness. If that hope is warranted, then utilitarians have strong reason to advocate respect for human rights, and cannot rightly renounce them. That, then, is the threatened paradox: utilitarians have strong reason to want the commonly respected core of human rights to be respected universally, even when respect for these rights appears to conflict with the demands of the general good. "Utilitarianism," though, whatever we take the term to mean precisely, is the doctrine that in some sense, the ultimate moral standard is the promotion of the general good. How can concern with the general good dictate that respect for rights takes precedence over considerations of the general good?

This challenge is sometimes met by formulating a "rule utilitarianism" that deviates from the prescriptions of standard "act-utilitarianism" when the principles it would be good to have recognized do not prescribe the act that would most promote the general good. The move to rule utilitarianism, though, may appear *ad hoc*, or a concession to irrational rule-worship. In this paper, I want to approach this perennial controversy by starting with the root idea of utilitarianism: that morality is a matter of the rational pursuit of the general good. What kind of utilitarianism emerges from this root precept?

PRAGMATIC INSTITUTIONAL DESIGN

Rights, I have said, on the view of a utilitarian liberal, are solutions to problems of institutional design, and are not, at the most fundamental level, part of the problem. They are good solutions in virtue of facts of human motivational psychology. What I now want to do is to back up from this claim about the moral status of rights, and examine the problem that faces a pragmatic designer of institutions. In doing so, I obliquely address standard problems of utilitarianism, but I do so by placing responses to them within the framework of a kind of problem that faces anyone trying to develop a theory of institutional design on a pragmatic basis. I want in this section to take up the project of pragmatic institutional design on its own terms and see where it leads, without regard, for the moment, to whether it leads to anything recognizable as principled political advocacy.

What is the problem of pragmatic institutional design? Here are some caricatures. The problem might be one of *scriptwriting*. The script would prescribe what each member of the institution should do, and be judged by the total amount of happiness that would be produced were those prescriptions followed. Imagine a script for a marionette show with the following novel features: the script is general, the happiness of the marionettes is affected by what the script has them do, and the test of quality is not aesthetic and not a matter of how the show affects an audience, but a matter of how happy the marionettes are as the performance proceeds.

Now, of course, one problem with the scriptwriting caricature is that it is hard to imagine people as marionettes without ignoring some of the central sources of happiness in life: the active pursuit of purposes. Another central problem is that no one has the power to get his script produced. The scriptwriting account ignores all matters of causation within a society: all design of systems of communication, coordination, and incentive. If we can write the script, why waste our puppets' efforts on getting each other to follow it? Either we choose among scripts on the assumption that the one we choose will be followed, or the scriptwriting account sets no well-defined problems to the designer of institutions.

Perhaps, then, the problem of institutional design is this: to design people and their relationships in such a way that the resulting mechanism produces good without further intervention of the designer. It is, in effect, an idealized problem of institutional engineering. The caricature of *institutional engineering* goes like this: an engineer designing a machine must know what his materials can do and how they would interact in various possible designs. He can deduce how machines of various possible designs could be expected to perform, and how reliably. He is given standards of cost and effectiveness for judging the expected performance of alternative mechanisms, including the costs of breakdowns, and he chooses the design that is the best, by these standards, of the alternatives he has analyzed. The institutional engineer is special in that he works primarily with people as his materials, and chooses a design on the basis of how much happiness it would produce.

As a caricature of mechanical engineering, what I have said abstracts from the problem of how to convince anyone to build the machine, and how to get people to use the machine as it was designed to be used. Institutional design involves the same problems. One cannot simply put properly designed people in their proper places and let the institutional machine work. Institutions depend on habits, accepted norms, and all the other aspects of human psychology that go to determine how people will act. Norms and habits can be affected by education and indoctrination, by discussion, praise, and criticism, by rewards and penalties – but hardly to industrial levels of precision.

Where institutions are to be designed, moreover, the designer is part of the design, or at least must speak to those who are part of the design as person to person. Rousseau (*Social Contract*, 1762, Bk. 2 Ch. 7), in contemplating the problem of institutional design, resorts to a *legislateur* of wisdom far greater than that of the people for whom he legislates, who wins the people to his laws not by reason, but by claiming to speak for the gods. The institutional designer's problem is how to proceed if no such claim will be believed.

Perhaps, then, the institutional designer must be a benevolent Machiavellian. A utilitarian, after all, acts to maximize expected utility – that is, the expected value of the consequence of what he does, where the evaluation counts equally the happiness of everyone. Now, writing and speaking about rights constitutes action, of a kind, and the rational utilitarian will judge what to say about rights, or what to do instead of talking about rights, by expected utility. If he affirms a right or denies one, he does so, and does so in the way he does, not because he believes what he is saying, but because doing so in that way has the highest expected utility of all the things he might have done at the time. On a given occasion, the benevolent Machiavellian may propagandize and manipulate, in the sense that he puts forth as his own, reasons he does not in fact accept for doing what he does think ought to be done. He may even advocate something he thinks ought not to be done – say to win favor, and thereby put himself in a position of more power to do good than he otherwise would be. The choice hinges on expected utility. He may, of course, speak honestly, giving his own reasons for conclusions he accepts – but only when honesty is the best policy on benevolent grounds.

This benevolent Machiavellian is no doubt not someone we would respect, much less trust, but that is not to the point now, which is to apply the utilitarian standard to what the benevolent Machiavellian does. Does utilitarianism prescribe a benevolent Machiavellianism? For a person with perfect self-control in the service of benevolence and perfect power to weigh evidence and ascribe expected utility to policies open to him, whose own good is not substantially dependent on a non-manipulative approach to human relations, the answer must undoubtedly be yes. A benevolent god will not have an admirable character by human standards. If this account of a benevolent Machiavellianism is, indeed, a caricature of utilitarian political advocacy, and a utilitarian morality of advocacy turns out to look at all like familiar morality, that will be because of human imperfection. That, alas, need not be a shaky foundation.

What goes wrong, from a purely utilitarian standpoint, when we drop the assumption of human perfection? In the first place, much of a person's happiness will depend on interpersonal relations that he experiences as reciprocally non-manipulative. This effect on his own happiness may, to be sure, be outweighed by his effect on others: perhaps kings, diplomats, and leaders of movements must sacrifice intimacy and plain dealing for the sake of others; but it could well be self-delusion to suppose that the rest of us face that choice. Consider also, though, matters of self-control. Is it not likely that starvation from human fellowship produces needs that cloud judgment, so that the benevolent Machiavellian risks becoming a Stalin? Most important of all, though, the benevolent Machiavellian with persuasive power needs some way of judging the expected utility of his words. The expected utility of his words will depend on considerations of great difficulty: on matters of evidence that can only be well judged with interpersonal support in an atmosphere of reciprocal honesty. The benevolent Machiavellian, then, seems caught on the horns of a dilemma. On the one horn, if he has little power to affect events with his social theorizing, then his own happiness and that of his intimates is of prime concern, and those are fostered by honesty. On the other horn, if he has any substantial power to influence events by his action or persuasion, then the fixity of his benevolence and the stability of the judgment that guides it are of prime concern, and those are fostered by honesty. Pure Machiavellian benevolence has poor utilitarian backing as a standard for a person of anything close to human possibilities and limitations.

What are the alternatives to Machiavellian benevolence as ways of working to bring institutions into existence? The achievement of consensus is one, institution by agreement is another, and using one's powers within existing institutions, such as the legal system, is another. Persuasion is important for all of these: persuasion to accept a principle, persuasion to enter into an agreement, and persuasion to exercise one's institutional powers in a given way. Now, persuasion itself draws on existing institutions, in which people play roles governed by norms: particularly on the institution we might call *dialogue*. The norms of dialogue are to be open about what one finds persuasive and to give serious attention to what the other side puts forth as possible considerations. The political advocate acts within an existing institution of dialogue, and the problem of how utilitarian advocacy is to proceed is a part of the general problem of how a utilitarian is to act within institutions.

THE RATIONAL PURSUIT OF AN END

J. S. Mill and Henry Sidgwick differed from many ethical theorists of today in that both took the fundamental problem of ethics to be the choice of an ultimate end. Utilitarianism as they conceived it is the thesis that the proper ultimate end is the same for each person, that that end is the "general good" or "good from the point of view of the universe," which is the sum of the goods of individuals, and that the good of each person is his happiness. How utilitarianism in this sense bears on conduct is a matter of what constitutes the rational pursuit of its end: what, the question is, would it be rationally to pursue the general happiness as one's ultimate end?

Consider, then, the general question of what constitutes the rational pursuit of an end. Sidgwick tackles this question first in his discussion of egoism, in the course of which he discusses whether the pursuit of pleasure can bring as much pleasure as can other pursuits. (*Methods of Ethics*, 1901, I.iv.2 and II.iii.2) If it cannot, the pursuit of pleasure is self-defeating; that, he calls the "Fundamental Paradox of Egoistic Hedonism." The argument for the paradox stems from Butler. Most pleasure, Sidgwick says, comes from the pursuit and attainment of goals that are distinct from the egoist's goal of his own happiness. A prime example is the pleasure of scoring a point in a competitive game. A player would get no great pleasure form scoring if he were not trying so hard to score, and although he plays the game for pleasure, in the heat of the competition he is not trying to score merely for the sake of the pleasure he thinks that will bring. He simply wants to score.

The "paradox" for egoism is this. A pure egoist is someone who desires nothing but happiness, a high balance of pleasure over pain in his life. Such a person, though, lacks the very kinds of desires from which most pleasures come. From the rational pursuit of happiness, then, will come a life of little pleasure, whereas having non-egoistic goals could lead to a life with much more pleasure and not much more pain. The rational pursuit of happiness is self-defeating.

Sidgwick dismisses this as no serious problem for egoism.

> It is an experience only too common among men, in whatever pursuit they may be engaged, that they let the original object and goal of their efforts pass out of view, and come to regard the means to this end as ends to themselves ... And if it be thus easy and common to forget the end in the means overmuch, there seems no reason why it should be

difficult to do it to the extent that Rational Egoism prescribes: and, in
fact, it seems to be continually done by ordinary persons in the case of
amusements and pastimes of all kinds. (II. iii. 2, p. 137)

Now, perhaps this reply concedes the objection. By definition, after all, an
egoist's sole goals are pleasure and the absence of pain in his life, and Sidgwick
concedes that a person who had only those goals would find little pleasure in
life. All Sidgwick has done, then, is to note what incorrigible non-egoists we
are: that even if we set out to be egoists, we would not keep at it, but would
soon be pursuing non-egoistic goals. What this shows is not that anyone can
enjoy life while remaining an egoist, but that no one will long remain an egoist.

The problem with this reply to Sidgwick is that it bypasses the kind of
egoism that matters. Suppose a man loves his wife and children, and finds life
fulfilling in ways that depend on his concern for their happiness. Suppose also,
though, that he would set out to wean himself of his love for them, and leave
them miserable and destitute if, on reflection, he thought he would find life
somewhat more fulfilling that way. Such a man, to be sure, will have many
desires that are not simply desires for his own happiness, and are not desires
for things simply as instrumental to his own happiness. He wants his family to
love him and to be happy. If on that account, though, we say he is not an egoist,
then we need a new name for the kind of person he is. What shall we call him?
His own happiness is, in an important sense, what he takes as the ultimate goal
of his conduct, for he fosters intrinsic desires when he thinks on reflection that
having them promotes his own happiness, and takes steps to rid himself of
desires when he thinks that doing so would foster his happiness. Indeed, that,
it seems, is what is involved in the rational pursuit of any long-range goal, be it
money, fame, pedagogical success, a winning season, one's own happiness, or
anything else. If that is not "egoism" in the strictest sense, we ought to change
the sense, so that we can apply the term 'egoism' to a theory that is worth taking
seriously.

What does all this tell us about the rational pursuit of the general happiness?
Clearly, the rational utilitarian, in the sense of the term that matters, will not
keep his attention fixed on the goal of the general happiness. He will take the
general happiness as his ultimate goal in the same way as a rational egoist takes
his own happiness as his ultimate goal. He will reflect from time to time on
himself and his situation, and consider the desires which in the ordinary
course of life he experiences as intrinsic. Those desires may well be ones that
stem from regarding actions as morally legitimate or illegitimate, equitable or
inequitable, proper or improper. They may well include the desires that
constitute commitment to a principle. A rational utilitarian will foster in
himself and others those attitudes, habits, and ways of deliberating the
fostering of which he thinks conducive to the general happiness, and work to

rid himself and others of moral attitudes, habits, and ways of deliberating when he sees that that has utility.

UTILITARIAN POLITICAL ADVOCACY

If what I have been saying is right, the puzzle of a utilitarian theory of rights hinges on a general question: What constitutes the rational pursuit of the general happiness within institutions? How should a utilitarian treat the accepted norms of dialogue? Now, in his participation in institutions, it follows from what I have said, a rational utilitarian will reflect from time to time about which tendencies of character and personal makeup work on the whole toward the general happiness in those institutions. The answer, of course, will depend on the nature of the institutions and the distribution of ways in which others are disposed to act in their institutional roles. Clearly in some cases, a rational utilitarian will violate institutional norms, whereas in other cases he will conform to them.

What utilitarian support, then, can be given for respect for human rights? In the first place, they may have a kind of "log-rolling" rationale. The utilitarian's reason for wanting human rights to be respected is his conviction that in most cases their violation detracts from the general happiness, that human judgment of what the exceptions are is notoriously unreliable, and that criticism that appeals to the promotion of the general good is ineffective compared to criticism that appeals to commonly recognized standards of human rights, because it is so highly debatable what best promotes the general good. The problem for a utilitarian advocate of rights is that he recognizes that anyone who investigates carefully would find a case, from time to time, that was exceptional, in that as far as he could see, it would further the general good on balance to violate one of the widely recognized human rights in that case. Suppose, though, that even careful investigators would come to little agreement with each other on which cases are the exceptions, and those who had not investigated with the care of experts would not agree on which of the experts to believe. Thus, although someone who investigated carefully might conclude that the ideal policy involves violation of a widely accepted human right, he might also conclude that no institution for deciding when that is so would do better than an institution of automatic condemnation of violations of certain recognized rights.

What, though, if the experts agree. Then the "log-rolling" rationale that I have been giving does not apply, and there is a case for refining our public understanding of what the universal human rights are. There is danger, though, in too much refinement. In human affairs, there is ordinarily no way to impose a rule unless the importance of keeping to the rule can be securely made to carry conviction. Even the clauses of a written constitution with a bill of rights work through human adherence: through legislative self-restraint, judicial review, or refusal of individual citizens to regard themselves as bound by purported laws they think unconstitutional. Even when legislators or judges adhere to the constitution itself, they can often talk themselves around provisions for which they find no satisfying rationale, and the aura of legitimacy on which legislators and judges depend requires that they act to a considerable degree on norms that they share with the rest of the community. If, on the other hand, the principle is to govern not through the provisions of a written constitution but by consensus, as is the hope for human rights secured by the power of world opinion, the point is apparent: a principle that applies to important matters will be followed only if the importance of keeping to it can draw conviction.

In this respect, there is a special virtue in principles that carry with them a strong non-utilitarian rationale. Principles like freedom from arbitrary arrest have a direct rationale in the dignity and security of each person protected. To qualify the principle with exceptions would be to undermine that rationale. "Why except this case?" it would then be asked, "and to what else does the same kind of reasoning apply?" Some principles, then, make more effective taboos than others.

What place does a non-utilitarian rationale have in utilitarian argument? Just this: People in general, utilitarians and non-utilitarians, can be strongly moved by a principle with a coherent rationale, and especially one that seems to fill in the dictum "To each his own." Utilitarians, to be sure, argue that being strongly moved is not enough for rational moral conviction. They claim that when we look at the principles that have such strong appeal and test them carefully against our more specific moral convictions, we find no coherent whole. With that, of course, intuitionistic opponents of utilitarianism agree, but whereas the intuitionists try to construct a coherent whole by a strategy of piecemeal adjustments, utilitarians look for a standard by which conflicts may be resolved. The utilitarian, though, is not a person unmoved by principles, but a person who has learned to distrust the principles he finds moving until he has tested them by the standard of utility.

A principle with a rationale that carries conviction may be of great utility. Suppose two alternative principles both have a high *acceptance-utility*: for each, its being adopted and followed by most people would have high utility. If one has much more natural appeal as a principle than does the other, there will be greater utility in supporting it even if it has slightly less acceptance-utility. It will not only be more convincing to others; it will command the utilitarian's own principled adherence more securely.

What bearing does this have on political advocacy and political commitment? Advocacy often at least purports to be governed by the norms of dialogue: sincerity and willingness to consider what others say. Sincerity in the advocacy of principles consists in advocating principles by which one is willing to be bound, either unconditionally or if enough others are. The questions to ask, then, are whether a utilitarian should abide by the norm of sincerity, and if so, what principle he should advocate under the constraint of this norm. The issue, here, is not whether to be sincere in all circumstances, actual or possible, but whether to be sincere in a discussion of political institutions when others, for the most part, are.

Now deception, as we know, has various psychological costs: it cuts a person off from some of the emotional rewards of human company, and it is likely to give him an artificial manner which makes him at once less convincing and less rewarding as a conversationalist. Insincerity in writing may be less costly psychologically, but it is hard to write insincerely and speak sincerely: the secret will out.

Perhaps the most important consideration, though, is the way insincere advocacy is likely to affect the advocate's judgment. If matters are easy to think through, this consideration will not apply, but then in most such cases, the greatest utility lies in advocating the clear basis of one's own conviction. In difficult matters, the thinker needs the exercise of sincere participation in dialogue, for sincere dialogue can help thinking in a way that delivering a sales talk cannot. Cultivating habits of sincerity will normally foster good habits of thought.

Now, whereas in matters of fact and evidence, sincerity is not achieved by adjusting one's beliefs to what one wants to assert, in matters of commitment to principle, it can be. That is to say, one can adopt a principle on the basis of the utility of advocating it. Of course, one cannot adopt a principle at will: commitment must be fostered and practiced. How well one can expect to be able to cultivate the various alternative commitments one might now choose to foster bears also on a utilitarian choice of principles: if commitment to either of two principles would have high utility, but one of the principles is felt as more compelling, that may be a strong point in its favor from a utilitarian point of view.

If, then, you are a utilitarian who thinks the facts of social psychology are as I have been supposing, here is why you should accept certain principles of individual human rights, advocate them, and foster your own commitment to them. The facts I have been supposing are these: for the most part, violations of the commonly recognized core of human rights detract from the general good. There may well be exceptions, but even with careful investigation, there will be much disagreement on what those exceptions are. Moreover, even if we can agree on a few exceptions, a principle without qualifications to provide for those exceptional cases may have a much stronger natural appeal than a principle meticulously qualified. Suppose, then, you have a choice between the following: (1) A simple principle of great natural appeal – say, the principle of freedom from arrest without probable cause and a speedy trial; (2) That principle with provisos for the rare kinds of cases where detention without trial, we all now agree, seems best calculated to promote the general good; and (3) No principle at all other than the principle of acting in the way best calculated to promote the general good. Questions of sincerity aside, advocacy of the simple principle may well have the greatest expected utility. For commitment to it is likely to be especially easy and firm, because of its compelling non-utilitarian rationale.

Now reintroduce considerations of sincerity. Should you (a) advocate the simple principle and accept it, (b) advocate the simple principle and accept an alternative, or (c) both advocate and accept an alternative? Recall that if you accept an alternative, you will in some ways have a more difficult time fostering your own commitment to it than you would have in fostering a commitment to a principle with strong natural appeal. If you both accept and advocate an alternative to the simple principle, you lose the advantage of natural appeal of the simple principle. If you advocate the simple principle but secretly accept an alternative, you lose the utility of sincerity, and gain little or nothing in utility from your commitment to the principle you think ideal. It is ideal, after all, only in that so far as you can determine, widespread, firm commitment to it would have greater expected utility than would widespread, firm commitment to any alternative. If you cannot even secure your own firm commitment to it, that is a poor utilitarian recommendation for the principle.

Principles are often rejected as dangerous, and courses of action are often rejected as violating principles it it important to maintain and foster. These lines of argument often seem to embody wisdom, but they seem available to the utilitarian only at the price of making him crafty and manipulative rather than wise. I have tried to explore what happens if we think of utilitarianism not as taking the form, "An act is right if and only if . . .," but as saying that everyone should take as his ultimate end the greatest total good of all sentient beings, and pursue that end rationally.

Utilitarians think that the justification of moral principles often requires sagacity: understanding of important aspects of human psychology, of social and institutional dynamics, and of the consequences of these for the rational pursuit of the general happiness. Here, what I have tried to do is not to provide utilitarianism with the social theory it needs, but to sketch the kind of argument a utilitarian might give for a commitment to human rights. There is nothing incoherent, I maintain, in the general form of a utilitarian argument for rights.

Philosophy, University of Michigan

Social Philosophy & Policy Vol. 1 Issue 2 ISSN 0265-0525

COMMENT ON GIBBARD
UTILITARIANISM VERSUS
HUMAN RIGHTS

JAMES FISHKIN

Rather than respond to Gibbard, point by point, I will comment on what I take to be the general spirit of his argument. The old consensus on some form or another of utilitarianism, a consensus that dominated discussions in moral and political theory only a few years ago, has now largely evaporated before the heat of distributional objections founded on justice, the "separateness of persons," and other concerns for the severe sacrifices that utilitarianism might require of some for the sake of greater gains to others (or for the sake of gains to a greater number of others).[1]

By attempting to develop a utilitarian basis for adherence to "core human rights," Gibbard is offering a variant of utilitarianism that holds out the promise of withstanding some of these distributional objections and, perhaps, of rehabilitating some form of the theory in a thorough-going way. After all, many of the standard anti-utilitarian arguments focus on the theory's ability to legitimate deprivations of what Gibbard calls core human rights.

> Liberty of person as opposed to enslavement, freedom from cruelty, freedom from arbitrary execution, from arbitrary imprisonment, and from arbitrary deprivation of property or livelihood, freedom of religion and freedom of inquiry and expression.

If adherence to these core human rights can be given a utilitarian basis, then many anti-utilitarian arguments can be dismissed.

I wish to argue that this strategy faces three basic difficulties. First, it takes more than Gibbard's list of core human rights to protect utilitarianism from strong distributional objections. Second, if the ultimate basis for institutionalizing one set of rights-defining practices rather than another is utilitarian, then those core human rights have a most uncertain basis. It is an open, quasi-empirical question whether other practices, abhorrent to rights advocates,

---

[1] For some insightful remarks on this general transition see H. L. A. Hart "Between Utility and Rights" in Alan Ryan (ed.) *The Idea of Freedom: Essays in Honour of Isaiah Berlin* (Oxford: Oxford University Press, 1979).

For one attempt to formulate distributional objections to utilitarianism and other key principles see my *Tyranny and Legitimacy: A Critique of Political Theories* (Baltimore: Johns Hopkins, 1979).

might not produce greater aggregate utility. Third, the core rights on his list may constitute major impediments, in themselves, to the manipulation of preferences and practices required by the rest of his argument. If one relies, as Gibbard advocates, on "the facts of social psychology" one will have to choose, under realistic conditions between utilitarianism and human rights. This is a choice Gibbard's paper has not equipped us to make.

1. Let us begin by imagining a society in which the practices on Gibbard's list of core human rights have been institutionalized – freedom from arbitrary execution and imprisonment, freedom from arbitrary deprivation of property or livelihood, freedom of religion, inquiry, and expression. The first thing to notice about these "core human rights" is that they are all formulated as freedom "from" certain kinds of coercive interference. They are forms of "negative liberty" if you will, or in Nozick's terms, they offer protection from certain kinds of "boundary crossings."

I believe that a consistent utilitarianism – even when applied within the confines of such core rights – is subject to some disturbing distributional objections. For example, let us suppose that the society institutionalizing these core human rights has no developed welfare state apparatus. Nothing on Gibbard's list would require such an apparatus. The basic structure of this state, let us assume, is more or less that of a Nozickian minimal state. Now, let us also assume that this state faces an economic situation rather like our own at present and that the state tolerates increasing unemployment, concentrated among the poor and unskilled and the members of various minority groups, in the interests of moderating inflation.

Nothing on Gibbard's list would mandate even the meager "safety net" tolerated by the Reagan administration. We might assume, however, that Gibbard means for utilitarianism to determine not only institutional design but also particular policies. However, if Gibbard's policymakers are consistent utilitarians, then whether anything at all is done for the poor, starving, and unemployed depends on a series of empirical issues. One factor supporting at least some redistribution is the degree to which there is declining marginal utility of income. But there are also weighty factors on the other side. Incentive effects may require substantial inequalities and they may sharply limit how much is available for redistribution. Furthermore, we can tip the balance of purely utilitarian calculations against potential welfare recipients (or job program recipients) by imagining strong patterns of racial or ethnic hatred such that large numbers of the better off would intensely resent any give-aways to the poor. Nothing in Gibbard's paper would rule out counting such "external" or "public-regarding" preferences.[2] Indeed, once a utilitarian

---

[2] For efforts to draw this distinction more precisely see *Tyranny and Legitimacy* 26–9 and Ronald Dworkin *Taking Rights Seriously* (Cambridge, Mass.: Harvard University Press, 1978) 234–5.

begins choosing among the preferences that are to count as utility, there are serious questions to be raised about whether he is still a utilitarian at all. But once such external preferences are included, severe deprivations and blighted life chances to the poor and the black may be balanced out, in utilitarian calculations, by the resentment and smug satisfaction of the rest of the population – particularly when the latter may also directly benefit from some moderation in inflation. The issue is quasi-empirical. However, we may easily imagine a world – not too distant from our own – in which strictly utilitarian calculations would support such disturbing distributional results – even when Gibbard's core human rights are fully institutionalized. His rights would protect people from arbitrary *deprivations* of property but they would not require adequate opportunities to acquire property or a means of livelihood in the first place. There is no one to single out for a rights violation if the "hidden hand" does not provide.

2. Now, let me turn to a somewhat stylized example of the kind of case for which Gibbard's proposal would seem perfectly adequate. My point will be that if utilitarianism is the ultimate criterion for determining which rights-defining practices are to be institutionalized in the first place, then the strategy may not even hold for such obvious cases – because one might imagine alternative practices outside Gibbard's proposed list which would, under some empirical conditions, produce greater aggregate utility. If Gibbard is ultimately a utilitarian, then he must face the prospect that some utilitarian calculations about which practices to institutionalize will, in some empirical contexts, yield practices that run counter to his core list of rights.

I borrow this stock anti-utilitarian example from Gilbert Harman.[3] Let us first imagine a doctor who must choose between concentrating on one patient to the exclusion of five others in an emergency situation or saving the five others. In this simplified situation, if we must choose between saving one life and saving five, many of us would support the utilitarian calculation that the five be saved. I say "utilitarian" because in introducing no further facts about the six patients, I am making it easy for a utilitarian to count them equally and to treat the saving of life as a place-holder for the production of a future stream of utility. Furthermore, this calculation would appear quite favorable to utilitarianism because by counting lives rather than utilities or dollars, I am permitting the utilitarian to avoid the well-known Paretian difficulties with interpersonal comparisons.

The second step in the example is to imagine the same doctor with five patients, each of whom requires a different organ (one a kidney, another a lung, another a heart, etc.). Without the required transplants, they will each die in the immediate future. The difficulty is that there is no available donor.

[3] Gilbert Harman *The Nature of Morality* (New York: Oxford University Press, 1977) 3–4.

There is, however, a patient in room 306 who has all the required characteristics and organs in good condition. He has checked in for a routine set of physical exams. If he were killed and the required organs redistributed, five lives could be saved at the cost of one lost.

Now, this is the point in anti-utilitarian horror stories when the rejoinders focus on the dangers of exceptions, the value of maintaining ongoing practices, and the disutility of a climate of fear that might be created if exceptions to an on-going practice – such as those defining the routine physical exam – were permitted. Much that Gibbard says along these lines is persuasive. Furthermore, his proposed right to protection from arbitrary loss of life or liberty might be held to protect the patient in room 306 – even when the utilitarian calculations might support taking his life in the interests of saving five others (and even when secrecy and deception might be employed to prevent fear and other forms of disutility from entering the calculation).

However, what is the criterion for deciding, in the first place, that one set of rights-defining practices rather than another is to be institutionalized? If it is utilitarian, as Gibbard implies, then he must face the difficulty that under some empirical conditions, alternative *practices*, even those antithetical to the concerns motivating his list, may yield greater aggregate utility.

For example, if the calculation takes place at the level of institutional design, it may very well turn out to be the case that a forced practice of involuntary organ donation may lead to more lives saved. Only a consistent consequentialism, insensitive to all distinctions between omissions and commissions, could lead us to consider such a horrendous practice. But utilitarian calculations might favor such a practice: (a) if the bulk of the population viewed themselves as potential beneficiaries; (b) if a substantial number of lives could be saved as a result; (c) if there were some reason why the bulk of the population could neglect or discount the possibility that they might turn out to be organ donors. This third condition might be satisfied if organ donation was concentrated unfairly upon some particular sector or group or if it were spread so widely by a lottery system that each person's chances of sacrifice were negligible (or about like those we face in auto accidents). Deception about the risks, per capita, of the practice is another possibility. Under such conditions, purely utilitarian calculations might very well support institutionalization of a practice requiring arbitrary deprivations of life quite as abhorrent as that demanded from the patient in room 306. Even if the donor were picked by a lottery rather than plucked from his routine physical, many of us would strongly object to his involuntary sacrifice – although that objection would have to be non-utilitarian under the conditions I have described.

3. Lastly, it is worth emphasizing that the results of utilitarian calculation – even at the level of institutional design of alternative social practices – will depend crucially upon the preferences and characters of the people whose

utilities are being calculated. Some of my objections could be set aside if people were imagined to be far less nasty, selfish, and resentful than I hypothesized. My point, however, is that if the preferences are as I imagined, then what Gibbard calls the "facts of social psychology" support utilitarian calculations that are distributionally objectionable.

One strategy of response might be to attempt a thorough-going reform of human psychology. If we simply assume universally benign preferences, then many of my objections will have to be set aside. But if we make sufficiently counter-factual assumptions, utilitarianism like most any other theory, can be made to yield almost any results. (I am reminded here of the Yiddish proverb, "if my grandmother had wheels, she'd be a trolley car"). The real issue is what utilitarianism will yield given a *realistic* consideration of the problem of institutional design. And, here, the very core rights Gibbard proposes to implement stand as a stark impediment to the manipulability of preferences in any on-going system. Freedom of thought, freedom of inquiry and expression, freedom from arbitrary deprivations, freedom of association[4] all of these freedoms make the process of preference and character formation difficult to control by "institutional engineers," "scriptwriters" or "Machiavellian" leaders. Free speech, for example, must protect the Nazis marching in Skokie, the Klan rallies in Connecticut, the distribution of pornography victimizing women and children, and hate campaigns against homosexuals, to mention only a few examples. As attached as I am to free speech, it must be admitted that in some empirical contexts it may foster and nurture precisely the preferences that support the most perverse utilitarian calculations. At the very least, institutionalization of these core rights (along with some related customary assumptions about the family – in particular the right of parents to influence their children[5]) renders the process of preference formation insensitive to centralized manipulation. Hence, a defender of Gibbard's position could not defend a pro-rights utilitarian calculation through a continuing manipulation of the preferences fed into the calculation – without also having to sacrifice the very rights whose protection was the point of the exercise. Once more, the choice comes down to utilitarianism *versus* human rights. It seems hopelessly unrealistic to imagine that the latter will always support calculations institutionalizing the former. I can only conclude that taking account of the "facts" of human psychology – the imperfections of human nature – leads us to a hard choice between ultimate principles rather than to their easy reconciliation.

Political Science, Yale University

---

[4] This last right is not on his list but I assume it is an oversight.
[5] For a discussion of this latter right and related issues of liberty see my *Justice, Equal Opportunity, and the Family* (New Haven: Yale University Press, 1983).

Social Philosophy & Policy Vol. 1 Issue 2 ISSN 0265-0525

LIFE, LIBERTY, AND PROPERTY

DAVID KELLEY

The words "liberty" and "liberalism" have a common root, reflecting the commitment of the original or classical liberals to a free society. Over the last century, the latter term has come to represent a political position that is willing to sacrifice liberty in the economic realm for the sake of equality and/or collective welfare. As a consequence, those who wish to reaffirm the classical version of liberalism – those who advocate liberty in economic as well as personal and intellectual matters – have invented a new word from the old root; they call themselves libertarians. Both in doctrine and in etymology, then, partisans of this view define themselves by their allegiance to liberty. Yet they spend most of their day-to-day polemical energies defending property rights and the economic system of laissez-faire capitalism that is based upon such rights. Evidently there is a strong link between liberty and property at work here. What is that link?

The history of political thought is full of ideas and controversies about precisely this question. My goal here is to raise the question in a specific form, one that I think captures a basic difference in approach between classical liberals and most libertarians today. The difference is not in the substance of the position – it is not a disagreement about how the ideal society would be constituted – but rather in the way the position is to be defended. The key question is: can the right to property be derived from the right to liberty?

Of course a property right *is* a right to a kind of freedom. My property right in my car is the right to choose freely how I shall use and dispose of it. But my right to that freedom is contingent on my ownership of the car, the fact that it is my property. This relation of ownership between me and certain objects, but not others, is what gives me a certain kind of freedom in regard to the first set of objects, but not the second. The question, then, is whether we can derive this relation of ownership from the premise of a right to liberty.

We can clarify the question by stating it in terms of principles. To ascribe a right to a person is to accept a principle which legitimates certain claims by that person, and imposes obligations on others to recognize those claims. Thus the *right to liberty* can be formulated as the principle: each individual ought to be free to determine his own actions (within certain constraints); and no one is permitted to force or coerce him to act in any way (except in certain circumstances). The *right to property* is more difficult to formulate as a principle. We cannot say: each individual should be free to use and dispose of certain objects as he chooses; and no one is permitted to use those objects without his permission, or to interfere coercively with his use of them. For this principle applies only when a person has acquired an object, has come to own it; and thus it fails to capture two points essential to the defense of a natural right to property. The first is that the existence of property rights does not guarantee that each individual will own property; the existence of such rights is perfectly consistent with my having failed to acquire anything. The second point is that certain actions of mine *ought* to confer ownership. That is: the principle of property should specify not only what sort of freedom is involved in owning an object, but also what sorts of actions are sufficient to create ownership. The abstract form of the principle is then: each individual ought to be free to take certain actions, in the appropriate circumstances; and, having taken those actions, he should be free to use and dispose of certain objects . . . (as before).

It is the function of a theory of property rights to fill in this abstract schema by specifying which actions, in what circumstances, should confer ownership over which objects. My question is whether any such principle can be derived solely from the principle of liberty. I think that many libertarians today would answer this question in the affirmative. In their view, the primary right is a right to freedom, a right against coercion, from which all other rights can be derived as implications. The sort of exclusive control over physical objects which is protected by a right to private ownership is seen as an essential element of freedom, so that the right of property is implicit in the right to liberty.

I believe that this is a departure from the classical liberal approach, in which neither principle – liberty or property – can be derived from the other, but rather both derive from an underlying principle that would normally be formulated as the right to *life*. That is, some fundamental end – life, happiness, self-realization – is an ultimate end, the source and standard of all values; society should be so organized as to allow people to pursue that end; and the rights to liberty and property, each in their way, are necessary elements in that organization.[1]

On this issue, I side with the classical liberals. I will not try to present here the case for private property I just described. I do not think it can be presented briefly, because there is no quick and deductive way to establish the relationship of means to ends at this level. My goal, rather, is to show that the libertarian approach cannot succeed. The central point at issue in my polemic will be that private property cannot be defended without a substantive

---

[1] For some examples, see n. 13 below.

commitment to certain values above and beyond the value of liberty. The system of private ownership cannot be supported solely by derivation from a principle of liberty. In the following sections, I will examine three contemporary arguments that attempt to do just that; I will show where the arguments fail, and where I think some reference to the underlying ends of human action is required.

I

Before we take up the first of these arguments, we need to introduce a framework that will serve us in examining each of them. We say that a person is free if he can choose his own actions. Intuitively, there are two key elements in this notion of freedom: the idea of a range of possible actions from which a person chooses; and the idea of the person as an agent who determines which of those actions will be performed. In regard to the first element, it may be argued that if we take into account all the causal factors, there is only one action possible to a person at a given moment. This is the thesis of determinism, and we need not debate the truth of it here, because the issue is *political* freedom, not freedom of the will. So we need a broader sense of possibility. Let us say that an action is possible for an agent, and thus within the range of actions from which he may be free to choose, if it is consistent with all of the agent's abilities.[2] Thus the action of standing up is on my list of possible actions right now; the actions of jumping twelve feet into the air, or solving a problem in multivariable calculus, are not.

We can say, then, that a person is free if nothing constrains his (second-order) action of choosing among the actions that are possible to him in the sense just defined. It is crucial here than only other persons can limit my freedom. If something other than interference by another person is the cause of my inability to take an action, then that action is simply not on my list to begin with, and the issue of freedom does not arise in regard to it. My inability to solve problems in multivariable calculus, for example, does not represent any lack of freedom on my part, since no one prevented me from acquiring that ability. (It should be clear, then, that I am concerned here with "negative" freedom, freedom *from* interference, and not with "positive" liberty, which *would* treat some inabilities as constraints on freedom.)

Let us turn now to the first of the three arguments I want to consider. So far I have been using "liberty" as a descriptive concept. A person 'A' enjoys *de facto* liberty if no other person 'B' interferes with 'A's' choice among the list of actions $a_1, a_2 \ldots a_n$, that are possible to him. This list of actions, however, is not

---

[2] This would of course be circular if offered as a definition of 'possible,' since 'ability' would have to be defined in terms of possibility. But I am not trying to define these concepts; I am merely specifying a range of possible actions.

coextensive with the list involved in 'A's' *de jure* freedom, the freedom to which he has a *right*. For as Hillel Steiner has argued, a system of rights must be "compossible": it must be possible for any person to take any action on his *de jure* list without interfering with the freedom of anyone else to choose any action on *his* list.[3] And each person's *de facto* list must be pruned to eliminate two sorts of incompossibilities. First, some actions on 'A's' list are acts of coercion against 'B'; these must be removed from 'A's' list if 'B' is to enjoy liberty. This sort of case poses no problem, since we are limiting 'A's' *de facto* freedom in order to have a workable *system* of rights to freedom.

But there is a second sort of case. An action a_i on 'A's' list and an action b_j on 'B's' list may involve incompatible uses of the same object or region of space. Neither of these acts is really coercive, since neither aims at constraining the other person's choice, or involves the use of physical force. But the two actions are not compossible, and so a compossible system of rights must not allow both actions to appear on their respective lists at the same time. And the only way to accomplish this, as Steiner argues, is to assign property rights to objects and regions. If 'A' is given title to the object in question, then a_i will remain on his list, but b_j will be removed from 'B's'. "A rule or set of rules assigning the possession or exclusive use of each particular physical object to particular individuals will, if universally adhered to, exclude the possibility of any individual's actions interfering with those of another in any respect."[4]

In short, any action must make some use of some objects in the world, and so a person cannot have a right to take that action unless he has the right to use those objects. The latter is a property right. Hence a system of property rights is required if we are to have a set of compossible rights to liberty, and in this way, it seems, we can derive property from liberty.

The problem with this derivation is that while Steiner has shown the necessity for some system of property rights, he has not shown the necessity of a system of private property rights in the full-blown sense designated by the term "ownership." *Any* system of rules that eliminates conflicts in the use of physical things would meet the formal condition of compossibility. Private ownership is one such system. But the bundle of rights that make up ownership can be divided, rearranged, allocated to different individuals. A material resource can be treated as a commons, for example, as the ocean waterways are treated today. That system allows each individual to use most regions of the oceans as a transportation route, and "rules of the road" serve to eliminte conflicting uses by specifying which of two boats must give way when a collision is impending. But the system does not give anyone the right to continuing possession, or the right to exclude others after one has left the

[3] Hillel Steiner, "The Structure of a Set of Compossible Rights," *Journal of Philosophy 74*, 767–75.
[4] Ibid., 769.

region. Again, a socialist economy in which all productive resources are publicly owned and administered by the state might very well meet the formal condition of compossibility, if the bureaucratic rules assigning authority over each resource were elaborated carefully enough; but this would certainly not be a system of private ownership.

Steiner would reply, in effect, that the bundle of rights constituting ownership cannot be divided up. Suppose, he says, that 'A' owns an object in a qualified way: there are certain actions he does not have the right to take regarding O. In that case, 'B' would not be forbidden by the system of rights from interfering with any such actions; 'B' would have the right to use O in ways incompatible with 'A's' (unprotected) use of O. Yet 'B' cannot have this right to use O unless *he* owns that object, not 'A'.[5] Steiner's argument, here, begs the question by assuming that 'A' and 'B' cannot both have (part) ownership rights in the same object, for that is precisely the question at issue: can the rights to engage in different uses of an object be assigned to different people, thus dividing up the bundle of users' rights which together constitute full ownership? I see no formal reason why not, so long as the system does not give 'A' and 'B' rights to take incompatible actions at the same time.

It is at precisely this point that the argument for private property must begin, not end. We need to know why the bundle of rights constituting ownership forms a natural unit. A system of private property allows an individual exclusive control over the objects he owns, including rights to use, exchange, or otherwise dispose of them as he chooses; but no control over the objects owned by others. A system of community property allows the individual to participate in collective decisions about the use and disposition of all objects, but offers him exclusive control over none. Both may yield compossible sets of rights. To justify a preference for the first over the second system, we need to appeal to substantive value judgments. We need to explain, for example, why the independence in action which the first system permits is crucial if individuals are to achieve their ends, while the sort of participation offered by the second system is not. Steiner's argument offers us no hint of any such explanation.

II

The second argument I want to examine turns on the concept of coercion, which has become perhaps *the* central concept in libertarian political theory. Many libertarians, indeed, regard a principle banning coercion as a kind of axiom from which all principles assigning rights can be derived. In effect, the fundamental right is the right not to be coerced, and specific rights can be

[5] Ibid., 772.

established by identifying specific forms of coercion. Property rights in particular are to be established by identifying certain actions involving physical objects as acts of coercion.

The problem with this approach is that it works only if we can identify a given act as coercive prior to and independently of any premises about the rights of individuals affected by the act – otherwise we would not be able to derive those rights from a ban on coercion. I will not consider here whether this is possible even in the case of the right to liberty, though I have my doubts. But I think it is clear that it cannot be done in regard to the right of property. In this case, what the libertarian must show is that prior to any recognition or acceptance of property rights, we can identify certain uses of a physical object by 'A' as acts of coercion against 'B'. But how are we to do this? If we already know that 'B' owns the object, then 'A's' taking the object or using it without 'B's' permission may be regarded as coercive: it prevents 'B' from acting in ways that fall within his *de jure* freedom. If we do not know whether 'B' owns the object, however, then we cannot tell merely by inspecting 'A's' action whether it is coercive. If I walk across a piece of land, or fence it off and plant it, there is simply no way to tell whether I have engaged in coercion without knowing whether the land belongs to someone else.

Eric Mack, for example, holds that "An agent's right to any object rests on his being so related to it that nonconsensually depriving him of it constitutes coercion. Hence it is the demand for noncoercion, for each person's liberty being respected, which underlies each person's moral titles. . . ."[6] The agent must be "so related" to an object – what relation does Mack have in mind? It would be circular, of course, for him to say that the relation to an object which makes deprivation of it coercive is the relation of ownership. Then what is the relation? At this point, Mack incorporates John Locke's labor theory of ownership. "The just acquisition of object O by person A involves an intentional investment by A of his time and effort which results in O's becoming an instrument of A's (ongoing though, perhaps, intermittent) purposes."[7] There are two elements in this relation: i) the fact that O is an instrument, a means to A's ends; and ii) the fact that A has "invested" time and effort in making O an instrument. The presence of (i) alone would obviously not necessarily make it coercive for someone else to deprive A of O. For one thing, O may be owned by someone else. But let us consider the case in which O is unowned; (i) by itself is still not enough. If an early American settler had formed the purpose of having two oceans to swim in, then access to a continent-wide strip of land would have been essential to his purpose, but

---

[6] Eric Mack, "Liberty and Justice," in John Arthur and William H. Shaw (eds.) *Justice and Economic Distribution* (Engelwood Cliffs, N.J.: Prentice-Hall, 1978), 189.
[7] Ibid., 188.

surely he did not acquire title merely by having that purpose, even if there was a continuous strip of unowned land.

Hence element (ii) is crucial: O must become an instrument of A's purpose *as a result of* A's investment of time and effort. The problem now is to understand why the "investment" of time and effort should so alter my relation to that object that another's unauthorized use of it is an act of coercion against me. The question can be put in terms of our framework. Let us assume that among the actions on A's *de jure* list are some which make use of unowned objects. A's right to liberty then includes the right to use those objects, and it would be coercive for someone else to interfere with A's action. This is a kind of property right, but not a right to private ownership of those objects, which would include the right to possess the objects and exclude others from them even after A has ceased that particular action. In order to establish the latter right, Mack would have to show that *after* A has acted upon O and made it suit his ends, it would be coercive for others to use the object without A's permission, even if A is not himself actively using it at that moment. Mack's argument might be formulated as follows. A's action a_i alters O in such a way that some further action a_{n+1} becomes possible – if, but only if, A can maintain exclusive control over O. The obvious example is that having planted, one may reap, so long as others keep off the field in the interim. A's own action has expanded his *de jure* list to include a_{n+1}, but that action can remain on A's list – A is free to choose a_{n+1} – only if others refrain from using O without A's permission. If others *did* take O or use it without permission, they would be preventing A from taking an action on his *de jure* list, and would thus be coercing him. A ban on coercion, then, requires the recognition of private ownership rights in such cases.

The problem with this argument lies in its key premise. If someone else uses O, then A is no longer able to take action a_{n+1}. But that is a violation of A's freedom only if a_{n+1} is on A's *de jure* list. Why *should* it be on his list? Well, if A is the one who made a_{n+1} possible, then he deserves to have it available to him. I consider that a good argument, but it is an argument from justice, not liberty. From the standpoint of liberty alone, the fact is that if a_{n+1} is to be on A's list, certain other actions involving O must be excluded from the lists of other people. Among these latter actions are some which were on their lists before A altered O. It may thus be argued that if a_{n+1} is to remain on A's list, others will suffer a diminution of freedom.

This, after all, is one of the major complaints against the Lockean theory of appropriation. The classical objection is that after the first generations have appropriated resources, none will be left for succeeding generations, and their freedom to act in the world will be vastly restricted. Here again, I think the classical liberal has a sound rejoinder. The purpose served by appropriation – i.e., the support of life, directly through consumption, or indirectly through production – can be served equally well if people are free to acquire ownership rights by trade. Indeed, over time, this second method serves the purpose much better than the first. But here again the argument goes far beyond any appeal to liberty *per se*; it rests on a value judgment about the ends to which the system of private property is a means.

This discussion has revealed, I think, that the concept of coercion is a complex one. The concept picks out a class – a natural kind – of actions. Some of the actions in the class, such as physical assault or confinement, can be picked out in a purely descriptive way. But surrounding this core subset of coercive actions, there are successive layers of actions that come to be included in the natural kind because they interfere with freedoms that we think people *ought* to have. Each time we extend the sphere of actions that are to be protected by rights, we also extend the class of actions that are to be considered coercive. But the actions that are included by extension under the concept 'coercion' cannot be picked out in any purely descriptive way; the criteria for identifying them as coercive are normative ones. And these normative criteria are based on antecedent judgments about rights. Thus we cannot reverse the logical order and identify rights by first determining which actions are coercive.

III

Yet another sort of argument linking liberty and property is implicit in Robert Nozick's discussion of distributive justice in *Anarchy, State, and Utopia*.[8] Nozick criticizes "patterned theories of justice" – theories which hold that wealth should be distributed in accordance with some dimension such as merit, need, effort, etc. Nozick's contrary position is that a given distribution is just if each person's holdings were justly acquired by original appropriation or by voluntary transfer from others. The distribution as a whole is just if each element in it is just; there is no reason why the whole should fit some global pattern. Nozick defends his "entitlement" view by arguing that the attempt to maintain any patterned distribution would require "continuous interference with people's lives."[9] For suppose that we start with a distribution that fits some ideal pattern (call it D_1). That pattern could not be maintained without restricting the freedom of people to exchange the goods they hold under D_1. Otherwise we have Nozick's famous "Wilt Chamberlain" problem: everyone voluntarily pays extra to watch Wilt Chamberlain play basketball, and he ends up far richer than D_1 would allow.

Nozick does not offer this argument as a defense of property rights *per se*. But the entitlement theory does embody a theory of property rights; any other

[8] Robert Nozick, *Anarchy, State, and Utopia* (New York: Basic Books, 1974).
[9] Ibid., 163.

theory of distributive justice involves limitations on property rights; and Nozick argues that any such limitations compromise individual freedom. The argument may, therefore, be interpreted – certainly it often *has been* interpreted – as an attempt to show that the right to liberty implies a right to property.[10]

In any case, the argument outlined above cannot stand alone as a defense of property rights without begging the question in essentially the same way that Steiner's and Mack's arguments did. Nozick's critique of patterned theories turns on an assumption he makes in the following passage:

> There is *no* question about whether each of the people was entitled to the control over the resources they held in D_1; because that was the distribution (your favorite) that (for purposes of argument) we assumed was acceptable. . . . If the people were entitled to dispose of the resources to which they were entitled (under D_1), didn't this include their being entitled to give it to, or exchange it with, Wilt Chamberlain?[11]

The clear assumption, here, is that a patterned theory gives people the right of full private ownership over the goods assigned to them by D_1, including the right to exchange them at will. But as Cheyney Ryan points out, a patterned theory might well hold that the rights assigned under D_1 are *not* those of full ownership. A person who has a job, for example, has certain rights vis-a-vis that economic good, but he does not have the right to sell it or give it away. A patterned theory might hold that the same should be true for all holdings.[12] To complete his argument, then, Nozick would need to defend his assumption. If we assume that people have full ownership rights in their holdings, then maintaining patterns will clearly involve intrusions into their freedom. But Nozick needs to apply his argument one level deeper, to back up his assumption that people do have ownership rights. That is, he must show that there is a diminution of our freedom if we do not have such rights in the first place. This is the point at which his argument fails.

My *de facto* freedom would certainly be limited if I cannot acquire ownership rights, but we have seen that *de facto* freedom will have to be limited in certain ways in any case. Coercive actions, for example, will have to be excluded to protect the freedom of others. How can we answer the claim that the same is true of limitations on private ownership? I am not free to sell my job, and could

---

[10] It is not surprising that many people *have* looked to this section of *Anarchy, State, and Utopia* to find Nozick's basis for affirming property rights, since he does not provide such a basis earlier in the book, where he lays out the framework of individual rights.

[11] Ibid., 161.

[12] Cheyney C. Ryan, "Yours, Mine and Ours: Property Rights and Individual Liberty," in Jeffrey Paul (ed.) *Reading Nozick* (Totowa, N.J.: Rowman and Littlefield, 1981), 329 ff.

not be given that freedom – i.e., could not be made owner of the job – without curtailing my employer's freedom to determine who will have it. Similarly, countless critics of private property have argued that a system which denies a person full ownership of his land or other resources may shorten his *de jure* list, but would expand the lists of others. The question becomes: which actions should be on whose lists? A principle of liberty, which says that people should be free to decide among the actions on their lists, will not answer this question.

This is, of course, the same problem I pointed out in the two preceding sections. The point of repeating it here is that Nozick's argument suggests yet another way to formulate what is missing from all three arguments. Nozick says that maintaining a pattern will require continual intrusions into the freedom of each individual, to prevent him from exchanging goods in certain ways. But a system of private ownership must prevent people from taking each others' property or using it without permission. Won't this also require continual intrusions into our lives? Nozick doesn't think so. I don't, either. But why? My *de facto* freedom is curtailed as much in the one case as in the other, since acts of theft and unauthorized use are certainly on my *de facto* list. The reason Nozick's point is persuasive, I think, is that we do not give actions of theft or unauthorized use the same *importance* as actions of using and exchanging our possessions freely.

It is implicit in the way I have conceptualized freedom that no distinction was made among the actions on 'A's' list, $a_1 \ldots a_n$, in terms of their importance. I did this deliberately, because the only way to weight these actions differentially would be in terms of their relation to a hierarchy of purposes, and we must not take any such hierarchy into consideration if we are to evaluate an argument which claims to rest solely on each person's right to choose among the actions on his list. It has transpired, now, that no such argument will succeed in establishing a right to private property. To establish that right, we *must* introduce the value premises which allow us to weight actions differentially. One example of the sort of argument I have in mind might run as follows.

If human life and happiness are values, then so is production. But production is a long-range, rational process. It requires continuous, connected activity, in the service of a plan, over lengthy periods of time. It requires technical judgments about the best means to achieve a given end, and economic judgments about the ends best served by a given set of means. People disagree about such judgments. People differ in the way they value the possible products, they differ in the way they prefer to spend the income from production, they differ in the terms of cooperation they find acceptable. If production is a value, then the ability to act upon these judgments – the ability to carry out long-range plans involving physical resources, without having to seek the permission or agreement of everyone else – must be highly weighted. And it is precisely the freedom to act in this way that ownership rights protect.

That freedom is not offered by a system of commons, or of collective ownership. Conversely, the sort of actions allowed by the latter systems, but excluded by a system of private property – e.g., having some (extremely limited) say over how others use the resources at their disposal – are of little or no importance, so long as rights are protected, cooperation is possible, and markets exist in which goods can be traded.[13]

What I have given is no more than a sketch of a line of argument for property rights, and a sketch of only one line of argument at that. But I think it is clear that this is the sort of argument required. We need to connect certain categories of action involving physical resources with basic ends and purposes if we are to provide a satisfactory foundation for property rights. It is only in this way, I think, that we can explain why certain actions on our *de jure* lists *ought* to have the consequence of conferring ownership rights over an object; why the bundle of rights constituting ownership does form a natural unit, protecting a set of actions which all belong together on an owner's *de jure* list unless he voluntarily subdivides his bundle and transfers certain rights to others; and why it is an intrusion into one's freedom, a form of coercion, for the state to forbid the kinds of actions that ownership rights protect.

Philosophy, Vassar College

---

[13] The empasis on production in the case for private property is a recurrent theme in the classical liberal tradition, from Locke's *Second Treatise* onward, E.g., John Stuart Mill's *Principles of Political Economy*, II 2. For a powerful contemporary argument of this form, see Ayn Rand, "What is Capitalism?" in her *Capitalism: The Unknown Ideal* (New York: New American Library, 1967).

Social Philosophy & Policy Vol. 1 Issue 2 ISSN 0265-0525

THE PRIMACY OF WELFARE RIGHTS

Martin P. Golding

This paper deals with three topics: (1) types of rights, (2) the development of the terminology of rights, and (3) the question of the primacy of welfare rights. Because these topics are interrelated, my exposition does not observe rigid boundaries among them. There is no pretence at all that any of these subjects is fully covered here; nor is it proposed, except for one writer, to touch upon the contemporary literature on rights, as noteworthy as some of that literature is. In order to gain entrance into the field, on which the writing has grown to massive proportions, I shall begin with an interesting historical phenomenon, some of whose philosophical import I want to explore.

I should say at the outset, however, that the general motivation of this paper is the problem of the significance of the language of "rights." Does it really make a difference, for instance, to speak of the "rights of man" rather than the "common duties of humanity"? Does the term "rights" add anything of special significance or is its only significance rhetorical and ideological? Can we dispense with the language of rights and still say everything we need to say about our moral relations? I confess to a moderate skepticism about the necessity of the language of rights in the last analysis. At any rate, this paper is intended as a contribution, however small, to this problem. The historical phenomenon with which I am going to begin will enable us to bring into focus the issue of the meaning of "rights."[1]

In the first chapter of his study, *John Locke and Children's Books in Eighteenth Century England*, Samuel F. Pickering traces the development of a genre of literature – not John Locke Comics – written for young ladies and gentlemen which was, as the title of one such book put it, an attempt to amend the world, to render the society of man more amiable.[2] This genre – animal books – was

---

[1] My interest in the specific, non-reducible functions of rights language – if there are any such functions – is part of a larger interest in the specific functions of the various terms of moral discourse and appraisal. This subject begins with Plato (Socrates?), *e.g.*, in the *Euthyphro*, which discusses the relationships and differences holding between "piety" and "justice." It is carried on in Aristotle's discussion of "justice" and the various virtues. On the other side, though, we may note the tendency to subordinate the various forms of moral appraisal to a single moral standard or bring them all under a single moral concept.

[2] Samuel F. Pickering, Jr., *John Locke and Children's Books in Eighteenth-Century England* (Knoxville: University of Tennessee Press, 1981), 15.

based on the premise that "first impressions" have an especially powerful influence on the mind and that proper habits of conduct are therefore to be inculcated in the early years. Furthermore, it was concluded, in order to instill the social virtues it is particularly important to wean children away from cruelty to animals, for cruelty to animals leads to a hardening of the heart which will later show itself in one's dealings with one's fellows. If the number of books devoted to the subject is a reflection of the pervasiveness and seriousness of the problem, one may fairly judge that cruelty to animals was, for the eighteenth-century English child, the moral – or perhaps immoral – equivalent of watching violence on television.

By the end of the eighteenth century a new and rather controversial note began to be introduced into the educational theory underlying this literary genre. It was not enough, it was said, to teach compassion to animals because of its character-building effects. To be sure, as one writer argued, "many of those brought to the scaffold for capital crimes" began their "progress in wickedness" as children who mistreated animals. What needed to be recognized, however, was that animals have rights, for the rights of animals like the rights of man are "deduced from the Light of Nature."[3] As another writer of animal books states, the time would soon come when men would "acknowledge the RIGHTS; instead of bestowing their COMPASSION upon the creatures, whom, with themselves, GOD made, and made to be happy!"[4]

The idea that animals have rights clearly was a minority position, and it met with sharp rejection. The most vigorous opponent seems to have been Mrs. Sarah Trimmer, perhaps the period's leading writer of children's books and also the leading Lockean educational theorist. The ascription of rights to animals, she held, was a confusion of the order of nature. Now the issue of animals' rights, itself, is not of interest to me here. What does interest me, rather, is the historical phenomenon of the emergence of a seemingly new moral claim and the attitude with which it was met. I say "seemingly" because the claim that animals have rights may well have been asserted before the end of the eighteenth century. Nevertheless, in that English context the claim provoked both anger and surprise. For the overwhelming majority of rights thinkers it was an entirely unanticipated claim.

The anger, I think, is easily understood. As indicated by one of the quotations I mentioned, the argument for animals' rights seems to have been this: Humans have rights because God made them to be happy; God made animals to be happy; therefore animals have rights. While this is a simplistic formulation it expresses the orthodox seventeenth and eighteenth centuries' view that rights have a theological underpinning, a view which, I believe, was

---

[3] Thomas Young, *An Essay on Humanity to Animals* (1798); cited in Pickering, 37.
[4] E. A. Kendall, *Keeper's Travels in Search of His Master* (1798); cited in Pickering, 38.

also held by Locke. The response to the argument, therefore, was along theological lines: the argument is mistaken because it overlooks the fact that God made animals for human use. Were the upholders of animals' rights seriously claiming that it is wrong to shear the wool of sheep?, that it is wrong to own animals? It certainly was readily agreed that it is *wrong* to torture animals and that men have a *duty* to be compassionate toward animals. But the assertion of animals' *rights* was perceived as carrying with it a definite danger, for it involves a "levelling" of man and beast, as Mrs. Trimmer wrote.[5] The ascription of rights to animals, therefore, could easily be seen as threatening the panoply of the natural rights of man; for instance, such rights as the right of property and those political liberties claimed as natural rights.

But why the surprise? The surprise was of course not occasioned by any unfamiliarity with the terminology in which the assertion of animals' rights was expressed: it was formulated in the familiar and accepted language of "rights." This situation should be compared with its mirror image, namely, the use of new moral terminology to express accepted and familiar claims. In this latter case it would appear that a kind of conceptual, and I think ultimately moral, reorientation is actually occurring and it is understandable that some surprise should ensue. But why in the former case?

Moral surprise is not an entirely unusual event. T. H. Green describes the case of the Greek slaveholder who becomes disabused of the Aristotelian doctrine of natural slavery when he enters into conversation with his slave on the basis of a common language.[6] By means of this special kind of interaction, prejudice and ignorance are broken down, and "moral progress," one might say, is achieved. Still, that the barbarian slave should come to be regarded as having a moral status equal to that of his Greek owner is something initially unanticipated.

The structure of the situation, however, is a familiar feature of moral and legal discourse. Certain normative qualities are ascribed to some person, action, thing, or circumstance on the basis of the possession of various properties. When it is shown that some other person, action, thing, or circumstance has these properties, it is then argued that it too has similar normative qualities. The conclusion, nevertheless, can be as surprising as it often is unwelcome. There is no doubt that the ascription of equality of moral status to the slave involves a considerable "reordering" of nature for the Greek as well as a revision of particular moral claims. Aside from the rejection of the doctrine of natural slavery, however, it is not clear how much of a shift is produced in the conceptual system of the accepted ethical theory.

[5] *Guardian of Education*, 1802, 1; cited in Pickering, 38.
[6] See T. H. Green, *Lectures on the Principles of Political Obligation* (New York: Longmans, Green and Co., 1941), sec. 140.

The surprise occasioned by the assertion of animals' rights is in a different case from the above. The novel ascription of rights to animals partly incorporated old moral prescriptions – that it is wrong to torture animals and that there is a duty of compassion to animals – in (by then) old moral language, but it must have gone beyond these prescriptions in some way. It was clear to the majority of eighteenth-century English rights thinkers that animals could not possibly have the rights that men have. And this was true independently of the theological claim that animals were made for human use. Despite the "territorialism" of animals, beasts cannot own property; they have no *animus domini*, intention to own, though they may have an intention to exclude others from their nests and dens. The extension of the terminology of rights to animals, it was feared, could have the effect of contracting its normative range – hence, the angry tone of the rejection.

But the surprise was partially the result of the received tradition of rights thinking and the particular concept of rights that it explicitly employed. The received tradition had left the eighteenth-century rights thinkers unprepared to consider whether there was a *kind* of right that animals would have, if they did have rights. In fact there was a more antique tradition of rights thinking that did recognize a different sort of right than the received conception, but it had slipped from ken. Although the eighteenth-century thinkers may ultimately have come to reject the proposition that animals do have this other sort of right, even if they had had this type of right in view, they might also have been led to consider whether there is any difference between saying, for instance, that it is wrong to torture animals or that there is a duty not to torture animals, on the one side, and saying that animals have a right not to be tortured, on the other: that is, the problem of the significance of rights language.

The natural rights tradition did, of course, assert that there are a variety of different rights that men have. In expounding what these rights are, the theorists probably were influenced by particular rights that were recognized in their own legal systems. Rights naturally fell into certain categories: for instance, the right to transfer property fell under the right to own property, from which the former was derived. Oftentimes the Latin terminology of jurisprudence was employed in expounding these rights, e.g., *ius in personam*, a term that, incidentally, was not used by the classical Roman jurists. Yet the received concept of what a right is, the explicitly acknowledged concept of rights, broadly took rights as being basically of one kind, namely, as *option* rights.[7]

Option rights correspond to spheres of individual sovereignty, as it were, in

[7] For the terminology of "option" and "welfare" rights see M. P. Golding, "Towards a Theory of Human Rights," *The Monist*, October 1968, 52(4), 521–49.

which the individual is morally free to act on the basis of his own choices. Depending on what the rights are, these spheres, and hence the rights, generally are conceived of as limited. Possession of an option right, furthermore, implies some kind of rightful control over the actions of others. Why anyone has option rights (if anyone has them), what these rights are, whether any of them are natural or human rights, what the limits of one's sphere of sovereignty are, are all questions of ethical theory. The concept of an option right of itself does not imply, for instance, that no one has the right to injure himself or others. It is a question of ethical theory whether or not this is the case.

The notion of option rights, as an explicitly recognized concept, was inherited by the natural rights theorists from the definition of "rights" given in the late middle ages and the Renaissance. These definitions do not express the oldest explicitly formulated conception of rights, but they were the ones which were influential. I have traced the development of these definitions elsewhere and shall not go into details here.[8] These definitions conceive a right in terms of *potestas*, power, or *facultas*, capacity or power, and they emphasize the "active" character of rights. The epitome of this tradition is a statement of Sir William Blackstone's in his *Commentaries on the Laws of England* (1765 et seq.):

> The absolute rights of man, considered as a free agent, endowed with discernment to know good from evil, and with the power of choosing those measures which appear to him most desirable, are usually summed up in one general appelation, and denominated the natural liberty of mankind (I, 125). . . . The rights themselves . . . will appear from what has been premised, to be no other, than that *residuum* of natural liberty, which is not required by the laws of society to be sacrificed to the public convenience; or else those civil privileges, which society has engaged to provide in lieu of the natural liberties so given up by individuals (I, 129).

From the phrases "power of choosing" and "residuum of natural liberty" and such phrases as "power of acting" and "free will" used in nearby places in the text, the historical roots of Blackstone's conception of rights are apparent, and this is an option-rights conception. It is also clear why it might be thought that beasts cannot have rights.

But option rights, arguably, are not the only kind of right: there also may be *welfare* rights. Welfare rights are entitlements to goods. They imply that the possessors of these goods have desires and/or interests, but the concept itself

---

[8] Martin P. Golding, "Justice and Rights: A Study in Relationship," in E. Shelp (ed.), *Justice and Health Care* (Dordrecht, Holland: D. Reidel, 1981), 23–36. See also the useful book by Richard Tuck, *Natural Rights Theories* (Cambridge: Cambridge University Press, 1979), and my review in *Political Theory*, February 1982, 10(1), 152–57.

does not entail that one has a right to everything one desires or that one has no right to what one does not desire. It is a substantive question of ethical theory whether or not one may relinquish or waive a welfare right, though of course one may refrain from claiming the object of such a right. Like an option right, possession of a welfare right implies some kind of rightful control over the actions of others. Questions of ethical theory parallel to those mentioned earlier arise here too: why anyone has welfare rights (if anyone has them), what these rights are, and so on.

Although any concrete right is likely to be a composite of welfare and option elements, the failure to distinguish between them can lead to moral confusion. It is claimed, for instance, that a woman has the moral right to abort the fetus she is carrying. Is this merely an option right, something she is morally free to do if she so chooses? If it is, it entails no claim to the provision of facilities or financial assistance to have an abortion, anymore than my right to drive a car implies a claim to be provided with gasoline. Clarification of the *kind* of right the alleged right to an abortion is, or of the elements of this alleged right, would be helpful in the present social context.

It is fairly plain, I think, that *if* animals have rights, these are welfare rights or something very much like them; and so, also, are the alleged rights that more recently have been claimed for trees and other natural objects. (I confess to being puzzled by the relative rights of the pine tree and the pine-tree beetle: which ones have precedence?) If the eighteenth-century rights thinkers had had welfare rights as clearly in view as option rights, they might not have been taken aback by the assertion of rights for animals, though they still may have rejected the claim. Their attention, however, was so fixated on option rights, partly because of the tradition they had received, that they overlooked the possibility of animals' rights as welfare rights. And this happened despite the fact that some of the rights recognized by many of these theorists could have been put into the welfare category. But the conception of a welfare right had failed to chrystalize for them.

The broad notion of welfare rights, in fact, is represented in an older tradition in the development of definitions of "rights." These other definitions are found primarily in the Glossators on Roman legal texts, which may partially explain why an explicitly recognized conception of welfare rights was lost until the nineteenth century, when it became clear that the claims that were being pressed in society as matters of alleged rights could not all be subsumed under an option-rights notion.

These older definitions[9] are interesting because they connect rights with justice; in fact they primarily occur in comments on the definition of "justice" given by Ulpian, a third-century Roman jurist, and contained in the first

---

[9] For a fuller discussion see my paper, "Justice and Rights."

sentence of Justinian's *Institutes*: "Justice is the constant and perpetual will of giving to each his own right (*ius suum*)." Placentinus expresses the prevailing twelfth-century view that rights flow from justice *tanquam ex fonte rivuli*, just like rivulets from a spring.[10] And *ius* is identified with *dignitas*, worth, or more often with *meritum*, desert or worth. This approach derives from Cicero, whose definition of "justice" is cited by Placentinus with approval: "Justice is that condition of the mind which, with the common utility being preserved, gives to each his own *dignitas*" (*De Inventione*, II, 53, 160).

I think it is no surprise that the oldest definitions of "rights" occur in legal texts. Although law and ethics contain a number of overlapping concepts, rights are the most legalistic of our moral notions because they cover the domain of *interpersonal claims* in a way that such notions as right, wrong, good, and evil do not. (The problematic notion is that of duty, which I shall discuss later.)

The fact that definitions of "a right" do not appear until the middle ages does not mean that the concept of rights was "discovered" or "invented" in that period. Nor does it mean that the term *ius* was not employed in option and welfare senses until it was defined in one or the other way. It is the case, rather, that the Roman jurists and moral philosophers did not take the trouble to define the rights-sense of *ius* because the concept did not have for them the systematic importance that it later attained in law and ethical theory. (The only definition in the classical sources is that of the jurist Celsus, in Justinian's *Digest*, 1.1, 1: "Ius is the art of the good and the equitable." But this is a definition of *ius* in the sense of "law" not in the sense of "a right.") It is important to recognize, I think, that much of what *we* would express in the terminology of rights was not expressed that way in the early sources. I want to illustrate this point and then remark on its theoretical significance.

The legal context can be illustrated by translations of the Bible. Genesis, chapter 23, tells the story of Abraham's purchase of a gravesite for Sarah, who had just died. "Give me," he says to the children of Ḥeth, "*aḥuzath* burying-place with you" (v. 44). Literally the Hebrew means "the possession of," which is adhered to in the Vetus Latina, *possessionem monumenti*. Jerome's fourth-century Vulgate, however, reads *ius sepulchri*, the right of a grave. This terminological development is reflective of a tendency in law – and I suspect in moral discourse, too – to move from relatively concrete concepts to more abstract ones, in this case from possession to a right. (Compare, also: mine and thine, property, the right of property, and property in rights.)

This tendency is present, for example, in Jewish law. The classical texts of the third through the sixth centuries hardly seem to know the abstract concept

---

[10] Cited in H. Kantorowicz, *Studies in the Glossators of the Roman Law* (Darmstadt, Germany: Scientia Verlag Aalen, 1969), 10.

of a right, while the mediaeval and especially the later sources employ it more freely. Interestingly, the notion first begins to turn up in Franco-German eleventh-century juristic rabbinic sources as something close to an option-right idea: the term is *koah*, the equivalent of *potestas* (power).[11] It is nearly astounding, though, that the later term for a right, *zekhuth*, means "merit" in classical rabbinic Hebrew.

To revert back to my Biblical illustration, I find it fascinating that the sixteenth-century Spanish philosopher, Francisco Suarez, explains that Jerome's *ius sepulchri* means *facultas sepliendi*, the capacity or power of burying.[12] Thus, Jerome first reads "a right" into the Biblical text and Suarez then reads this expression in terms of his own "active," option-rights conception. This "reading in" is something we all do; sometimes it is quite harmless, but sometimes it can be misleading – especially in the case of "rights," if the terminology of rights has special significance.

An old illustration of this phenomenon (interpreting a source that lacks an explicit concept of rights in terms of a rights notion) is Socrates' situation in the *Crito*. Socrates wants to know whether it is just or unjust, right or wrong, to escape his sentence. We easily translate his question into rights terminology: Does he have the right to escape his sentence? When we do this we are going from an "objective" notion of rightness to a "subjective" notion of rights possessed by individuals, to use the nomenclature of continental jurisprudence. I do not particularly care for this terminology, but I think it hints at a very fundamental distinction and helps in identifying the domain of morality to which rights are unique – if there is such a domain. I shall return to this issue shortly.

The word "right" has a dual use and, therefore, an ambiguity that can bedevil the ethical theorist. A similar duality is had by the Latin word *ius*. While Roman legal texts generally employ the word in an objective sense (in which *ius* means "the law" or "the right") they also employ it in the sene of "a right" that someone has, though less frequently so in the earlier sources. The Roman moral philosophers, on the other hand, very rarely use the term in a subjective or personal sense. The outstanding example is Cicero's important work – it is said to have influenced Kant – *De Officiis*, concerning duties, which is based upon Stoic sources. The term *ius* occurs well over 100 times in this book, and in at most a few cases is it ever used to refer to "a right" rather than "the right."

One of these cases is instructive. Cicero states that only the Stoics, Academicians, and Peripatetics have anything to teach us about duty. Certain

[11] See, e.g., Rashi's comment on *Makkoth*, 3a, s.v., *kaytzad shamin* (in standard editions of the Babylonian Talmud).
[12] Francisco Suarez, *De Legibus* (Madrid: Consejo Superior de Investigaciones, 1971), 24.

skeptical philosophers, on the other hand, would "have the right" (*tamen haberunt ius suum*) to discuss duty if they had left us any power of choosing between things, so that there might be a way of finding out what duty is (I, 6). This reference to a right sounds very much like what Professor Alan Gewirth calls an "intellectual right," but I do not think that this really is the case. Until I read Professor Gerwith, I confess, I had never heard the expression "intellectual right."[13] I like the term, but it seems to me to be an entirely unnecessary addition to our language. Whether or not a particular conclusion follows from given premises is a matter of objective standards of reasoning, and there is no need whatever to speak of someone's "having the right" to draw some inference. On the other hand, it is a matter of moral right, and not any so-called intellectual right, whether or not someone has the right to express the conclusion to others, or whether others have the right to prevent him from expressing it. The notion of an intellectual right is parasitic on the idea of "what is right."

In the last analysis this proposition may also be true of moral, natural, or human rights. The problem of the significance of rights language would thereby be compounded. Still, it may be possible to locate the domain of morality proper to rights. My earlier illustrations, from a legal and a moral context, of the importation of rights into sources in which they do not initially appear raise the question of the indispensability or dispensability of rights-discourse. The emergence of the terminology of rights in the law seems to be virtually inevitable because of the law's concern with interpersonal claims. This fact provides an important clue to the nature of rights language generally.

Before proceeding with this point, I want to go back to our eighteenth-century English friends and animals' rights. I earlier maintained that the surprise with which the assertion of animals' rights was met was partially due to the negelect or unawareness of the possibility of welfare rights. Another factor, I think, was the belief that other moral notions than that of a right are quite adequate to govern man's behavior toward animals. This circumstance is exemplified in Samuel Pufendorf's *De Iure Naturae et Gentium* (*Of the Law of Nature and Nations*, 1672, expanded edition 1674). This large tome, written by a seventeenth-century writer born in Saxony, was published in English translation in 1710, and was a great success. (It had been available earlier in a French translation.) Before Pufendorf gets to a treatment of rights, he has extensive discussions of man's duties, to himself and to others. Of particular interest is his expression of grave doubts on whether the killing of animals is permitted. He concludes that the killing and use of animals is allowed, but he says that it nevertheless is beyond dispute "that the Abuse of this Power, and especially such as is attended with foolish Cruelty and Barbarity, deserves to

---

[13] Alan Gewirth, *Reason and Morality* (Chicago: University of Chicago Press, 1978), 69f.

come under Censure" (IV, iii, 6).[14] The English rejectors of animals' rights fully agree with this statement. The fact that they also agree that such abuse of animals also "tends to the prejudice of men" (i.e., has detrimental effects on character) as Barbeyrac, the French translator, notes, does not at all derogate from the separate wrongfulness of mistreating animals.

Putting aside the case of animals and focusing instead on the moral relations of human beings, I think it is noteworthy that such an important natural rights theorist as Pufendorf was able to write a book on ethics in which the notion of rights plays a very subsidiary role. I refer here to his 1673 book *De Officio Hominis et Civis* (*On the Duty of Man and Citizen*), the French translation of which appeared in many editions from 1707 on. Topics in which one might expect "rights" to be the key term are instead expounded in terms of "duty." For example, Pufendorf talks about the duties attendant upon the ownership of property rather than about the rights of ownership. (I suspect that the title of the French *Declaration of the Rights of Man and Citizen* was deliberately chosen in opposition to Pufendorf's title.)

I think it is clear that moral discourse can go quite a distance without employing the quasi-legal conception of rights. This also is evidenced by the great ethical systems of the ancient world in which the notion hardly appears, though I should concede that it sometimes is lurking below the surface. It is plain, at any rate, that these antique systems are conceptually very far from any kind of "rights-based" morality and that their transmutation into such a morality would have constituted an ideological shift of a radical sort. To the extent that these sytems did employ a notion of rights, which was almost not at all, they tended to cash it out in terms of such "objective" ethical notions as "the just," "the right," and "the good." (A good example is Cicero's *De Officiis*.) It cannot be denied that it is only with the coming of the middle ages, and in fact more towards the end of that period, that we find the upsurge of rights thinking and a tendency to displace other ethical concepts by that of rights. This upsurge, I believe, is partly due to the infusion of legal ideas into ethics and political philosophy and partly due to the concomitant rise of individualism and the nation-state. Still, even though the ancients managed quite well without the concept or terminology of rights, one is justified in wondering whether they thereby also left part of the domain of morality fallow.

If we focus attention on the idea of duty I think a bit of progress can be made toward understanding the nature of this domain and the significance of rights language. Let us put aside so-called duties to oneself and begin with duties to (or of) humanity, as they were termed. These duties obviously are other-regarding; or to put it a bit differently, they govern conduct that is other-

---

[14] Samuel Pufendorf, *Of the Law of Nature and Nations* (London: 3rd edition, 1717), trans. by Basil Kennet, with the notes of J. Barbeyrac, Bk. IV, 144.

affecting. Of course, this is also true of other moral concepts. For instance, it would be unjust or wrong for Socrates to escape his sentence, and the wrong committed would be a wrong *to* the *polis*. But it is quite impossible, here, to go through the gamut of other-affecting applications of our moral notions. The focus on duty is sufficient and also the most germane.

Now, it is important to recognize that there can be other-affecting duties that are *not* correspondent to a right held by the affected party, that is, the beneficiary of the duty. "Duties of humanity" is an apt description of them. Since I want to use it to make a point, I offer the following as an example. According to Jewish law, an individual is duty-bound (*ḥayyav*) to rescue someone in danger of loss of life, if there is no substantial risk to his own.[15] This is a *personal duty* of the would-be rescuer's, and there is no suggestion that the would-be victim has a right to be rescued. This duty should be compared with another one that the individual has, namely, the duty to rescue someone's possessions that are in danger of being lost (e.g., by being swept away by a river), if there is no danger to oneself. In this case, the owner may waive the rescue of his possessions, and thereby absolve the would-be rescuer of the duty. The case, therefore, has a feature often associated with one's having a right, namely, the power to waive it if one so chooses. (Compare, however, "inalienable rights.") And it would not be misleading to say that the owner has a right to the rescue of his possessions were it not for the fact that the emphasis would be misplaced: the duty is still conceived of as a personal duty. (In the former case, the duty of rescue cannot be waived. There is a duty to let oneself be rescued, so to speak).

It appears that an other-affecting personal duty, a duty that is not rights-related, is possible insofar as such a duty is imposed by law or is a *naturalis obligatio*, a natural duty imposed by morality or "objective right." Other-affecting duties, however, have no application in a universe inhabited only by a single, isolated person. On the other hand, the *concept* of a personal duty, itself, is perfectly intelligible for such a universe, and could have applications as long as deliberate activity were possible therein. A single person could have duties in respect of himself. (Such a being may only be able to engage in mental acts. I suppose it could then have the duty to think "clear" or "clean" thoughts.)

Personal duties, of whatever kind, might not exhaust the domain of dutiful conduct, however. They would not exhaust it if there were duties that had as their *ground* the rights of the recipients or beneficiaries of the dutiful conduct. If we choose to speak in the modern way and talk of other-regarding personal duties as being correlated with the rights of other parties, we should be clear that these rights are *normatively subsequent* to the duties; while in the case of the

---

[15] For an extensive treatment see Aaron Kirschenbaum, "The 'Good Samaritan' and Jewish Law," *Diné Israel*, 1976, 7, 7–86.

other other-affecting duties, the duties are normatively subsequent to the *rights*. In more general terms, the distinction between personal duties and rights-related duties turns on the way each type is justified.

It is just this area of rights-related duties which was given short shrift in ethical theory until the emergence of an explicitly defined notion of a right. Until that time the tendency was to conceive of duties in personal terms and to subordinate them to "objective" notions. The best example of this is Stoicism, as presented in Cicero's *De Officiis*. The general tendency, as I argued earlier, was to bypass the language of rights at large. Even in the law, where the use of the language of rights and duties would be natural, the opportunity to employ it was often passed up. Thus, in Roman law "obligation" (*obligatio*) is defined as "a tie of law which binds us according to the rules of our civil law to render something" and it arises, as Gaius says, through consent or commission of injury (*Institutes*, III, 88). The use of the langauge of correlated rights and duties would be natural here, but "obligation" is taken as designating the parties' situation as a whole and as arising through law.

Of course, rights-related duties, duties that are grounded on the rights of others, lurk below the surface of the classical theories. Aristotle's idea of the virtue of particular justice, which concerns fairness in one's dealings with others, comes very close to the concept, though it is not explicitly construed as deriving from a right of others to a given share or a given conduct. Yet it seems more than an accident that Aristotle's discussion of distributive justice probably was the *urtext* of the earliest explicit definitions of *ius*, which were given in terms of *dignitas* and *meritum* (worth and desert). These definitions derive from Cicero, whose own definition of "justice" as giving to each his *dignitas* stems from Aristotle's principle of "each according to his *axion*" (worth or merit). As I noted, these early definitions are close to a welfare notion of rights – a suggestive if not a theoretically determinative fact.

The distinction between personal duties and rights-related duties, as I said, turns on the way in which each type is justified. In trying to spell out the difference, it is important to keep in mind that the concept of a personal duty has sense for a universe of a single, isolated individual (though there may not actually be any duties in such a world), while the concept of rights-related duties has no sense for such a universe – and neither does the concept of rights. The question of whether or not Robinson Crusoe has rights does not arise before the arrival of Friday. It would be completely idle to speak of Robinson's rights, and *a fortiori* of his rights "against the world" (assuming that the actions of those who have no contact with him have no affect on him). The concept of rights is inherently interpersonal; it presupposes claimers and claimants. These considerations have important theoretical consequences.

First of all, rights, and rights-related duties, can arise only in a social context, and that context may even have to be of a fairly specific sort, which is a subject I cannot go into here. In asserting the necessity of a social context, I perhaps am prejudicing the question of animals' rights, because humans and animals hardly stand in the same "social" relations that humans can toward each other. (In older language, there is no "common right" between humans and animals.)[16] This thought, I believe, underlies the occasional statement in the classical natural rights literature that humans have no rights *against* things or animals; our rights *in* things or animals are rights against other humans. It is clear, in any case, that if the case for rights as between humans cannot be made, we will never succeed in establishing animals' rights against humans, and I think that the necessity of a social context of some sort is an element of this case.

For this reason I would take exception to Professor Alan Gewirth's attempt to derive rights from the generic features of action, if I understand it correctly. Consider the situation of Robinson Crusoe before the arrival of Friday. Robinson of course acts, and I am willing to grant that freedom and well-being are necessary conditions of his action: they are necessary goods for Crusoe, to use Gewirth's terminology. Still, it cannot be maintained that Robinson either has or does not have rights to freedom and well-being, for the question does not arise. The "dialectically necessary method" whereby Gewirth argues that a prudent, self-interested agent *must* claim rights[17] has no foothold in the situation of Robinson Crusoe. It may be true that the "necessary content of morality is to be found in action and its generic features,"[18] but rights cannot be derived from the generic features of action alone. Once Friday arrives the situation changes and Robinson now *can* claim rights, and perhaps he also must claim them. I think, in any case, that the more important issue is why Friday should concede any rights to Robinson.

The inherently interpersonal character of rights is a clue to the significance that rights language has as a minimum, namely, that rights language exists as a device for making claims and demands against others. (The fact, however, that people *make* claims doesn't mean that they *have* claims.)[19] This is a feature that moral rights language shares with legal rights language. The quasi-legal character of moral rights explains, I think, why some writers have thought that rights belong to that part of morality which can be physically enforced. Although I am not sure that one may not be rightfully compelled to perform one's other-affecting personal duties, I think it plain that one's possession of a right, whether welfare or option, does imply some kind of legitimate control

---

[16] See, e.g., St. Augustine, *The Catholic and Manichaean Ways of Life* (Washington: Catholic University of America Press, 1966), trans. by D. A. and I. J. Gallagher, Ch. 17, 102. This translation reads "common rights," but see the original in J. P. Migne (ed.), *Patrologiae Latinae* (Paris: 1844–), v. 32, 1368.

[17] *Reason and Morality*, 42–47.

[18] *Ibid.*, 25.

[19] See my paper "Towards a Theory of Human Rights," cited above, n. 7.

over others. So, while someone's having a duty does not necessarily entail that anyone else has a right, having a right does entail that someone else has a duty, the special kind of duty I have called "rights-related." Unless this were the case it is hard to see what special function would be served by the introduction of the terminology of rights into moral discourse. Admittedly, welfare rights pose a problem in this connection, for it is not always clear on whom it is incumbent to fulfill a welfare-rights claim. Perhaps, though, welfare rights impose some sort of duty on everyone.

In any case, the archetypical option right, the Hobbesian-Seldenian "right of nature," a right that passes no obligation,[20] is a phony right. The proposition that men have rights but do not stand in moral relations to each other (as in the "natural condition of mankind") undercuts the use of rights language. It is only by equivocating on the term "a right" that Hobbes is able to move his argument forward. The objection to Hobbes is well-stated by Pufendorf:

> . . . not every Natural License, or Power of doing a Thing, is properly a *Right*; but such only as includes some Moral Effect, with regard to others, who are Partners with me in the same Nature. . . . For 'tis ridiculous Trifling to call that Power a *Right*, which should we attempt to exercise, all other Men have an *equal Right* to obstruct or prevent us.[21]

Once we move from the situation of the isolated individual to that of human beings (or beings like humans in certain significant respects) in social interrelationship the question of rights becomes meaningful. At this point it becomes possible to assert and to deny that men have various specific rights and also to deny that they have any rights at all. At this point we can ask, Why should Friday concede to Robinson any of the rights the latter happens to claim? Why should he not, instead, deny these claims and even deny that Robinson has any rights at all?

Caution is required in approaching these questions. For there are at least two different respects in which rights claims can be conceded and two different ways in which a rights claim can be denied.

First of all, a rights claim can be conceded without its being acknowledged as a claim of right. It may, for instance, merely be *acceded to*. Friday thus may have good prudential reasons for acceding to Robinson's rights claims as claims or demands while not admitting them as rights claims. If Robinson and Friday each need and desire the cooperation of the other in order to achieve his own ends, they might enter into trade-offs that would be advantageous to each, these trade-offs being dependent upon imaginable variations in their respective circumstances. But, again, the bargained concessions need not be

---

[20]   See the book by Richard Tuck (cited above, no. 8), at 111.

[21]   *Of the Law of Nature and Nations*, III, 5, 3; in Kennet trans., Bk. III, 48.

acknowledgements of moral rights. In addition, a claim can be conceded as a matter of *grace*. David Hume speculates[22] that we would not be under restraints of justice to creatures who are very much weaker than we are, "nor could they possess any right," but I suppose that we could be gracious towards them. It is partly to forestall this possibility that Hobbes postulates a natural equality of strength among men in the construction of his rights theory. (In the legendary Wild West, the equivalent of the Hobbesian state of nature, the Smith and Wesson .44 was called the "Equalizer.") And in more orthodox constructions of rights theories an equality of moral status is postulated in order to forestall the merely gracious accession to a rights claim. This postulate, again, would prejudice the case of animals' rights. I probably should own up to the fact that I don't think that animals and other natural things, and also artificial things like buildings and art objects, have rights.[23] But I am not certain that the postulate of moral equality is required for a rights theory. Finally, of course, a rights claim can be conceded because it is acknowledged *as such*. Whether this occurs depends upon the special kind of reason for the concession, which I shall take up shortly.

A rights claim can be denied in two ways: in a *weak* way and in a *strong* way. Denial, as I conceive it, is a combined pragmatic-semantical notion. The weak denial of a proposition merely says that the proposition is *not true*, and it does not commit the denier to the assertion of some counter-claim. The strong denial of a proposition, on the other hand, does so commit him. This distinction, I believe, is important in the area of normative discourse, in which the notion of commitment plays a role, in the sense of what a person is committed to as a result of accepting or denying various claims. Thus, the weak denial of a proposition of the form

(R) A has a right to interfere with B's liberty

merely states that (R) is not true. The weak denial of (R) does not entail (does not commit one to) the counter-claim

(S) B has a right not to be interfered with by A

or the counter-claim

(T) A has a (rights-related) duty of non-interference toward B.

I take it that the moral skeptic, who denies that there are any rights and duties at all, is prepared to deny all three of these propositions; that is, he weakly

[22] David Hume, *An Inquiry Concerning the Principles of Morals* (New York: Library of Liberal Arts, 1957), 21 (Sec. III, Pt. 1).

[23] See M. P. and N. H. Golding, "Why Preserve Landmarks? A Preliminary Inquiry," in K. E. Goodpaster and K. M. Sayre (eds.), *Ethics and Problems of the 21st Century* (Notre Dame, Ind.: University of Notre Dame Press, 1979), 175–90.

denies them; he declares that none of them is true. The strong denial of a normative proposition, however, does entail (does commit one to) the assertion of a counter-claim. Thus, the strong denial of (R) entails (S) and (T).

If we now ask why Friday should concede any of Robinson's rights claims (or vice versa) or why he should not deny any of these claims (or vice versa), our concern must be with concession *as* a rights claim and with denial in the strong sense. Anything less will not take us fully into the realm of moral discourse and would leave us unprovided with a basis for moral rights. The focus of our attention, nevertheless, must be on the question of why a rights claim should be conceded as such, for this is the more fundamental issue.

Now, it is important here to keep in mind the distinction mentioned earlier between personal duties and rights-related duties. For it might be maintained that Friday should concede a rights claim of Robinson's because Friday accepts some personal duty-proposition that commits him to conceding some rights-proposition. This may very well be the case in the last analysis. But if it is the case, we should probably have to admit that the terminology of rights has no special significance and does not mark out a particular domain of moral conduct. Secondly, I do not think it adequate to say that Friday should concede a rights claim of Robinson's because Friday makes rights claims against the latter. This conventional and generally proper move in moral argument is inadequate because Friday might not make any rights claims; he may merely make claims and demands that he expects or hopes will be acceded to for any of a number of reasons, and he may deny Robinson's rights claims in the weak sense of the term. This assertion is contrary to Professor Gewirth's thesis that rationally self-interested individuals must make rights claims, against which thesis I have expressed objections elsewhere.[24] In any case, underlying our initial question is the further question, Why rights at all?, Why isn't the rest of our moral language enough?

In order to answer the question of why Friday should concede Robinson's rights claim as a rights claim, I think it is useful to consider how he might come to so conceding it. In order to grasp this process, we must be careful not to confuse it with any of the other ways in which a rights claim purportedly can be accepted.

It seems to me that there just is one way in which this concession can come about (aside from its being entailed by another rights claim which he concedes), a way that has two analytically separable steps. The first step consists of the recognition that the object claimed by the other as a matter of right is an

[24] Martin P. Golding, "From Prudence to Rights: A Critique," in J. R. Pennock and J. W. Chapman (eds.), *Human Rights*, NOMOS XXIII (New York: New York University Press, 1981), 165–74. I have not succeeded in convincing Professor Gewirth of the error of his ways. See his reply in *idem, Ethics, Economics, and the Law*, NOMOS XXIV (New York: New York University Press, 1982), 178–88.

element of, or a means to, the other's *personal good*. The second step consists of the acknowledgement that this good is genuinely *a good*, that is, the good-of-Robinson's is a good-to-Friday. By this I, of course, do not mean that it is good for Friday to acknowledge Robinson's personal good or that Robinson's good is something that Friday necessarily has a stake in.

It is the combination of these two steps which provides the clue to the special kind of justification that marks off the domain of rights-related duties from other other-affecting duties. The ground of Friday's duty is located in Robinson's personal good that is also taken to be a genuine good. This, however, is not to say that Robinson's personal good is a genuine good because it is his personal good. For Friday can be as mistaken in the second step as he can be in recognizing that the claimed object is an element in, or a means to, Robinson's personal good. Nevertheless, having taken these two steps Friday has committed himself to conceding Robinson's rights claim as such. These steps mark out the domain of "subjective right."

Admittedly, the above account, which for purposes of the present exposition has had to focus upon a simple, two-person situation, is a highly abbreviated description of the process that is uniquely involved in the concession of rights claims. (The account also can explain what is meant in saying that someone "implicitly" has a concept of rights even though rights language is not available to him.) Much remains to be filled in. In particular, further clarification is needed regarding the idea of a personal good. The important point, however, is the centrality of this idea in the concession, as such, of rights claims.

Strictly speaking, taking the described steps commits one only to conceding a *presumptive* right to the claimed objects. Much more is required before it can be maintained that the other party *has* an unqualified right to those objects. Plainly, an object claimed by one person as a matter of right might also be claimed by another person, so these conflicting claims will have to be arbitrated in some way. There is, in fact, a long list of items that need to be established before it can be maintained that anyone has rights. Most of these items are the traditional matter of ethical theory. The above steps provide a clue as to the starting point of the inquiry. They are only the beginning of wisdom on the subject. And much filling in needs to be done to take care of rights against the government, so-called group rights, and so on. (I am not announcing any of this as if it were news.)

One thing nevertheless can be said. If there are any rights at all, there are welfare rights. This assertion, I think, follows from the location of the ground of rights in a personal good that also is a genuine good. Furthermore, it follows, I think, that the notion of welfare rights has a theoretical primacy, conceptually and normatively, over option rights. I have no doubt that liberty is an element in, and a means to, a human being's personal good. So, if there are any human rights at all, there are also option rights. Still, I see no reason whatsoever for respecting liberty as such, or for conceding option rights as such, that is, as something separate from an individual's personal good. (Of course, there can be prudential reasons and reasons of political or social expediency for respecting individual liberty.) The primary notion that underlies any theory of rights is that of welfare. I do not think that this idea is very far from those early definitions of "rights" given in terms of *dignitas* and *meritum*. Welfare rights, therefore, also appear to have historical priority.

I realize I have not said anything at all about the content of rights, if there are any rights. This issue, however, was not the subject of my paper. It is my strong suspicion, if I may say so, that many currently asserted rights claims, both welfare and option, are at best presumptive rights.

This paper has proceeded on the assumption that the language of rights has a special significance within moral discourse and marks out a special domain of morality. This assumption may be false, and perhaps we do not require the terminology of rights in order to say all we need to about our moral relations. It could be argued that there is a personal duty to promote the personal good of another if it is a geniune good, so that the need for the language of rights is obviated. We can weakly deny rights claims without being moral skeptics. But I rather doubt that I should give up claiming rights for myself.

There is a story told about John Dewey. Dewey was an ardent supporter of women's suffrage. He went to participate in a suffragist parade, picked up a sign, and marched along. Everytime he passed a group of men, he noticed that they would break out in howls of laughter, and this became quite embarrassing. When he put down the sign at the end of the parade, he saw the reason for the laughter. The sign read: "If men can vote, why can't I?" If other people claim rights, why shouldn't I?

Philosophy and Law, Duke University

Social Philosophy & Policy Vol. 1 Issue 2 ISSN 0265-0525

THE RIGHT NOT TO INCRIMINATE ONESELF

ALAN DONAGAN

The Fifth Amendment to the Constitution of the United States contains the following words: "No person . . . shall be compelled in any criminal case to be a witness against himself." In laying down this restriction on what government may do, the Constitution creates a legal right: the right to be free from coercion by any organ of government to testify against oneself – to incriminate oneself.

A moral question can be asked about this constitutionally grounded legal right: Are political societies morally obliged to recognize it? Or, in other words: Is a civil society that does not accord to those in its jurisdiction the right not to incriminate themselves so far morally defective?

Before attempting to answer this question, it is well to clarify the conception of morality by reference to which it is asked. Disputants who differ radically about what a moral issue is cannot expect to make much progress in settling any given moral issue. Fortunately the conception of morality I had in mind in speaking of moral obligations and moral defectiveness, and will have in speaking of moral permissibility and impermissibility, moral right and wrong, will be familiar to anybody with an elementary knowledge of the history of moral philosophy. Briefly, my metaethics is rationalist. I take there to be unconditional requirements of practical reason; and I take an action of a certain kind to be morally required in a situation of a certain kind if and only if any rational being in a situation of that kind would act contrary to practical reason if he did not perform an action of that kind. And I take an action to be morally permissible if and only if *not* doing it is not morally required.

What kinds of action *are* morally required? Briefly, again, my normative ethics is fundamentally Kantian – a teleologically based deontology. There are certain kinds of beings – rational agents – whose existence is of absolute worth, a good beyond price. Such beings are self-subsistent ends. Practical reason requires of any rational being that he respect the status of every rational being, including himself, as an end. And that involves not only noninterference with their morally permissible activities, and helping them when he can and they are in urgent need, but also goodwill to their morally permissible projects that is expressed in some rational plan of beneficence. However, evil may not be done that good may come: plans for beneficence are not rational if they entail impermissible interference with others, or refusal of help to those in urgent need. This view of morality is of course controversial, like every other view of it; but one cannot investigate questons about what is morally required without taking a position on what morality is.[1]

In inquiring whether civil societies are morally obliged to recognize the right not to incriminate oneself, I must confine myself to societies in which neither the criminal law itself nor the laws governing criminal investigations, trials and punishments are grossly unjust. How the injustice of the laws of a political society may affect the duties of those within its jurisdiction is far too complex to be considered here. Hence what follows will have to do with self-incrimination in societies of which neither the criminal law nor the systems of criminal investigation, trial and punishment are radically unjust. They need not be ideal; but they must not be such that their normal working would do serious injustice.

So far is it from being obvious that the legal right against self-incrimination has a moral foundation that at first sight the opposite is true. Given a fundamentally just system of criminal law, it is tempting to hold that anybody who has violated the law is morally obliged to confess and to submit to whatever punishment may be legally imposed. In Dostoevsky's novel, *Crime and Punishment*, Raskolnikov found confession and submission to punishment necessary for expiating his crime. And if confession – self-accusation – is a moral duty, what moral objection can there be to organs of government requiring anybody in their jurisdiction to testify as a witness in a criminal trial or investigation, even if his testimony should be against himself? How can it be morally wrong for an organ of government to compel somebody to do what it is his moral duty to do? The same conclusion seems to follow from a Rousseauist conception of a just criminal's own will: if a criminal wills that there be a criminal law forbidding certain of his own actions and ordering a certain punishment for them, must he not in consistency accuse himself? And should not Kant, whose theory of the moral law as autonomous was influenced by Rousseau's theory of the general will, also have concluded that, when public law ordains reasonable punishment for grave violations of the autonomously legislated moral law, criminals are bound by their own will to accuse themselves?

To the best of my knowledge, neither Rousseau nor Kant drew the conclusion which seems to follow from their theories; nor do I assert that Dostoevsky held that Raskolnikov's self-accusation to the public authorities was a moral duty, as distinct from a felt need to relieve by confession the guilt which his nihilistic theories dismissed as rationally unfounded. Why did they not assert that duty of self-accusation?

[1] In my *Theory of Morality* (Chicago: University of Chicago Press, 1977), I have developd the conception of morality here outlined.

A clue can be found, I believe, in the treatment of the topic by the medieval Christian scholastics. To them, as to Rousseau and Kant, the moral law is a set of requirements of practical reason, called 'natural law' because human beings recognize it by virtue of their nature as rational. The positive law of civil societies (called 'human law') ordains criminal sanctions on some violations of the moral law, because it is judged contrary to the common good that refraining from such violations should be merely a matter of personal conscience and public opinion. Apart from criminal sanctions, the duties of an individual with respect to a violation of the moral law were held by Aquinas to be contrition (regret for the violation and the intention of making amends), confession to a priest and submission to his judgment of what form those amends should take, and satisfaction or actually making those amends.[2] In those branches of Christianity that abandoned the practice of sacramental confession, the second of these duties was reduced to the duty to make a just self-judgment of what form the amends should take. Although, from a religious point of view, carrying out these duties does not suffice to rid us of moral guilt, divine grace being also needed, from a human point of view, contrition, confession (or just self-judgment) and satisfaction are all one can do – they are our whole human duty. Even the religious traditions that imposed private confession as a religious duty did not require that there be any public confession if amends would be made without it. For example, Aquinas held that sufficient amends are made for stealing something secretly if restitution (and, where necessary, recompense for the temporary loss) is made through an intermediary such as the priest who heard the confession.[3]

When violation of part of the moral law is forbidden by positive human criminal law, and a punishment prescribed, the scholastic view seems to have been that the only additional duties that are incurred are external: one must, as morality requires of members of a civil society, comply with the law. It is morally wrong to resist officers of the law, or to commit perjury in court, or to obstruct the processes of criminal justice. But, as Aquinas implicitly maintained, nobody is bound to expose his own crime (*nullus tenetur crimen suum detegere*).[4] You may not perjure yourself if a lawfully asked question will expose your crime, but you are not bound to initiate such exposure. The reason for this is plain. An essential element in the moral ground for supporting the civil institutions that promulgate and administer criminal law is that criminals typically are not contrite and do not render satisfaction for their wrongdoing. Supporting those institutions requires that you *submit* to criminal conviction and punishment even though you are contrite and have made amends for your crime; but it does not require that you *offer* yourself to such

---

[2] St. Thomas Aquinas, *Summa Theologiae*, III, 90, 3 *c*.
[3] Ibid., II-II, 62, 6 *ad* 2.
[4] Ibid., II-II, 62, 6 *obj.* 2.

conviction and punishment. You are morally bound to contrition and rendering satisfaction for your crime because crimes are also moral wrongs. But that, in the terminology of Rousseau and Kant, you autonomously legislate support for the institutions of the criminal law, in order to impose sanctions on typical violators of a moral law you also autonomously legislate, binds you to no more than conformity to those institutions and activity as a citizen in support of them. Both these requirements are consistent with concealing crimes which you repent and for which you have made amends.

This traditional Christian position, whether in its Catholic form or in its Protestant one, seems to be essentially sound. The rigorist doctrine that criminals are bound to accuse themselves to the public authorities is false. It therefore may be true that the constitutional right against self-incrimination has a moral foundation. But it has not yet been shown. That criminals are not bound to incriminate themselves does not entail that they have a right not to incriminate themselves. That they are not bound to incriminate themselves presupposes that they are not lawfully asked questions which they are lawfully bound to answer, to which truthful answers would incriminate them. We must now investigate that presupposition.

In Roman law, and in jurisdictions which accept the *Code Napoléon*, some procedures in criminal cases are inquisitorial, and witnesses can be lawfully required to answer questions so framed that, if they have acted criminally, truthful answers will incriminate them. Traditional Christian teaching did not object to that. It was with Roman Law in mind that Aquinas laid it down that when a judge *secundum ordinem juris* requires a witness to answer a question, it is not permissible for him to state a falsehood or to withhold truth in answering it (*non . . . licet ei vel falsitatem dicere vel veritatem tacere quam confiteri tenetur*). There are indeed restrictions on the questions a judge may put to a witness, for example, he may not ask a priest questions about what has been told to him in sacramental confession; but those restrictions do not, in Roman law, forbid asking questions to which truthful answers might be self-incriminating.[5]

Is there anything morally wrong with a system of criminal justice that permits such questioning? If there is, nothing we have so far considered has shown it. In arguing that those who have committed crimes are not morally bound to accuse themselves and submit to punishment, it was assumed as a premise that, apart from external support for a morally acceptable system of criminal justice, the only moral duties of those who have committed crimes are contrition and amendment. But plainly in some cases amends cannot be made without public confession. If you have destroyed somebody's good name by perjury, you cannot restore it without public confession that you perjured yourself. Again, when somebody else has been judicially convicted of a crime

<hr>

[5] Ibid., II-II, 69, 3 *c.*

of which you are guilty, it may be impossible for you to carry out your duty to correct whatever miscarriages of justice you can except by accusing yourself. In such cases, self-incrimination is a moral duty. Nor is that all. *Prima facie* it is a moral requirement upon any system of justice that it not jeopardize the direct ends of justice – namely, that cases be correctly decided, that the articles of the substantive branch of the law be carried out, and that only due obligations be imposed – by excluding from consideration the best evidence available. So Jeremy Bentham argued in his monumental, posthumous *Rationale of Judicial Evidence*.[6] Except for the special case of evidence by a Catholic priest about sacramental confessions made to him, Bentham maintained that the direct ends of justice are indefensibly jeopardized if the best available evidence is excluded from consideration in a judicial proceeding on any ground other than that the inconvenience of procuring that evidence "in the shape of vexation, expense, and delay" preponderates over "the mischief attached to a sacrifice of the direct ends of justice."[7] Now the best evidence respecting an issue in a criminal case may often be that of the criminal himself, and hence, if truthful, self-incriminating.

Taken as it stands, Bentham's position does not presuppose a utilitarian theory of morality, and is not even consistent with one. Not only does it not depend on the utilitarian principle that it is everybody's duty to maximize utility, to which anti-utilitarians object as false in principle and impracticable in application, but it implicitly excludes most utilities from consideration. The direct ends of justice on the one hand, and avoiding the evils of vexation, expense, and delay, are the only utilities that are recognized as relevant, although obviously they are not the only ones involved in most legal cases. For example, the disutility of inflicting a legally prescribed punishment on a criminal who has already repented and made what amends he can, is dismissed as irrelevant. Why? The answer seems plainly to be that Bentham takes only the ends of public justice to matter here: the direct ends of justice on the one hand, which include that of deciding cases correctly; and on the other what might be called its indirect end, that no suffering or inconvenience that would have to be inflicted in order to secure its direct ends be such that their infliction would be a greater violation of justice than sacrificing those direct ends. In Bentham's argument, the only 'inconveniences' that are held to justify

---

[6] Jeremy Bentham, *Rationale of Judicial Evidence*, (London: Hunt and Clarke 1827). In five volumes.
[7] Jeremy Bentham, *Rationale of Judicial Evidence*, vol. 4, 480. Bentham did, indeed, allow the exclusion of irrelevant evidence; but he maintained that the mischief of hearing such evidence 'is resolvable *in toto* into the mischief producible by vexation, expense, and delay' (ibid., 571). Of the special case of excluding evidence by priests about sacramental confessions, Bentham remarked: 'The advantage gained [by coercing priests to give such evidence] in the shape of assistance to justice, would be casual, and even rare; the mischief produced by it, constant and all-extensive' (ibis., 589).

the 'mischief' of sacrificing the direct ends of justice are injustices: and punishing the guilty who have discharged all the moral obligations arising from their guilt is not an injustice. So interpreted, and I can think of no other way to interpret it, Bentham's principle, "Be the dispute what it may, – see everything that is to be seen; hear every body who is likely to know any thing about the matter; hear every body, but most attentively of all, first of all those who are likely to know most about it, the parties,"[8] seems to have been inspired, not by utilitarianism, but rather by that *gemeine sittliche Vernunfterkenntnis* to which Kant also turned.

What reasons have been offered for rejecting Bentham's non-exclusionary principle in the case of self-incriminating evidence – or, as he called it, of 'self-disserving' evidence? Since Bentham's own list of the 'preferences' upon which the exclusion of self-disserving evidence is justified contains the elements of the only reasons known to me that are even plausible, I begin with it. It is composed of five items.

(1) "[T]he old sophism, the well-worn artifice, sometimes called *petitio principii*, and which consists in the assumption of the propriety of the rule excluding self-disserving evidence], as a proposition too plain to admit dispute."[9]

(2) "The old woman's reason. The essence of this reason is contained in the word *hard*: 'tis hard upon a man to be obliged to criminate himself.'"[10]

(3) "The fox-hunter's reason. This consists in introducing upon the carpet of legal procedure the idea of *fairness*, in the sense in which this word is used by sportsmen. The fox must have a fair chance of his life: he must have (so close is the analogy) what is called *law* . . . In the mouth of the lawyer, this reason, were the nature of it seen to be what it is, would be consistent and in character. Every villain let loose one term, that he may bring custom the next, is a sort of bag-fox, nursed by the common hunt at Westminster."[11]

(4) "Confounding interrogation with torture: with the application of physical suffering, till some act is done; in the present instance, till testimony is given to a particular effect required."[12]

(5) "Reference to unpopular institutions" – those mentioned by Bentham being the English prerogative courts of Star Chamber and High Commission, abolished by the Long Parliament and forbidden by the Bill of Rights, and the "Romish Inquisition."[13]

---

[8] Bentham, *Rationale of Judicial Evidence*, vol. 5, 743.
[9] Ibid., 229.   [10] Ibid., 230.
[11] Ibid., 238–39.   [12] Ibid., 240.
[13] Ibid., 241.

Of the reasons listed, (1) is patently objectionable – disputes cannot be settled by either side's putting forward the truth of what it asserts as indisputable; (3) and (4) also succumb to elementary but decisive objections. The fox-hunter's reason may be demolished by agreeing that the law of evidence must be fair, but denying that fairness to a defendant is the same as fairness to a hunted fox: ensuring that he has a chance to escape an adverse verdict, even though he is demonstrably in the wrong. And the identification of interrogation with torture is shown to be false by pointing out that being required to answer a question is not the same as being required to give a particular answer to it. It is true that a false answer to a question put to a witness under oath may lead to a prosecution for perjury; but if that be torture, then all questions asked of witnesses under oath are asked under torture.

Bentham of course acknowledged that a party to a case who is compelled on pain of contempt of court to give answer which, if truthful, would incriminate him, is exposed not only to the punishment for perjury to which an extraneous witness would be, but also "to a sort of punishment intrinsic to the cause, viz. loss of the cause: as where a defendant, in consideration of false responsion, evasive responsion, or obstinate silence, is concluded to be guilty."[14] But threat of neither punishment, extrinsic or intrinsic, is threat of torture. Punishments are tortures only if what is punished is failure to give a particular answer to a question – usually either a confession of guilt, or an answer implying such a confession, such as naming alleged confederates or giving information about incriminating matters of detail.

By separating (2), "the old woman's reason" from (5), "reference to unpopular institutions," Bentham made it easier to dispose of both. For the case of his non-exclusionary principle is persuasive only to the extent that the criminal law itself, and the institutions by which it is administered, function justly. By separating the argument that it is "hard upon a man to be obliged to incriminate himself" from any reference to unpopular institutions, he enabled himself to ascribe any evils that arise from the combination of the non-exclusionary principle with defects in the criminal law or legal institutions to those defects alone.

In most political societies there are movements to impose penalties on propagating unpopular opinions, usually on the ground that such propagation may subvert the political order itself. When those movements are successful, in order to avoid odium and other non-legal sanctions, some will conceal that they hold the opinions it is forbidden to propagate. In addition, proof that a defendant holds such opinions may, in the minds of judges and juries alike, be tantamount to a presumption that he has propagated them. Now, when a defendant has been discreet, the only way in which he can be proved even to

---

[14] Ibid., 240.

sympathize with the opinions in question may be out of his own mouth. A well-entrenched and popular principle that self-incriminating evidence cannot be compelled will not only be a defense against some of the abuses of laws against the propagation of opinions, it may even blunt the zeal of those who advocate such laws, whose intention often is to harass any who even passively sympathize with opinions they hate. One may generalize: many kinds of legal offence that will often be provable only by compelling self-incriminating evidence ought not, morally speaking, be legal offences at all; and most offences for which there ought to be legal sanctions can be proved, if at all, without recourse to such evidence. This appears to be a moral reason of some weight why it should be illegal to compel self-incrimination.

Against it, Bentham's argument is simply that any injustice that arises in such cases proceeds, not from compelling self-incrimination, but from "the substantive branch of the law: it consist[s] in the converting into a ... crime the act of him who makes known, to use the words of scripture, the reason of the truth that is in him."[15] In one respect, this is unanswerable. If the problem is abstract, 'How, without regard to what may be practicable in a given case, to eliminate the injustices arising from compelling a defendant charged with illegally propagating certain opinions to testify against himself?' the solution is plain – to abolish the offense. But if the problem is practical, 'How in societies subject to agitation to prohibit the propagation of opinions deemed subversive, to forestall the injustices that are apt to result?' part of the solution may well be to establish a legal principle forbidding compulsion to self-incrimination. By separating his consideration of the old woman's reason from all reference to unpopular institutions, Bentham purchased a polemical advantage at a price he would certainly not have chosen to pay: that of setting aside practical considerations.[16]

A parallel may help here. In the 1960's the U.S. Supreme Court forbade the use in criminal cases of evidence obtained by constitutionally forbidden searches, even when that evidence was both necessay to the prosecution and would have been decisive. The chief reason given for this was that the only effective way to deter some police officers from conducting such searches is to frustrate their purpose in conducting them. Bentham would presumably have objected: the solution is to prohibit unreasonable searches, not to exclude the best evidence from legal proceedings. But this begs the practical question: What if prohibiting unreasonable searches (as was done before the Supreme Court's action) fails to prevent them? What if the only way, in practice, to

---

[15] Ibid., 258.
[16] Leonard W. Levy has explored the complex practical considerations by which the prohibition of compelling self-incrimination has been justified in his *Origins of the Fifth Amendment* (New York: Oxford University Press, 1968). I owe this reference to David Luban.

prevent the injustice of unreasonable searches should be now and then to incur the mischief of failing to convict the guilty for want of the best evidence?

Moreover, even in his separate treatment of "the old woman's reason" Bentham seems to me to have lapsed into one of those "easy speeches that comfort cruel men."

> What then is the hardship of a man's being thus made to criminate himself? The same as that of his being punished: the same in kind, but inferior in degree: inferior, in as far as, in the choice of evil, there is less hardship than in the certainty of it. Suppose, in both cases, conviction to be the result: does it matter to a man, would he give a pin to choose, whether it is out of his own mouth that the evidence is to come, or out of another's?[17]

This was not the hardship that impressed itself most urgently on those who were horrified by compelled self-incrimination; that hardship was rather one pointed out by Franciscus Memmius, in arguing against the Roman Inquisition's practice with those accused before it, of exacting oaths to speak the truth, even if it should incriminate them.

> It was, according to Memmius, a form of torture more cruel than physical torture because it tormented one's soul by tempting a man to save himself from punishment by perjuring himself . . .[18]

This is horrible, as David Luban has well written, because even though a man is guilty, "it smites him through his human condition, not through his guilty condition. It treats the tenacity of survival as mere weakness."[19]

Horrifying though this hardship is, it should not be exaggerated. It is not severer than the hardship inflicted when, by compelling them to testify for the prosecution, a court tempts an accused's intimate friends – friends who in other circumstances would give up their lives for him – to perjury. And it is sheer hyperbole to describe it as more cruel than the extremes of physical torture – torture that breaks a victim's mind as well as his body. But Bentham goes further. He contends (falsely, I believe) that

> in proportion as you exclude this or that quibble, this or that device of technical procedure, by which a certain proportion of the whole number of delinquents are saved, and the probability of punishment in case of delinquency thereby diminished, you would put it in your

---

[17] Bentham, *Rationale of Judicial Evidence*, vol. 5, 230–31.

[18] Levy, *Origins of the Fifth Amendment*, 24. I owe this particular reference also to David Luban.

[19] David Luban, 'Corporate Counsel and Confidentiality,' typescript, Center for Philosophy and Public Policy and University of Maryland School of Law (1981), 34–35. (This paper is forthcoming in a volume edited by Frederick Elliston, *Whistleblowing: Conflicting Loyalties in the Workplace*).

power to make a correspondent and proportionable reduction in the magnitude of your punishment.[20]

If this were true – if abolishing the right not to incriminate oneself would, without working additional injustices, so increase the proportion of just verdicts of guilty to crimes committed that punishments could be reduced while deterring as many or more potential criminals from crime – then not even the hardships caused and the secondary benefits forgone would justify retaining it. But Bentham offers no evidence for what on its face is an extremely improbable assertion: unless his unsupported impression is to be accepted as evidence.

To compel anybody to give evidence against his will in a criminal trial, especially if the accused is near and dear to him, is a grave hardship; but, since everybody is morally obliged to support the direct ends of justice, if those ends would be jeopardized by allowing him not to testify, compelling him to testify does not fail to respect his status as a rational being. Compelling somebody to testify against himself, for the reasons given by Memmius, works an even greater hardship. But if the sacrifice of the direct ends of justice resulting from forbidding such compulsion were as great as Bentham maintained, without producing serious evidence, then to compel defendants to testify could not be held to fail to respect them as rational beings. The ground for prohibiting such compulsion, therefore, is not that by its very nature it violates the respect due to human beings as rational. Rather, it is that it is part of everybody's duty of beneficence to support institutions by which, as far as may be, the respect due to human beings as rational will be secured to them; and that, in the circumstances actually prevailing in most civil societies, the history of legal institutions, popular and unpopular, appears to show that while prohibiting the civil authorities from compelling self-incriminating testimony does not seriously jeopardize the prosecution and punishment of the guilty, permitting them to compel it has gone hand in hand with all kinds of moral outrages, from the use of torture to prosecutions directed not to conviction but to bringing the accused into obloquy. In practice, the combination of Bentham's "old woman's reason" with his "reference to unpopular institutions" is a convincing argument for the Fifth Amendment's prohibition.

Any civil society that allows its authorities to compel anybody to be a witness against himself in a criminal case has, without significantly promoting the direct ends of justice, omitted to establish in its legal system a principle that affords some security against moral outrages that otherwise there is reason to fear will occur in times of stress. Compelling a person accused of a crime to be a witness against his will inflicts on him a horrifying hardship; but inflicting that hardship is not in itself a moral wrong, being no different in kind from

[20] Bentham, *Rationale of Judicial Evidence*, vol. 5, 234.

compelling somebody to be a witness against somebody near and dear to him. A civil society that permits its authorities to compel self-incriminating testimony may perhaps avoid doing moral wrong to anybody: it may scrupulously respect the dignity of all rational beings in its jurisdiction. And a civil society that does not permit it may well commit all sorts of moral outrages against unpoplar persons. I do not maintain that the Swedish system of criminal justice is as a whole morally inferior to the American one. Yet societies of the latter kind are in one respect morally superior to those of the former: they have provided a morally permissible safeguard – and one for which no alternative is in view – against moral wrongs to which, in practice, all civil societies are prone. It is therefore the moral duty of citizens of any state – an 'imperfect' duty of beneficence – to support measures, such as the Fifth Amendment, that provide that safeguard.

The right not to incriminate yourself is not a moral right. It is not always morally permissible to refrain from incriminating yourself; for you may not be able to carry out the moral duty to give satisfaction for wrongs done except by incriminating yourself (for example, to bring to an end a continuing crime, where that can only be done by exposing it and incidentally your part in it). Hence if the argument of this paper is sound, it is a citizen's moral duty to uphold a legal right which in some cases it would be morally wrong to exercise. That this is not inconsistent should be obvious on reflection. One may have moral duties to uphold rights (property rights are a good example) which may be abused. It is of the first moral importance, therefore, *to distinguish between legal rights with a moral foundation, and moral rights.* Just as it may be morally wrong to do with your property what you have a morally based legal right to do, so it may be morally wrong to exercise your morally based legal right not to incriminate yourself.

In so arguing it will be evident that, while I hold that the U.S. Constitution's Fifth Amendment protection against self-incrimination can be morally defended, I am not tempted to confound the legal system of the United States, or any other, with a moral system. Law and morality are inseparable, in that it is a moral duty to promote the establishment of a just system of law. But even an ideal system of law will legally permit many kinds of moral wrongs, because there are many such wrongs – breaches of personal good faith, for example – for which there is no conceivable legal remedy.

It is therefore, in my opinion, a grave error to think of even an ideal system of criminal justice as being such that it is morally permissible to take advantage of every legal permission it accords. It is morally wrong for somebody whose perjury has resulted in a wrongful conviction to stand on his constitutional right not to incriminate himself and refrain from confessing his perjury, if only by such a confession can the miscarriage of justice be corrected. Only a belief in magic could make it plausible that systems of justice such as those in even the most enlightened and decent of actual political societies are so constructed that the working of any of them will in all cases ensure justice for all parties, provided only that they take full advantage of everything it permits them. It is true that in the United States, most parties to legal transactions do not take advantage of everything their legal system permits. But would the system be tolerated by the public at large if everybody treated it in the spirit of a rogue labor union or an unscrupulous financial manipulator?

If I am right in suspecting that even reasonably just and decent legal systems, like that of the United States, survive because most members of the societies in which they are established are themselves reasonably just and decent in exercising their legal rights, then an inference drawn by interested legal professionals (such as the Defense Lawyers' Association) from the legal right of a client in a criminal case not to incriminate himself is utterly invalid. That inference is that a lawyer, as his client's *alter ego*, has not only a moral right, but also a moral duty, to do for his client whatever that client has a legal right to do for himself, and would do, had he the necessary legal knowledge. Has his client a guilty secret, which, by the Fifth Amendment, he cannot be compelled to disclose? Then he, as lawyer, on learning that secret from his client, has not only a moral right, but even a moral duty both to keep that secret, and to advise his client how most effectively to prevent its disclosure. It does not matter that the client himself may have no moral right to keep that secret, as when its disclosure is necessary if he is not to wrong a third party. Here, the applicable moral principle seems to be plain: if a client's legal right to do something does not confer on him a moral right to do it, he cannot transfer a moral right to do it to his attorney. Neglect of this principle seems to me to have vitiated much recent work in jurisprudence on the confidentiality a lawyer owes to his clients.[21] But that is another story.[22]

Philosophy, University of Chicago

[21] I have explored this matter further in 'Justifying Legal Practice in the Adversary System,' typescript prepared for the Maryland Center for Philosophy and Public Policy Working Group of Legal Ethics (1981), publication forthcoming.

[22] Of the various valuable comments made at the Conference on my working draft, for which I desire to express my gratitude, those that have made most difference to this revision were by Alan Gewirth, Alan Gibbard, and Steven O. Ludd.

Social Philosophy & Policy Vol. 1 Issue 2 ISSN 0265-0525

MODERATING RIGHTS*

RICHARD E. FLATHMAN

Rights might be regarded as an objectionable and even a dangerous feature of moral, political, and legal arrangements. It is an element of all (Hohfeldian) types of rights that Able's having right X entails requirements or prohibitions for Baker. These restrictions hold against Baker at Able's discretion, that is unless Able excuses Baker from respecting them. Nor are the restrictions merely decorative. We must presume that they are established because of the expectation that Baker would otherwise be disposed to interfere with the action Ms. Able's right warrants her in taking.[1] Thus as writers as early as Spinoza have stressed, rights are powers – one might even say weapons – that Able may use against Baker. Of course, as a practical matter these "weapons" are frequently ineffective. Ms. Baker may willfully ignore her obligations and prevent Ms. Able from enjoying her entitlements.[2] But such occurrences, as common and as unfortunate as they are, do not materially ease the task of justifying rights. It is only insofar as rights are effective, and hence only insofar as anyone will have reason to defend them, that they are weapons in Able's hands.

It is true and important that rights may also influence, channel, and even limit Able's actions. There is first the point, inadequately appreciated by communalist critics of rights (such as Alasdair MacIntyre[3]), that rights integrate individuals into the society or polity in which the rights are established.[4] In addition, to give Able a right to do X may make it less likely that Able will do some more objectionable action Y. To give workers a right to strike may reduce the likelihood that they will wreck factories. It may be asking

---

*Earlier versions of this paper were presented to sessions of the Western Canada Chapter of the Conference for the Study of Political Thought, the Inter-American Congress of Philosophy, a National Endowment for the Humanities Seminar at The Johns Hopkins University, and to graduate seminars in political philosophy at Johns Hopkins. I am grateful to participants in these sessions, and especially to my colleague David Sachs, for their comments and suggestions.

[1] Wesley, N. Hohfeld, *Fundamental Legal Conceptions*, W. W. Cook (ed.) (New Haven: Yale University Press, 1919). I have discussed Hohfeld's distinctions and defended the claim about Able's discretion in my *The Practice of Rights*, esp. Ch. 2 (New York and London: Cambridge University Press, 1976).

[2] This theme is stressed in Stuart Scheingold, *The Politics of Rights* (New Haven: Yale University Press, 1974).

[3] Alasdair MacIntyre, *After Virtue* (Notre Dame: University of Notre Dame Press, 1981).

[4] See Flathman, *op. cit.*, esp. Ch. 9.

too much to expect factory owners to relish the constant threat of strikes. But they might prefer this circumstance to more anarchic conditions with which it might be compared.

But if rights are "taming" or "domesticating" devices, or devices employed in the hope of achieving some valued end or goal that can be defined independently of the rights themselves and used to discipline the exercise of the rights, they may also encourage excesses of a sort that Hobbes and others have associated with a "wild" or "savage" condition. This is in part because many rights are "open-ended" or "unlimited" in at least the respect that if Ms. Able has a right to do or to have X she can do X as often as she wishes and she can have, as far as her right is concerned, as much of X as she can get. If our union has the legal right to strike, we can legally do so as often as we think will serve our interests. Or to take the generic instance that most dramatically illustrates the dangers of this feature of rights, my right to hold property allows me to imitate such exemplars as Lord Thomson, the Rockefellers, etc. I can accumulate so much capital that I cannot spend as fast as I "make," acquire so many newspapers as to monopolize the flow of information to millions of people, own vast estates that sit unused for months or years at a stretch, and exclude whole generations from experiencing art objects of unique beauty by hoarding them in private places. In Blackstone's perhaps flamboyant but by no means uninfluential formulation, by virtue of her right, Able acquires "sole and despotic dominion . . . over the external things of the world, in total exclusion of . . . any other individual in the universe."[5]

This extreme version of rights theory can be put in the cadence of a once notorious slogan – "Extremism is the exercise of rights is no vice." As thus understood, some critics see the practice of rights as lacking in principles of moderation. Thus, we have a number of familiar plaints about rights: the "Weimar plaint" about extremists using their political rights to sabotage a civil order; the "Dickens plaint" about the well-heeled grinding down the impoverished by holding them to the letter of their obligations *vis à vis* contractual rights; the "Rachel Carson" or "Sierra Club plaint" about property holders treating their rights as licenses to despoil the commons.

Arrangements that give one person or group such powerful weapons in competitions and conflicts with others, that give one person or group so much as an approximation to "sole and despotic dominion" over the goods available to human kind, are, on the face of things, objectionable and dangerous arrangements.[6] It may be possible to justify such arrangements. But they are

---

[5] William Blackstone, *Commentaries on the Laws of England*, Book II, Ch. I, 2nd paragraph.

[6] In slightly less polemical terms: From a deontological perspective, while rights do much to protect, support or even guarantee the freedom of Ms. Able, they thereby impinge upon, interefere with, or restrict the freedom of Ms. Baker. From an axiological or classical utilitarian perspective, rights may guarantee that Able can act so as to maximize her personal utility as she conceives it, but they thereby put the greatest good or aggregate utility at risk.

arrangements that cry out for explicit, systematic, and – I would add – cautious justifications.

So at least it would seem from the foregoing, admittedly discursive remarks. And yet, to quote Blackstone once more, "There is nothing which so generally strikes the imagination and engages the affections of mankind" as do rights.[7] Of course, there has long been lively dispute as to what should be established and maintained as rights, who should have those rights, how they should be interpreted, and so forth. But the idea that rights as such, rights of any sort, may be lacking justification seems to be in danger of losing its foothold to the steadily rising waters of general enthusiasm for them. Rights are widely and deeply admired and the thought that they – the institution or device itself – might be without justification is entertained only by those who are radically alienated from, deeply disaffected by, beliefs and values fundamental to most contemporary Western societies and cultures.

The impressions just sketched are reinforced by recent writing about rights in moral, political, and legal philosophy. Numerous philosophers have not only accepted but celebrated what I have characterized as the immoderate characteristics of rights. Of course they do not use this language. But they insist on what in less polemical language might be called the distinctively independent standing and stringency of at least certain rights. That is, they insist both that certain rights are independent of considerations such as ends and purposes, and that they constitute warrants for doing or having some X that parties other than the right holder either cannot override at all (that are, for all other parties, dispositive, all things considered, reasons for the right holder doing or having X) or can override only by appeal to some other, conflicting right. In the most unqualified of the recent presentations of such views, that is Robert Nozick's, rights are asserted as moral givens and it is argued that all other moral and political issues must be resolved within the "side constraints" set by those rights.[8] Other recent versions of natural or human rights theory, for example Hart's and Gewirth's[9], offer a derivation for rights, but the most basic of the rights derived are treated as moral, legal and even political "trumps" which properly defeat or even exclude all apparently competing considerations. [10] If we don't understand and accept that rights are trumps, we simply haven't grasped and accepted the idea of rights. Sophisticated as the expressions of the "affections" of these theorists may be, there is no denying that their affections are deeply "engaged" by (what they understand to be) the idea of rights.

---

[7] Blackstone, *op. cit.*

[8] Robert Nozick, *Anarchy, State, and Utopia* (New York: Basic Books, 1974).

[9] H. L. A. Hart, "Are there any Natural Rights?". *Philosophical Review*, 64 (1955), 175 ff; Alan Gewirth, *Reason and Morality* (Chicago: University of Chicago Press, 1978).

[10] See Ronald Dworkin, *Taking Rights Seriously* (Cambridge: Harvard University Press, 1977).

In the present essay I continue my efforts[11] to qualify these tendencies of thought. I do not do so from an anti-right position such as MacIntyre's communitarianism or numerous of the versions of Marxism. Nor is it my intention to argue from or for any of the versions of utilitarianism that so thoroughly subordinate rights as to deprive them of distinctive character or significance. Although skeptical about the justifiability of a number of the rights most prominent in our society (especially some forms of the right to property), I regard the practice of rights as among the valuable features of legal, political, and moral life in modern Western societies. Although wanting to delineate and defend a more qualified view of the logic of rights than is presented in the insistently deontological accounts to which I have referred, I share the view that rights are distinctive and distinctively stringent entities. In the language of my title, I want to moderate not to abolish, and I want the entities that I moderate to be recognizable as rights.

The question that I want to address, then, is whether it is possible to accommodate the independence and distinctive stringency of rights while nevertheless avoiding the "immoderation" that seems to be attendant upon them.

I

I begin with a passage from a recent paper by T. M. Scanlon, one which is promising from the standpoint of moderating rights but which will be regarded as most unpromising indeed, by many theorists of rights. "In attacking utilitarianism, one is inclined to appeal to individual rights, which mere considerations of social utility cannot justify us in overriding. But rights themselves need to be justified somehow, and how other than by appeal to the human interests their recognition promotes and protects . . . . Further, unless rights are to be taken as defined by rather implausible rigid formulae, it seems that we must invoke what looks very much like the consideration of consequences in order to determine what they rule out and what they allow."[12] On this view, a right will be established and maintained only if it is consonant with or perhaps even contributive to the satisfaction of human interests that can be identified without reference to the right. In interpreting and enforcing established rights in particular circumstances consideration will be given to the consequences, presumably for human interests, of moderating rights at least in the sense of coordinating their exercise and enforcement with a variety

---

[11] See Flathman, *op. cit.*, and my paper "Rights, Utility, and Civil Disobedience," in J. Roland Pennock and John W. Chapman, eds., *Ethics, Economics and the Law* (*Nomos* XXIV) (New York: New York University Press, 1982). The present paper draws on material from the *Nomos* essay. I am grateful to the editors and publishers for permission to use it here.

[12] T. M. Scanlon, "Rights, Goals and Fairness," 93. In Stuart Hampshire (ed.), *Public and Private Morality* (London and New York: Cambridge University Press, 1978).

of other considerations that are valued in the society or group in which they are established. It must be admitted, however, that Scanlon's formulation confronts us with formidable difficulties. Scanlon is saying that a theory of rights must be consequentialist and in some sense teleological. In our time most theorists would take this to mean that such a theory will be utilitarian. But among numerous difficulties imputed to utilitarianism, one of them is just that no genuine form of that doctrine can provide a theoretically secure place for, or even a coherent account of, rights. Accepting for the moment a dichotomy widely regarded as exhaustive of the forms of utilitarianism, in its unqualified act-utilitarian versions utilitarianism tends to lose hold of the concept of rights, and wittingly or otherwise, to end up in the anti-rights camp. Rule-utilitarianism, by contrast, finds itself losing hold of its consequentialism and sliding toward a deontological position in order to "take rights seriously." If the program implicit in Scanlon's remarks is necessarily utilitarian, there are well rehearsed reasons for thinking that it cannot be carried through.

The most insistent formulations of these reasons have been presented by theorists who identify with the tradition of natural rights or human rights thinking. In the least qualified versions of this position, of which the most notable of the recent, secularized formulations is Robert Nozick's[13], it is asserted that rights simply are the starting points, the unfounded foundations, of morality (and of those parts of law and politics that are or should be subordinate to morality). Because they are not founded on or derived from anything independent of themselves, there can be no question of justifying or disproving, modifying or even interpreting, them in anything like the manner Scanlon suggests. And because they are starting points in this strong sense, they are stopping points in an equally strong sense. The entire independence and the absolute stringency of at least those rights that are "natural" is guaranteed.

The usual objection to this version of the natural rights position is that it is merely dogmatic; deprived of the religious suppositions that gave it credibility at earlier periods, it now presents itself as a form of instuitionism which, as with all others, provides no basis for resolving any disagreements or conflicts that may arise among intuitions.[14] Other formulations, for example H. L. A. Hart's and Alan Gewirth's, attempt to escape this objection;[15] they offer quite elaborate arguments intended to validate the belief that certain fundamental

---

[13] See Nozick, *op. cit.*
[14] Cf. Thomas Nagel's criticisms of Nozick in "Libertarianism Without Foundations," *Yale Law Journal*, 85 (1975) 136. There are other ways in which Nozick's argument might be construed, one of which makes it more closely akin to views of G. E. M. Anscombe that I take up and largely endorse below.
[15] See Hart and Gewirth, *op cit.*

rights are independent of and properly dominant over considerations of the kinds adduced by Scanlon.[16] If convincing, these arguments would provide non-arbitrary grounds on which to determine the content and distribution of at least the most basic rights as well as philosophical justification for rejecting views that subordinate rights to (or even coordinate them with) other kinds of considerations. In short, if arguments such as Hart's and Gewirth's go through, Scanlon's enterprise is doomed to failure. In the terms I have been using, the philosophical project of moderating rights would be shown to be misbegotten. The understandings that I have wrongheadedly characterized as immoderate would be in fact deep truths.

In an earlier version of this paper I attempt to show that the arguments in question are unconvincing.[17] In severely abbreviated summary (of an already compressed discussion), I contend that there are two possibilities: either (1) the claims are merely dogmatic (as in Nozick's case); or (2) the natural rights are justified by appeal to some beliefs or values independent of the rights and it is both logically possible and practically probable that those considerations (whatever they may be) will be ill-served by the distinctive institution or practice of *rights*. In the only philosophically interesting case, that is (2), it of course follows that no argument has been given for the entire independence and unqualified stringency of the so-called natural rights.

I will not elaborate these rejoinders and objections here. Because I find them convincing (there are of course numerous other such rejoinders to natural rights theory), I am prepared to pursue my project of finding a philosophical basis for "moderating" rights. But the difficulties with theories of natural and human rights do not obviate the fact, known to us as participants in the practice of rights (if not simply as speakers of languages that include the concept of rights), that rights are distinctive and distinctively stringent moral, legal, and political entities. Whatever our assessment of theories of human or natural rights, rights are widely regarded as potent entities and are valued and sought for that reason. There are numerous settings in which Ms. Able's showing that she has a right to do or to have X will settle the disputes that prompted her to invoke that right. If we denied these facts, or lacked a tolerably orderly account of them, we would not be in a position to determine whether we had moderated rather than distorted or failed to accommodate them.

[16] In Hart's case rights are dominant only in the realm or dimension of morality that is their home. He allows that there is another realm, the home of concepts such as the common good and the general welfare, the pursuit and service of interests and purposes, that has its own independence and integrity.

[17] The version of the paper to which I am referring was distributed in mimeo to participants in the Human Rights Conference sponsored by the Social Philosophy and Policy Center, Bowling Green State University, October 7–9, 1982. A limited number of copies are available from the author.

A brief but incisive paper by G. E. M. Anscombe will help us in this regard.[18] She gives an account of the features of rights (and of rules and promises) that have been my concern, namely their independence and their stringency. Her discussion of the stringency of rights begins with a puzzle about them. How can it be that the fact that you have a right (or the fact that I have made a promise, or that there is a prescriptive rule) creates an obligation for me; that owing to your right I *must* act in a certain manner or *must* refrain from a certain action or actions? These "musts" and "can'ts," which certainly are a characteristic of rights, are puzzling in part because they are obviously not the "musts" of physical necessity or impossibility. They are typically if not invariably invoked when it is quite obvious that in fact I *can* do or refuse to do the required or forbidden action. They are further puzzling because the necessity or impossibility seems to result from or be created by nothing more than a certain form or combination of words. But "How on earth can it be the meaning of a sign that by giving it one purports to create a necessity of doing something – a necessity whose source is the sign itself, and whose nature depends on the sign."[19]

In attempting to resolve these puzzles, Anscombe takes up Hume's view that the necessities attendant upon promises (and rights and certain rules) are "naturally unintelligible" and can only arise and be understood as part of a system of human conventions. For Hume this means two things: first, there is no natural object or event that is known to us by perception and for which (or for the image or sensation of which) the words "promise," "right," and "rule" stand; second, even if there were such an object or event it (our perception of it) could not of itself give rise to that "inclination to perform," that sense that one must perform, that is perhaps the most distinctive feature of promises, rights, and rules. Both the "object" and what we call the sense of duty or obligation attendant upon it are artifacts of human decision and agreement.

In respect to Hume's first point, Anscombe extends her argument to all "words and their relation to their meanings." All uses of words involve something conventional – namely rules and rule following. For this reason, language can never be "naturally" intelligible in Hume's sense. When we realize the ways in which the very meaningfulness of language depends on rules, we appreciate that words themselves, words as such, cannot be the source of that "inclination" or sense of duty which attaches to rights, promises, and prescriptive rules. Quite apart from psychological considerations such as Hume invoked, we could make no sense of the notion of duty or any particular duty. Of course words are typically used in the course of and as a

---

[18] G. E. M. Anscombe, "Rules, Rights, and Promises," *Midwest Studies in Philosophy* 3, (1978), 318–323.
[19] *Ibid.*, 320–321.

vital part of creating, discharging, and enforcing duties. But what matters, what generates and allows us to understand the "inclination" or duty, is not particular words or marks, signs or symbols, but the rules or – as Hume would say – conventions followed by those who use the words. It is because the activities of making and keeping promises, establishing, exercising, and respecting rights, adopting, obeying, and enforcing laws, are rule-governed that there is that sense of necessity, of stringency, attached to them.

To understand the stringency of rights, then, we must examine their place in rule-governed activities and practices. Doing so reminds us that there are a very large number of activities that involve "musts" and "can'ts" that have nothing to do with physical or natural limitations and necessities – that are asserted and acted upon just when and in part because in their absence we would be quite at liberty to do or refrain from doing the forbidden or required action. Such "modal pairs"[20] are a feature of every human activity that involves language. Any number of activities, moreover, involve rules over and above those governing the language used in the course of and as a part of engaging in them.

Let us pause to note that in this perspective the "musts" and "can'ts" that are a prominent part of rights present themselves as less distinctive, more ordinary, than they have been made to appear by moral and political philosophers. "It is part of human intelligence to be able to learn the response to . . . [these "musts" and "must nots"] without which they wouldn't exist as linguistic instruments and without which these things [and many others!]: rules, etiquette, rights, infringements, promises, pieties and impieties would not exist either."[21] They "are understood by those of normal intelligence as they are trained in the practices of reason."[22] In their generic character they are puzzling – or rather mysterious – only in the exceedingly deep sense in which we might find human intelligence and the practices of reason mysterious.

The foregoing observations indicate that Anscombe's analysis of modals is pertinent to the independence as well as the stringency of rights. This is also true of a further aspect of her discussion to which I now turn. It is very often the case that "musts" and "can'ts" are "accompanied by what sounds like a reason."[22] In the case of rights, the statement that Baker must do X or can't do Y is commonly followed by a phrase such as "it's Able's." "You must pay Ms. Able $50, she is entitled to it under the terms of your contract with her." The second clause in each of these statements is a reason for the "can't" and the

    [20] Anscombe employs the notion of modals in analyzing pairs such as "necessary, possible," "must, need not."
    [21] Anscombe, *op. cit.*, 321.
    [22] *Ibid.*, 323.
    [23] *Ibid.*, 321.

"must." But it is a reason of a special kind, "a 'reason' in the sense of a *logos*, a thought . . . [I]f we ask what the thought is, and for what it is a reason, we'll find that we can't explain them separately. We can't explain the 'You can't' on its own; in any independent sense it is simply not true that he can't (unless 'they' physically stop him). But neither does 'It's N's' . . . have its peculiar sense independent of the relation to 'You can't.'"[24] A "can't" or a "must" and its *logos* are interdependent or interwoven. If we separate them, try to understand or assess either of them alone, they lose their "peculiar sense," the sense they have in the activity or practice of which they are part. "If you say 'You can't move your king, he'd be in check', 'He'd be in check' gives the special *logos* falling under the general *logos* type: a rule of a game."[25] If you say to a police officer, "You must permit Able to speak, it's her right under the First Amendment," "it's her right . . ." gives the special *logos* of a constitutional right falling under the more general *logos* types "a right" and "a constitutional right limiting public authority." Those who know chess will understand that, and why, "You can't move your king"; anyone familiar with rights and with constitutional practice in, say, the United States will grasp that, and why, the police officer must permit Able to speak. Persons unfamiliar with these games and practices will be puzzled by both.

As I suggested, this notion of a reason in the special sense of a *logos* deepens the respects in which rights (but, again, also many other arrangements and practices) are stringent and independent. There is a reason not to move the king and not to prevent Able's speech; these "musts" and "can'ts" are not arbitrary. But in both cases the reason is internal to the game or practice and is so interwoven with "its own" "must" or "can't" as to be inseparable from it. The point, of course, is that it is not to be thought that the notion of a "reason" in the general sense of "something independent [of the particular practice and the 'must' or 'can't' in question] which someone puts forward as his reason for what he does"[26] is sufficient to understand or assess the "musts" and "can'ts" of rights. The *logos* of a right only "appears to be a reason" in this wider sense (the sense exemplified by, say, "serves human interests," "maximizes utility," or "is necessary to human freedom and well being.") Being distinct from reasons in the wider sense, the reasons for (or better, the reasons of) the "musts" and "can'ts" of rights at once embody and manifest the independent standing and stringency of the latter.

II

Anscombe's account is a description of rights not a derivation, explanation or justification of or for them. She assembles reminders of features of rights that

[24] *Ibid.*, 322.
[25] *Ibid.*, 322.   [26] *Ibid.*, 322.

are familiar to us as participants in practices and relations that involve rights. Her intention in assembling these reminders is not to advance a general theory but to dissolve or at least diminish any puzzlement that may overtake us if we attempt to derive, explain, or give a general justification for rights. Rights are no more puzzling than a large genus of other features of human affairs with which they share a number of characteristics; what might be the puzzling character of a particular right disappears when we attend to its specific characteristics or differentiae, above all its *logos*.

If, as I believe, Anscombe's account is essentially accurate, it yields tests that have to be satisfied if we are to "moderate" *rights*. A theory that failed to incorporate "musts" and "can'ts" and their internal relationships with a *logos* would simply not be a theory of rights as we know them. With these tests in mind, I return to the project of coordinating rights with other desiderata and thereby – or to that extent – moderating them. I continue my pursuit of this objective in two stages. First, I consider features of utilitarian theories, particularly John Stuart Mill's as recently construed by David Lyons, which, despite being teleological and consequentialist, seem more consonant with Anscombe's description than Scanlon's. Second, I draw comparisons between rights on the one hand and authority and the theory and practice of civil disobedience on the other. Authority has many of the characteristics Anscombe finds in rights and for this reason might seem equally unamenable to accommodation in and thereby moderation by theories such as Scanlon's and Lyons' Mill. Yet, the theory and practice of civil disobedience, which typically if not invariably gives substantial weight to teleological and consequentialist considerations (or at least to considerations "independent" of authority, laws, and rights), has been judged by many – including many philosophers – to accommodate the basic characteristics of authority while affecting valuable analogous understanding concerning rights. In short, I argue that there is available a version of teleological and consequentialist theory that can meet the tests posed by Anscombe's description of rights and which, if accepted and acted upon, would moderate rights in much the way that civil disobedience moderates authority.

If described in what is by now orthodox terminology, Lyons' recent essays concerning Mill interpret him as a "rule" or "restricted" utilitarian rather than a proponent of the "act" or "unrestricted" version of that theory.[27] But in my view, Lyons' account calls attention to aspects of Mill's theory that are

---

[27] David Lyons, "Human Rights and the General Welfare," *Philosophy and Public Affairs*, 6, (1977) 113–129; "Mill's Theory of Justice," in A. I. Goldman and J. Kim (eds.), *Values and Morals* (Dordrecht: Reidel Publishing Co., 1978); "Utility and Rights," in J. Roland Pennock and John W. Chapman (eds.), *op. cit.* My discussion of this last paper is based in part on the original draft version, primarily on the published version. References are to the latter unless otherwise indicated.

inadequately appreciated in recent reformulations of utilitarianism as well as in exegetical and historical studies. The most important point, which has strong affinities with the view of Anscombe just discussed, is made through a comparison with the much less subtle utilitarianism of G. E. Moore.

In Moore's view, all moral questions are properly decided by determining which among the available courses of action will "promote intrinsic value to the maximum degree possible." The principle "Always act so as to maximize intrinsic value" replaces equally forward-looking and undifferentiating imperatives such as "Act so as to maximize pleasure and minimize pain" and "Act so as to achieve the greatest happiness of the greatest number." According to Lyons, Mill's advice is that we "begin" our practical moral judging and deciding "at the other end." As with his predecessors and successors in the utilitarian tradition, Mill is a teleological theorist who aims to achieve certain objectives or end-states. But he does not use these basic purposes as engines of a reductionism that wipes out the many differences among moral concepts, questions, and issues. In Lyon's words, "He considers . . . what forms of judgment must be accommodated by a moral theory and then applies his basic values within the . . . constraints" established by those forms of judgment."[28]

The key phrases here are "forms of judgment" and "must be accommodated." Examples of forms of judgment are the concepts, arrangements and practices of justice, obligation, and rights. In the paper of primary interest here, Lyons concentrated on the form of judgment that is a legally established right. His discussion stresses the settled characteristics, the defined limits and implications of this "form." By virtue of Mary's right (which is to the exclusive use of a garage that comes with a house she has rented and the private driveway leading to the garage) there are a number of actions that she can take or not entirely at her discretion, certain restrictions and obligations fall to everyone other than Mary unless she releases them from them, and there are more or less clearly defined exceptions to what she can and they must and must not do (for example ambulances can use or block the driveway, without Mary's permission, when responding to emergencies). In Anscombe's terms, "because the driveway is hers (to use)," Mary not only can but may act in certain ways, and for the same "reason" certain "musts" and "can'ts" hold for or apply to other persons.

The notion that these forms "must be accommodated" is complex, involving at least two different (albeit related) senses of "musts." The first of these is conceptual. We might say that the form of judgment determines the appropriate descriptions or characterizations of the actions of Mary and others in respect to the driveway. Whatever else might be said about those actions, some

---

[28] Lyons, "Utility and Rights," draft version, 28.

of them are the exercise or enforcement of the right, others the violation of the right or the discharge of obligations in respect to the right. Persons who fail to recognize the correctness and acknowledge the relevance of these descriptions quite literally "do not know what they are talking about."

This "must" holds regardless of one's attitude toward or assessment of the right. Jane might think that Mary's right is indefensible and should be abolished – even that all rights should be abolished. And she might decide to "respect" the right only if forced to do so. If she convinced others of these views she might succeed in getting the right abolished. But *what* Jane is against is not some pattern of movement or conduct that can be identified without reference to rights; what she is against is the right. If Joan doesn't understand the notion of a right, if, say, she is from a culture that lacks rights, she might object to the fact that Mary is the only one who uses the driveway. But Joan would not be against the same thing that Jane is against.

According to Lyons, Mill recognized such conceptual "musts" and built recognition of them into his theory. He may not have been aware of the number and diversity of such "musts," but insofar as he was aware of them he made it a criterion of the adequacy of his theory that it accommmodate them.

The second sense of "must" is more clearly and directly normative. Rights must be accommodated by a moral theory when, and because, they are justified by whatever criteria of assessment the theory employs. Accordingly, there are some theories that neither must nor can accommodate any rights whatsoever. I suggested above that this is true, at least as regards rights of individuals, of certain forms of communitarianism and Marxism. It is also widely held to be true of "extreme" utilitarianism. Proponents of these theories who find themselves in a society in which some number of rights are morally or legally established are conceptually bound by the first kind of "must." And there might be tactical, instrumental, or prudential grounds on which they would sometimes or even regularly choose to conduct themselves in ways consonant with or required by those rights. But they could not regard themselves as morally or legally entitled to the havings or doings protected by the rights or as bound to the obligations that correlate with the rights of others. Whenever "violating" those rights served their basic values they would be bound by their theory to do so.

On Lyons' interpretation, Millian rule-utilitarianism attempts to accommodate the normative "must" of at least some rights. But it succeeds in doing so – even in respect to legal rights – only in a limited and finally inadequate sense. It does generate what by its own criteria are convincing justifications for the institution or practice of rights as one of the features of some societies and for establishing some specific rights. Confronted with the view that there should be no rights whatever, or with arguments against familiar rights such as to habeas corpus, trial by a jury of one's peers, various rights to property, and so forth, Millian-style utilitarians are able to make rejoinders that are forceful and consistent with the basic features of their theory. In respect to justifying institutions and practices, Millian utilitarians can easily march in the ranks of the pro-rights company.

The difficulty with Millian theory, Lyons argues, presents itself when the justification for the institution of rights or for a particular right must be brought to bear on conduct within the confines of the institution and concerning a particular right. Why should such a utilitarian respect a right in circumstances in which refusing to do so would better serve the general welfare? The justification for (as distinct from the conceptual grasp of) the institution and each of the rights of which it consists is its contribution to the general welfare. If refusal to comply with its requirements yields greater utility, the utilitarian is bound by his theory to refuse. In Lyons' view, this means that rights lose their standing as independent and distinctively stringent normative considerations.

Or rather this is a widely held view of the upshot of rule-utilitarianism. Lyons' analysis, although finally endorsing this assessment, is more complex. He considers the possibility that the utilitarian reasons for the right or other "form of judgment" give the utilitarian "reason to conform to the rules of the institution" in particular cases. It is possible that the usual objection against utilitarianism (as I just summarized it) ignores "the direct practical implications that the justification of social rules or institutions has for a utilitarian."[29] If we take this view of it, "utilitarianism gives rise . . . to conflicting considerations." It would remain true, however, that utilitarian arguments for the institution of rights or for specific rights "would not show that direct utilitarian arguments concerning [particular cases of] conduct are excluded."[30] They "would show only that such arguments must be weighed within utilitarianism against arguments flowing from the utilitarian justification of those institutions."[31] And in Lyons' view to show this much is not enough to defend utilitarianism. There is nothing in the theory that requires a right-thinking utilitarian to resolve such conflicts in favor of respecting the right.

Lyons' conclusion suggests that utilitarianism could be said to accommodate rights only if it did "exclude" direct utilitarian arguments from reasoning about particular cases of rights. Perhaps this is his view about the class "direct utilitarian arguments." But Lyons is not a natural or human rights theorist à la Nozick or Gewirth. He allows the possibility of morally defensible violations of morally justified rights, and he does not restrict this possibility to cases in which there is a conflict between or among morally justified rights. Thus, an adequate moral theory, one that successfully accommodated rights,

[29] Lyons, "Utility and Rights," 129.
[30] *Ibid.*
[31] *Ibid.*

would not have to – or rather could not – "exclude" all considerations external to or independent of rights themselves (of their *logos*) or the justification for them. Accordingly, Lyons' objection to utilitarianism is not that it allows the possibility of morally justified violations of rights; rather, it is that the theory makes it too easy to justify such violations. Although not an "absolute," a right "provides an argumentative threshold against objections to my . . . [*exercising*] it, as well as a presumption against others' interference."[32] Even on the most sympathetic interpretations of the most refined versions of utilitarianism, that theory cannot accommodate this feature and hence it cannot accommodate the "form of judgment" that is a right. Thus, we cannot look to utilitarianism as a way of at once accommodating and moderating rights.

Lyons claims that this conclusion is required by "the common understanding" of rights, particularly the notion that justifications for violation of rights must cross an "argumentative threshold." As should be evident from my reliance on Anscombe, I have no quarrel with the idea that there is such a common understanding and that a theory of rights should encompass and be responsive to it (albeit having grasped that understanding, a theorist might want to challenge it). Nor do I see any reason to deny that the common understanding includes something like what Lyon calls an argumentative threshold. If there were no such threshold, if any argument whatever justified violating any rights, the obligations attendant upon rights would amount to no more than the requirement that one give reasons for those of one's acts or omissions that affect the right-holder in respect to the subject or content of her rights. The difficulty with the notion of an argumentative threshold as Lyons deploys it is that it requires no more than this. For this reason the notion is not so much wrong as it is unhelpful. It is, perhaps, conceivable that we could give it greater specifity in respect to *this*, *that*, or the next right. If we did so, and if concomitantly we performed a Millian utilitarian "calculus" as to whether we should respect or violate the right in the circumstances in question, it might turn out that the latter always – or very frequently – led us to conclusions at variance with the former and hence with the "common understanding." Even these operations would not establish Lyons' conclusion that Millian utilitarianism *must* diverge from what the common understanding requires. But in any case Lyons has performed no such operations. His discussion of the common understanding and the implications of Millian utilitarianism are in equally general terms – terms far too general to support his conclusion.

I myself have no intention of performing a series of operations such as I have just tried to imagine. (Indeed, the notion that one could settle the question whether utilitarianism can accommodate rights by such an apparently

---

[32] *Ibid.*, 111, italics Lyons'.

inductive procedure is, for more than one reason, at least faintly absurd.)
Rather, with Anscombe's more elaborate account of the common understanding of rights in mind, I will use a discussion of authority and civil
disobedience to expand somewhat on features that Lyons attributes to Millian
utilitarianism, particularly its understanding and handling of relationships
among the conceptual features of forms of judgment, justifications for such
forms of judgment, and reasoning about conduct within the setting of forms of
judgment. I do not hope *to prove* that this understanding is correct. But I hope
to show that it is more plausible than Lyons – to say nothing of more militantly
anti-utilitarian writers – allows.

My first point can be viewed as an objection to Lyons' way of distinguishing
between conceptual and normative reasons why forms of judgment must be
accommodated. In the example on which Lyons relies, the practical question
to be decided is whether an "official" (evidently an executive official such as a
policeman or sheriff as opposed to a judge) who is of Millian utilitarian
persuasion should acknowledge and discharge an obligation to enforce Mary's
legal right to the exclusive use of the driveway. Lyons explictly makes two
assumptions about his official and implicitly makes a third. The first is that the
official has no doubt that Mary's right is legally established – for example, in
his mind there is no question about the constitutionality of the right. Secondly,
he assumes that the official believes that the right is justified by the normative
standard of Millian utilitarianism. To use Lyons' terminology, in the official's
view the right is not merely a legal right, it is a legal right with "normative
force." The third, unstated assumption is that the system or practice of
authority under which he holds his position as an official, and the particular
provisions of that practice that authorize him to enforce Mary's rights, are also
justified by Millian utilitarian criteria. The rules and conventions that establish
and partly constitute his authority are not merely legal or constitutional rules,
they are legal and constitutional rules with "normative force."

Owing to the first assumption, if the official understands the forms of
judgment in which the question of enforcement arises, he thereby knows that
the queston before him is whether, *qua* official exercising authority, he ought
to enforce a right. Lyons is correct that as a Millian utilitarian the official will
be concerned that his actions maximize the general welfare or happiness.
Unlike the Moorean utilitarian, however, he will understand that the question
is whether the general happiness will be served by his decision, *qua* official, to
enforce or to overlook violations of *a right*. If he doesn't formulate the question
in these terms, if he doesn't use these descriptions of himself and of the issues
before him, he "doesn't know what he is talking about."

Putting the matter this way specifies and extends considerations that, as
Lyons allows (albeit inadequately) are very likely to support a decision to
enforce Mary's right. The official's belief that the right and the authority have

normative force *is* the belief that the general welfare is served by the existence of these arrangements and practices. Lyons is correct that this belief does not itself require (the propositions which state this belief do not entail) the concluson that the general welfare will best be served by enforcing the right in every particular circumstance. But first, and in the spirit of Lyons' account and of the accounts that most antiutilitarians give of this point, if the official's belief is based on utilitarian criteria we must asume that it developed out of and has been sustained by experience with cases involving rights and authority. If the belief is in fact well-grounded, it is to be expected that it will hold for most future cases as well. If the official thought that it was an altogether open question whether the general welfare would be served by enforcing rights, if he thought that it was as likely as not that the general welfare would be served by allowing violations of rights, he would thereby demonstrate that he did not in fact hold the belief that Lyons attributes to him.

But this way of putting the matter, while perhaps appropriate concerning Benthamite reasoning, fails to appreciate a distinctive characteristic of Millian utilitarianism as Lyons describes it. We can appreciate the position better if we return to Anscombe's discussion and a Wittgensteinian thought that is consonant with it. It is a feature of rights that they "must" be respected. This feature, as we might put it, is a rule of the larger practice of rights of which any particular right is a part. And if, to introduce the Wittgensteinian thought, "rule becomes exception and exception rule; or if both become phenomena of roughly equal frequency – this would make our normal language-games lose their point."[33] Of course, exceptions are made to rules; of course "musts" and "must nots" are not always performed. But the notion of rules and of rule-governed practices such as rights and authority cannot be understood in merely contingent, probabilistic terms – in terms of nothing more than the likelihood that participants will find the arguments for following the rules convincing in this case or that. Someone who thought of them in such terms would misunderstand them. If Lyons is correct that Millian utilitarianism understands and seeks to accommodate such forms of judgment, then someone who thought of them in the manner assumed in Lyons' attack would not be a Millian utilitarian.

There is a more specific point here that will lead into the discussion of civil disobedience and the ways in which a Millian utilitarian *would* go about deciding whether to violate a right. It is a conceptual fact that officials (in the sense of Lyons' example) act only within their authority. Acts not within their authority are either private and hence without official standing or (if done "under color of" their authority) *ultra vires* and subject at least to nullification

---

[33] Ludwig Wittgenstein, *Philosophical Investigations*, I, para. 142 (New York: The Macmillan Company, 1953).

and very often to punishment.[34] It is a further conceptual fact that legal rights set limits on the authority of all officials. An action that violates a legal right is therefore either *ultra vires* or not an official action.[35] If an official is to act officially, she can do no other than respect rights. Hence, in this case the "musts" and "can'ts" are yet stronger than those described by Anscombe. In Wittgenstein's terms, in this case *there can be no* exceptions to the rule.[36]

III

We must not lose sight of the point on which Anscombe agrees with Hume. All of these "artificial" or conventional "musts" and "can'ts" are to be understood by contrast with physical necessities and impossibilities. The considerations I have been discussing do not settle what a Millian utilitarian (or anyone else) who among other things is an official *will* do, they only settle what, conceptually speaking, any person *qua* official, can do.

Neither do they properly *settle* what a Millian utilitarian who among other things is an official ought on balance and morally speaking to do. It is unquestionably part of the common understanding that an act by an official that violates a legal right is null and void. Millian utilitarianism accommodates this feature. Moreover, anyone who believes that the institutions of authority and legal rights, as they exist in her society, are valuable features of moral and political life, has excellent reasons for avoiding all *ultra vires* acts, and particularly for avoiding acts that are *ultra vires* because they violate legal rights. The combination of these distinguishable but by no means unrelated considerations amounts to a powerful argument that officials ought to respect and enforce rights. It is not too much to say that anyone who denies this does not *understand* the practices of authority and rights as we know them. On Lyons' account, Mill understood them.

Lyons is nevertheless correct; on a Millian utilitarian view understanding and accepting these practices does not and cannot properly *settle* the moral

---

[34] I follow Lyons in ignoring complications presented by the fact that his official is considering whether to enforce a right against encroachments by others. My discussion in the text holds without qualification for cases in which the official is considering an action which would itself violate the right. But I leave aside questions about the discretion that police officers, sheriffs, etc., have in deciding whether to enforce a person's rights against encroachment by other private citizens. It is not always the case that failure, or even refusal, to do so is *ultra vires*.

[35] This is the one respect known to me in which rights truly are "trumps" or "side-constraints." Of course anyone familiar with the processes of interpreting the scope of rights will realize the extent to which this truth is a formalism. (I would not say a mere formalism.)

[36] We might think of this aspect of the relationship between authority and right as what Wittgenstein calls a "paradigm" in a language-game. See Wittgenstein, *op cit*. I, para. 50, where he is discussing the role of the hermetically sealed metre bar in Paris. But note his further comment; "But this, of course, is not to ascribe any extraordinary property to it [the metre-bar], but only to mark its peculiar role in the language-game of measuring with a metre-rule." *Ibid*.

question whether a person who is an official ought to enforce or respect a particular legal right in a specific set of circumstances.

Is Lyons, therefore, also correct that Millian utilitarianism fails to accommodate legal (and hence also moral) rights? Assuming that the foregoing discussion presents a correct account of Millian utilitarian reasoning, does that reasoning violate the common understanding concerning rights?

Imagine that someone claims to believe that authority is in principle a justifiable institution by Millian utilitarian criteria and also to believe that a particular instance of that institution, the authority of the government under which she lives, is justified by those criteria. She claims, that is, to subscribe to that authority. She nevertheless insists that it is both conceptually and normatively proper for her to obey (or to enforce if an official), admittedly *intra vires* laws and commands only when doing so, in the circumstances under which the question arises in practical form, maximizes the general welfare. This combination of views, most of us would hold, is incoherent; the last claim contradicts, and as a practical matter nullifies, the claims that precede it.

It might be thought that this incoherence could be avoided in one of only two ways. Our utilitarian must either commit herself to the view sometimes known as legal absolutism or she must forthrightly embrace philosophical anarchism. Either the authority of a law is a sufficient, a conclusive, reason for acting as the law requires or it is irrelevant to the question of how to act and acts must be chosen and justified on their (directly utilitarian) merits.

Neither legal abolutism nor anarchism, however, seem to me to map the "common understanding" of this matter. Many people see merit in the institution of authority and recognize that subscription to it commits them to treating the authority of laws or commands not only as a *logos* in Anscombe's sense but as a weighty, indeed ordinarily a decisive, reason – in Anscombe's wider sense – for acting as the laws and commands require. But they also believe that they ought to subject the content of laws and commands to critical scrutiny. More important, here, a not inconsiderable number also hold that they are sometimes morally justified in disobeying or refusing to enforce substantively objectionable laws while continuing to avow, both sincerely and cogently, subscription to the authority of the government that promulgated the laws.

The views just sketched will be recognized as rudiments of the theory of civil disobedience. This theory, it seems to me, addresses the same question (albeit in a somewhat different institutional setting) that Lyons raises about the compatibility of Millian utilitarianism with legal rights. Mill claims to understand and to accept as justified the institution of rights and obligations as they present themselves in the societies about which he is thinking; civil disobedients claim to understand and to accept as justified the institution of authority as it presents itself via the governments under which they live. Mill recognizes that accepting rights and their attendant obligations entails regarding these as weighty, ordinarily decisive reasons for action; civil disobedients take the same view of the practical import of their acceptance of authority. But both Mill and civil disobedients hold out the possibility, at once logical or conceptual and normative, of refusing to draw the practical inferences that (they not only concede but insist) are strongly supported by the reasoning that justifies the institution. In this respect, Mill and civil disobedients agree with Anscombe. Someone who doesn't understand that "it's N's right" or "it's a law" is the *logos* of a "must" or a "can't" does not understand the institutions of rights and of law. But: "Of course, *once these linguistic* practices exist, we can detach the two parts from one another and 'It's N's' can appear as an independent reason, for example, a reason why one will not do something."[37] Lyons' view that this feature of Mill's theory vitiates Mill's claim to accommodate rights and their correlative obligations implies that Anscombe does not accommodate rights and that civil disobedients cannot, consistent with their overall position, accommodate authority.

I am inclined to agree with this conclusion as regards act-utilitarianism (which, as Lyons points out,[38] does not settle the question whether act-utilitarianism is the theory we ought to adopt). But the conclusion seems wrong concerning the more complex, conceptually sensitive, mode of utilitarianism he finds in Mill. Let us return to the theory of civil disobedience to see whether it can help to arbitrate this disagreement.

Civil disobedients do not merely avow or claim, abstractly as it were, to respect authority. They take some pains to show that their commitment to authority carries specifiable import for their thought and action. The several versions of the doctrine pursue this objective in varying ways, but most of them do so at least by:[39]

1. treating questions about subscription and obedience, nonsubscription and disobedience, as distinct and distinctively important questions – as questions that have their own conceptual form and that involve reasoning of the kinds Anscombe has described.

2. accepting that there are circumstances in which a well-grounded adverse judgement about the substantive merits of a law or command does not provide a sufficient justification for disobedience. The familiar distinction between a single seriously objectionable law and a recurring pattern of such laws is perhaps the most dramatic manifestation of this view, but in almost all

[37] Anscombe, *op. cit.*,. 322, italics Anscombe's.
[38] Lyons, "Utility and Rights" (original version), 7.
[39] The following summary is taken, with minor modifications, from my *The Practice of Political Authority* (Chicago: University of Chicago Press, 1980), 121–22.

versions of the theory it is accompanied by less categorical maxims
that counsel restraint and circumspection when deciding whether
to engage in civil disobedience.

3. accepting a variety of constraints on the modes of conduct that will
   be employed in the course of disobedient action. Among the more
   important of these are that the action will be done openly not
   conspirationally and without the use of physical violence.

4. insisting that their own adverse judgments about laws and command do not deptive officials of the authority to attach and enforce
   legal sanctions for disobedience to or refusal to enforce them.
   "You broke a law" remains the *logos* of "You must pay a fine" or
   "You must go to jail." Adverse judgments about laws and commands, in other words, do not themselves (directly) deprive the
   latter of their authority. The only implication that follows from
   such judgments is that the obligation to obey or to enforce them,
   which ordinarily follows (the civil disobedient insists) from the
   fact of their authority, is called into question as a conclusive
   reason for obeying them. It remains a reason for obedience to
   which serious-minded persons must give considerable weight
   (which it does not do, for example, for the anarchist or the
   revolutionary). But if the judgment that the laws are strongly
   objectionable coincides with a number of other judgments about
   matters such as the likely consequences of the acts of disobedience, including the likely effects of acts of disobedience on the
   viability of the practice of authority, that judgment is accepted as
   contributing to a justification for disobedience.

On this understanding, justifying disobedience will not be notably easy.
Authority remains a potent concept, one that yields "musts" and "can'ts" that
cannot be understood or assessed apart from the rule-governed practice in
which it has its sense. In these ways the theory and practice of civil disobedience can be said to accommodate authority and law. The familiar
criticism that civil disobedients either do not understand authority or aim to
destroy it (that they are in fact revolutionaries or anarchists) is belied by the
details of the thought and action of civil disobedients. In the light of its details,
the criticisms to which I allude tell us more about what the critics would like –
for reasons that are independent in Anscombe's sense – authority and law to
be than they tell us about what that understanding is and what is consonant
with it. The question arises whether this is not equally true of critics of "civil
encroachment" concerning established rights.

There are two morals to be drawn from these considerations, one primarily
conceptual and theoretical, the other more broadly moral and political. As to

the first, authority is parallel with rights at least in the Anscombian sense that both involve rules that are understood to create "musts" and "can'ts" that are interwoven with reasons in the sense of a *logos*. In other words, both are independent and stringent. As evidenced by the fact that it concerns, involves, and defends illegal acts, the theory and practice of civil disobedience introduces such independent reasons into the practice of authority; it appeals to such reasons as grounds for diminishing the stringency of the "musts" and "can'ts." Although controversy continues concerning it, it has been quite widely accepted that civil disobedience is nevertheless conceptually and theoretically compatible with authority. (Note that insofar as we are talking about legal rights, a practice of authority that countenances civil disobedience has very likely also countenanced instances of civil encroachment on rights. Many – though not all – acts of civil disobedience encroach on legal rights.)

Rights and authority are not fully parallel. And the only undeniable commonality between civil disobedience and Millian utilitarianism is that both entertain considerations "independent" of practices and institutions in the course of thought and action within and concerning them. Thus, even the entire disappearance of controversy concerning civil disobedience would not *prove* that Millian utilitarianism is conceptually and theoretically compatible with the common understanding of rights. But neither has Lyons (or, to my knowledge, anyone else) *proven* the contrary. The purpose of the comparison I have introduced is to give greater plausibility to the view that Millian utilitarianism can accommodate rights.

If I have succeeded in this – to turn to the moral and political upshot of my story – it may now be possible to address more directly the question whether we *ought* to understand rights so as to admit of the kind of thought and action that Mill recommends. *Should* we be open, should we be receptive, to the idea that Baker might consider, for purposes of deciding whether to respect or enforce a right of Able's, the possibility that the exercise of that right is unjustifiable in the circumstances at hand?

My suggestion is that we should. I suggest that openness to such thinking and acting would moderate rights in much the same manner that openness to civil disobedience moderates authority. Practices of authority that are open to civil disobedience afford participants a range of socially approved responses not otherwise available in the same sense. Presented with a law or command that is at once legally valid and substantively objectionable, participants in the practice are not forced to choose among obedience, merely criminal disobedience, or revolutionary action. Other participants recognize the differences between civil disobedience and the latter two alternatives; their responses to disobedients reflect that recognition. Most importantly, argumentation about the merits of the law or command not only continue after its adoption or promulgation but take on added forcefulness and drama. It is more difficult for those who support the adopted law or command to say "Well, that's settled, let's go on to other things." It is even more difficult for them to say "We won that one, let's go out and win another." In these ways, civil disobedience enhances the seriousness of moral and political discussion – perhaps especially the seriousness attached to the arguments of those not in positions of authority and power.

In a practice of rights open to "civil encroachment" and perhaps even "civil non-enforcement," alternatives would be comparably enlarged and enhanced. Presented with Able's right claim, Ms. Baker could concede that the right was well established and generally well justified and yet experience social accept-ance or legitimacy as she attempted to dissuade – perhaps even to prevent – Able from exercising the right in the circumstances at hand. If the right was legal, Baker would have to "take the consequences" of refusing to respect or enforce it. But those consequences would not necessarily include the moral opprobrium – and hence the sense of wrong doing, guilt, and shame – that strict deontological theories attach to violations of rights.

Of course, such a practice would also eliminate or qualify some alternatives that would be assured by understandings of rights according to which they are yet more strongly independent and stringent. In particular, in such a practice it would be more difficult for Able to "stand on her rights," to dismiss or brush aside arguments that they should not be exercised in this or that circumstance. She would have to anticipate not only Baker's persistence but the possibility that Baker might enjoy sympathy and support from others in the community. Rights would alter the character of discussion about what should and should not be done, but validly asserting a right would not necessarily end that discussion.

The terms "civil encroachment" and "civil non-enforcement" are not in general use and may seem menacing. Understood as I have described them, however, the thinking and even the acting to which they refer are familiar enough and no reason for disquiet. I have argued that Millian utilitarianism and civil encroachment have in common the willingness to entertain "inde-pendent" reasons in deciding how to act in respect to rights. On this view, civil encroachment is a mode of action opened up and sometimes justified by Millian utilitarian thinking.[40] I have further argued that Millian utilitarianism is consonant with the common understanding of rights. If I am correct in these contentions, an increased willingness to consider civil encroachment would not itself represent a change in – certainly not a threat to – the practice of rights. If anything were menaced by such a development it would be mis-

---

[40] Of course there are other modes of thinking – those that appeal to religious considerations would be an example – that entertain and invoke "independent" reasons. Millian utilitarianism is only one of a number of possible bases for civil encroachment.

understandings that encourage extremism in the exercise of rights and give rights an undeservedly bad name. If I am correct in thinking that extremism in the exercise of at least some rights is prevalent, an increased incidence of announced and defended civil encroachment might benefit the practice of rights in much the manner that civil disobedience has benefitted the practice of authority.

Political Science, The Johns Hopkins University

Social Philosophy & Policy Vol. 1 Issue 2 ISSN 0265-0525

COMMENT ON FLATHMAN
DIFFICULTIES WITH FLATHMAN'S MODERATION THESIS

CHARLES R. BEITZ

Professor Flathman's main aim in this interesting paper is to set forth what we might call the "moderation thesis." It holds that there may be occasions when the best thing to do, all things considered, is to violate a right – at least if the violation takes the form of what Flathman calls "civil encroachment" or "civil non-enforcement." Moreover, it would be desirable, in a society whose practices include rights, for this belief to be generally accepted, so that those who engaged with good reason in "civil encroachment" would receive the sympathetic support of the community.

Let me begin by trying to explain the source of the problem to which this thesis is a response. As Flathman notes, rights have a discretionary character: if I have a right to do or to have something, it is up to me whether to do it or to have it. Having a right, I am entitled to make a choice. Since we cannot say, in advance, what choice I will make, we cannot say, in advance, what will be the state of the world after I make it. But since it seems plain that some states of the world are more desirable than others, it will always be possible that the consequences of my choice will be worse, on the whole, than the consequences of some other choice that I might have made but did not. To moderate rights is apparently to act in ways that redress or compensate for the undesirable results of their exercise.

Now, it is important to see that Flathman's problem arises independently of the *content* of any particular right. Thus, it would be incorrect to object that bad things happen only when the rights that people exercise are unwarranted, or unwarrantedly broad – that is, when a society's practices recognize the wrong rights. One might be misled about this by some of Flathman's examples involving property rights, where the bad results (for example, Lord Thomson's newspaper monopoly) seem clearly to be due to society's failure to limit legal rights in ways required by their moral warrant. But undesirable results could be produced by the exercise of rights even in a society in which all rights were so limited. As long as rights retain their character as *rights* – that is, as entitlements to choose – this possibility remains.

Flathman apparently wishes to argue that the moderation thesis applies even in such an ideal society. Surely, it is only in that context that there is any occasion for puzzlement – in nonideal circumstances, only the most implausibly extreme deontological views would lead to rejection of the thesis. (Even Locke thought it permissible to violate *positive* rights when doing so promised to improve the prospects of respect for *moral* rights.) I am troubled by two aspects of Flathman's argument. First, I do not believe that he succeeds in escaping from the dilemma that he creates for himself by accepting both Anscombe's analysis of rights and Lyons' version of Mill. Second, I do not believe that he says enough about the moral basis of rights to show either why rights are of such great moral importance or how we should decide whether violating a right on any particular occasion would be justified. I will comment briefly on each point.

Flathman says that any philosophically adequate explanation of the moderation thesis must still account for certain special and peculiar features of rights, which he calls their "stringency" and "independence." His interpretation of these ideas is based on a short, and not altogether clear, paper by Elizabeth Anscombe. At the risk of oversimplifying, the "stringency" of rights is taken to refer to their conclusiveness as sources of reasons for action: if I say "you can't have that; it's mine," the claim that "it's mine" is normally all that needs to be said to explain why you can't have whatever it is you are threatening to take. The "independence" of rights refers primarily to their anti-consequentialist force: "it's mine" singles out a limited class of reasons as relevant to the justification of the claim, "you can't have that," and excludes as irrelevant various other classes of reasons, including generalized result-oriented ones.

The difficulty arises when Flathman suggests that Millian utilitarianism can justify rights with these properties of stringency and independence. He notes that his position differs from that of David Lyons, whose interpretation of Mill he otherwise adopts. But Lyons' position seems more plausible to me than Flathman's. There is no disagreement that the structure of Mill's theory of rights, for all its subtlety, is ultimately teleological. I do not believe that any plausible theory with such a structure can make good the claim that justified rights are in principle immune to justified violation under all circumstances; yet this is apparently what Anscombe's analysis requires. As far as I can see, Flathman's only defense rests on the analogy with authority. Just as people can consistently accept authority and advocate civil disobedience, he says, they can consistently believe in rights with the extreme stringency and independence that Anscombe wants and yet advocate civil encroachment. I don't think the analogy proves Flathman's point. Civil disobedience, and (I assume) "civil encroachment," are precisely refusals to take rules and rights as conclusive reasons for acting, and they are typically justified by considerations beyond those that rules and rights pick out as relevant. So, apparently, either Anscombe's extremism or Mill's consequentialism has to go. Which should go is a difficult question; it raises the related issues of whether the Anscombe view is a faithful report of the meaning of the concept of rights in commonsense moral thought, and whether it is in fact necessary for a theory of rights to accommodate the concept exactly as we have it in commonsense moral thought. Both are interesting issues, but since Flathman doesn't pursue them, I won't either.

Let me turn, instead, to the second difficulty I mentioned, which has to do with the obscurity of Flathman's own account of the importance of rights. As I said, I think there is too little here to make clear how a correct theory of rights would work, and hence, too little to guide deliberation about whether violating a right on some occasion would be justified, all things considered. I don't disagree with the thought that a broadly Millian account is what we want; but I don't think that Flathman can be allowed to conclude that the moderation thesis is true without developing, rather than simply referring to, such an account.

I realize that this is no small order; perhaps in the short space I have left, I can at least advance a suggestion or two about how an explanation of the value of rights might be developed in such a way as to shed light on the occasions when violating a right might be justified. I believe that Flathman is correct in following Mill's lead here: unless one thinks that rights are self-evident (whatever that means), attributions of rights will always stand in need of justification. The justification must end somewhere, and it is unlikely to end convincingly in yet another right. For we may always ask why people have *that* right, and the reply, if any, will probably refer to something besides rights: interests, for example, or needs, or perhaps, as Mill thought, some complex interpretation of utility. (I note, parenthetically, that this is the truth in the remark that Flathman quotes from Scanlon's paper on "Rights, Goals, and Fairness," and since it seems wholly sympathetic to Flathman's own position, I am curious why he does not pursue the line that Scanlon suggests.) I do not mean to say that the justification of rights must be ultimately utilitarian; only that it must refer in some way to the consequences of the social recognition of rights. Those consequences might, of course, enter moral thinking in a variety of ways; I am not prepared to argue that they must enter in the utilitarian way. However this may be, we should consider what it is about rights that might explain their stringency and independence of direct consequentialist reasoning.

Now, it seems to me that a complete justification of any particular right will be complex in the sense of referring both to the substantive interest that the particular right protects and to the features that the right has as a right. At the same time, any justification will be open to question if it fails to take account of the costs of recognizing the right, including both the harm likely to be done over time by the exercise of the right and the opportunity costs to others flowing from their forbearance. As I said, I am not prepared to offer any general view about how these costs and benefits should be weighed and compared. The immediate problem, however, is how the special features of rights *as rights* enter the picture. It seems to me that there is no alternative to exploiting the especially intimate connection between rights and choice: as I have noted, having a right, I have an option to do or not do, to have or not have, the thing to which I have a right. Normally, having a choice is itself a good thing, for reasons both of efficiency and of autonomy, and, therefore, the simple fact that a right is a *right*, and so allows me a choice, should play a role in explaining why rights are important. And the value of the dependable expectation that choices will be available under appropriate circumstances will, then, be the source of the claim that rights should not be violated for consequentialist reasons. Of course, it remains to say why we should accord such great weight to reasons of efficiency and autonomy, especially since their ultimate impact will be to screen out more broadly consequentialist appeals. More critically for Flathman's thesis, it remains to explain *why* and *at what point* the screening-out of these broader aspects should be overcome and "civil encroachment" could permissibly be contemplated. I confess to some doubt about whether this threshold will allow such things as "civil encroachment" in any but the most extreme and unusual circumstances, provided, that is, that we confine ourselves to ideal theory. Fortunately, I lack the space to give a very satisfying answer to these questions.

Political Science, Swarthmore College